THE EDWARDIAN CRISIS

British History in Perspective
General Editor: Jeremy Black

Please note that a sister series, *Social History in Perspective*, is available covering the key topics in social and cultural history.

British History in Perspective
Series Standing Order: ISBN 0–333–71356–7 hardcover/ISBN 0–333–69331–0 paperback

You can receive future titles in this series as they are published by placing a standing order. Please contact your bookseller or, in case of difficulty, write to the address below with your name and address, the title of the series and the ISBN quoted above.

Customer Services Department, Macmillan Distribution Ltd
Houndmills, Basingstoke, Hampshire RG21 6XS, England

THE EDWARDIAN CRISIS

BRITAIN 1901–14

DAVID POWELL

palgrave

Published by
PALGRAVE
Houndmills, Basingstoke, Hampshire RG21 6XS and
175 Fifth Avenue, New York, N. Y. 10010
Companies and representatives throughout the world

PALGRAVE is the new global academic imprint of
St. Martin's Press LLC Scholarly and Reference Division and
Palgrave Publishers Ltd (formerly Macmillan Press Ltd).

Outside North America
ISBN 0–333–59542–4 hardback
ISBN 0–333–59543–2 paperback

Inside North America
ISBN 0–312–16093–3

This book is printed on paper suitable for recycling and
made from fully managed and sustained forest sources.

A catalogue record for this book is available
from the British Library.

Library of Congress Cataloging-in-Publication Data
Powell, David, 1956–
The Edwardian crisis : Britain 1901–1914 / David Powell.
    p. cm. —(British history in perspective)
    Includes bibliographical references and index.
    ISBN 0–312–16093–3
1. Great Britain—Politics and government—1901–1910. 2. Great
Britain—Politics and government—1910–1936. I. Title.
II. Series.
DA570.P69   1996
941.082'3—dc20   96–15375
                                                  CIP

10   9   8   7   6   5   4   3   2
10   09 08 07 06 05 04 03 02

Transferred to digital printing 2001

Printed and bound in Great Britain by
Antony Rowe Ltd, Eastbourne

CONTENTS

Glossary

ASRS	Amalgamated Society of Railway Servants
BSP	British Socialist Party
ILP	Independent Labour Party
LEA	Labour Electoral Association
LRC	Labour Representation Committee
MFGB	Miners' Federation of Great Britain
NUWSS	National Union of Women's Suffrage Societies
SDF	Social Democratic Federation
TUC	Trades Union Congress
UVF	Ulster Volunteer Force
WSPU	Women's Social and Political Union

PREFACE

Seen from the vantage point of the late twentieth century, across what J. B. Priestley described as the 'vast dark chasm' of two world wars, Edwardian Britain evokes contradictory impressions in the mind's eye. One is that of the 'long summer afternoon', the leisurely swansong of an aristocratic society bathed in the afterglow of Victorian splendour. The other is of a time of mounting discord overshadowed by the lowering clouds of approaching war. Both of these images are more than usually shaped by the wisdom of hindsight, just as 'Edwardian Britain' (which should, logically, end with the death of Edward VII in 1910) is, in a sense, the retrospective creation of historians who know what happened after 1914. Yet they remain the starting points from which most studies of the period take their cue, and the idea that the immediate pre-war years constituted some kind of emergency or 'crisis' in British history has been widely discussed. The great French historian, Elie Halevy, wrote about the way in which 'domestic anarchy' had spread in Britain before 1914.[1] This theme was developed with seductive fascination by the young George Dangerfield, whose book *The Strange Death of Liberal England* was first published in 1935.[2] Dangerfield argued that, far from being the quiet haven of social peace affectionately remembered by those wishing to return to pre-war 'normalcy' after 1918, the Edwardian period was itself a time of mounting conflict and instability, in which many of the unsettling post-war changes had their roots and in which British society was suffering from a deep-seated malaise that was symptomatic of a sea-change in the national psyche. The tensions of the pre-war years, with their increasing violence and political extremism, were evidence, he believed, of a loss of respect for the rule of law and for the institutions and conventions of parliamentary government; in short, of a fatal weakening of the spirit of moderation, compromise and social harmony which had been among the distinguishing characteristics (in his view) of the 'liberal England' of the middle and later part of Queen Victoria's reign.

Dangerfield's concept of a generalised crisis has generated considerable controversy among historians. Recently there has been a tendency to dismiss his account as impressionistic and misleading.[3] There nevertheless remains lively disagreement as to the nature and direction of events in the 'lost world' of pre-1914 Britain, over which the writings of Dangerfield and Halevy continue to cast a long shadow. What the present study sets out to do, therefore, is systematically to re-examine the components of the Dangerfield/Halevy thesis in the light of subsequent research and to attempt a fresh assessment of the severity or otherwise of the 'Edwardian crisis' in relation both to the short-term and the longer term perspectives of British history in the nineteenth and twentieth centuries. In so doing it will not only touch upon specific issues of thematic concern but will also engage a number of broader areas of historical debate. For example, did the First World War accelerate or divert the currents of change in pre-war Britain? Was the Liberal party, which formed the government for most of the Edwardian decade, in any sense in irretrievable decline before 1914, faced as it was with a dual challenge from left and right? Above all, did the surface excitements of the Edwardian years – over constitutional and fiscal reform, women's and workers' rights, Irish Home Rule – signify a deeper crisis of social or political relations, or were they merely passing problems whose coincidence was unconnected to any single, common cause? The emphasis throughout is on domestic affairs and space precludes any detailed treatment of foreign policy, but in this last respect it might be instructive to make comparisons between what was happening in Britain and the experience of countries like Germany or Russia, where internal problems of equal or greater seriousness were occurring – problems which may have played their part in influencing the conduct of international relations and thus in precipitating a more profound catastrophe of which, whatever their gravity, the conflicts of 1901–14 were but the forerunners.

In writing a book of this kind, I have obviously relied heavily on the research of other historians, which I have done my best to acknowledge in the endnotes and the guide to Further Reading. I am grateful to Jeremy Black, the series editor, for inviting me to undertake the work and to the publishers for their continuing support. My thanks also go to successive generations of students in Ripon and York who have endured my enthusiasms and helped to shape my thinking on the topic. Needless to say, any errors or eccentricities of interpretation are entirely my own.

INTRODUCTION

The Victorian Legacy

Queen Victoria died on 22 January 1901, at the end of a reign which had lasted for sixty-three years, seven months and two days.[1] The occurrence of her death at the start of a new century, after a reign of such length and distinction, imparted a special significance to the accession of her heir, the ebullient and avuncular Prince of Wales, who became King Edward VII. Contemporaries were conscious at once of a generational shift, a change in the style of monarchy which was felt to reflect a change in the temper of the nation at large – a quickening of the pace of life, a relaxation of conventions and an impatience with restraints, an openness to new ideas, new fashions, new experiences.[2] Historians, too, have often seen the distinctiveness of Edwardian Britain as lying in the extent to which it marked a departure from Victorian norms. Yet the differences between Edward's short reign and the closing years of Victoria's did not represent a complete break with the past. Before any attempt can be made to assess the depth of the Edwardian crisis it is necessary first to consider the legacy bequeathed to the Edwardians by their Victorian predecessors and to outline some of the problems which the citizens of the new century inherited from those of the old.

The Victorian legacy was a mixture of achievement and uncertainty. In the mid-nineteenth century Britain had been the pre-eminent global power: the hub of a world-wide empire and the world's leading manufacturing and commercial nation, whose colonies and trade routes were protected by the largest navy the

1

world had ever seen. By the time of Victoria's death, pre-eminence was no longer assured. Britain was still immensely powerful, but on the economic and imperial fronts alike her earlier supremacy was coming under increasing threat. A second generation of industrial powers, most notably Germany and the United States, were overtaking Britain as a manufacturing nation and putting pressure on her command of world trade. Although Britain's economy was still growing in absolute terms, and her role as the centre of the international finance system was as yet unrivalled, the long process of relative decline which was to be such a feature of the twentieth-century British experience was already under way by 1901. Similarly, Britain's colonial and naval supremacy had been challenged in the era of the 'new imperialism' from the 1870s onwards. Germany's Navy Laws of 1898 and 1900 foreshadowed an intensifying naval arms race. Competition for colonies and the desire to protect existing territories had in the 1890s led Britain to the verge of war with Russia and France. Meanwhile the internal problems of main-taining the Empire were graphically illustrated by the South African War of 1899–1902, a conflict provoked by Britain's desire to incorporate the Boer republics of the Transvaal and the Orange Free State into a British-dominated South Africa in order to forestall the breakdown of British control over a region which was seen as economically and strategically crucial to the Empire's future. The war was a supreme test of Britain's ability to sustain an expanding empire with finite financial and military resources and it drove home in urgent terms the growing precariousness of Britain's international position compared with the mid-Victorian heyday of fifty years before.[3]

If the international situation looked more uncertain towards the end of Victoria's reign than it had half a century earlier, there were also mounting troubles on the domestic scene. After the near-revolutionary upheavals of the early part of the nineteenth century, the mid-Victorian period had been a time of com-parative social and political stability, an 'age of equipoise' in which Britain benefited from the rising prosperity generated by the industrial revolution and the stable government provided by established representative parliamentary institutions. Britain alone of the West European nations had escaped the trauma of revolution in 1848 and seemed to be following a unique path of development based on social harmony, economic growth and generally liberal (if not always Liberal) government. However, the stability and peacefulness of the age of equipoise proved to be at best transitory, at worst illusory. The later nineteenth century once again saw widespread popular protest which in some ways echoed the Chartist outbreaks of the 1830s and 1840s. In addition to discontent arising from economic and social causes, there was more organised political protest from those denied a full share in power by the mid-Victorian dispensation. Finally there were signs of rifts in the ranks of the governing class which inevitably weakened the consensus on which the political stability of the country had hitherto rested.

Perhaps not surprisingly at a time when national and great-power rivalries were undermining Britain's position abroad, the first focus of domestic instability was provided by an upsurge of nationalism within the British Isles, as the move towards a more centralised, unified state was contested, with varying degrees of fervour, in the non-English parts of the supposedly 'United' Kingdom. Ireland was the principal source of disturbance, as it had been intermittently since the 1780s. Groups such as the Fenians used terrorist tactics in an attempt to force the British government to make concessions to nationalism in the 1860s. In the 1870s and 1880s a strong constitutional Nationalist party, under the leadership of Charles Stewart Parnell, campaigned for the granting of Irish Home Rule. British ministers thus found themselves having to apply coercion to Ireland to suppress terrorism and popular unrest while searching for a framework of political compromise which would keep Ireland within the Union. Ireland, moreover, was only part of a wider problem. In Scotland and Wales there were equally strong, though less violent, currents of nationalist feeling which challenged the policies of the Victorian state and the social, religious and political predominance of the anglicised ruling elites who mono-polised the institutions of central and local government.

The growth of nationalism was just one of the tendencies towards conflict which disrupted the social and political consensus of the mid-Victorian years. Another, which took on a sharper form as the century progressed, was discontent among the working classes. Although it occasionally revealed itself in violent outbursts (as in the riots of the unemployed in London in 1886 and 1887), this was more a problem of accommodation than one of public order. The industrial Labour movement which grew up after 1850 was overwhelmingly moderate and non-revolutionary in outlook. Even so, there were over two million trade unionists in Britain by the early 1900s. Groups like the miners had shown their capacity to cause economic disruption by taking strike action and in the 1890s a serious gulf seemed to be opening up between workers and employers as industrial relations steadily worsened. Meanwhile there were signs that socialist ideas were supplanting the previously dominant Liberal-radicalism of the Labour movement, indicating the adoption of a more assertive, class-conscious approach to political and industrial activity. Keir Hardie and other socialists founded an Independent Labour Party in 1893 which later joined forces with the trade unions to form the nucleus of the modern Labour party after 1900. Here again was evidence to suggest that the mid-Victorian dispensation was being undermined, this time by processes of economic and social change, with the result that the late Victorians were more sceptical than their predecessors about the possibilities of cooperation between social classes and more fearful about the prospect of class war.

Old certainties were being similarly challenged in a third area, the position of women. Victorian society was heavily male-dominated, patriarchal in structure and masculocentric in orientation. The conventional roles of women, especially middle- and upper-class women, were strictly defined. But in the second half of the nineteenth century significant pressures for change were at work. From the 1850s and 1860s an increasingly influential women's movement pressed for reforms across a broad front, including legal rights for married women, easier access to divorce and improved educational and employment opportunities. Women began to enter the professions. They played a part, as voters and elected representatives, in local government and, by the turn of the century, they were becoming more vocal in their demands for the parliamentary franchise. The formation of the National Union of Women's Suffrage Societies in 1897 and the Women's Social and Political Union in 1903 made 'Votes for Women' the centrepiece of the campaign for women's rights in the Edwardian era. To talk at this stage of a 'women's rebellion' or a 'sexual revolution' may be going too far, but it can at least be seen that the more visible unrest of the Edwardian period had its roots in previous decades and that, in this as in other cases, there were unresolved problems carried over from one century to the next.

It was significant, too, that movements such as nationalism, socialism and feminism came to the fore at a time when the political system as a whole was entering a transitional phase. In the mid-nineteenth century politics was still the preserve of a narrow, mainly aristocratic elite. Parties rested on an informal, often familial, structure of influence and there was a large measure of agreement within the governing class on the broad lines of national policy. In the 1860s, however, this system began a long process of transformation, from the basically aristocratic to at least the quasi-democratic. The franchise was extended in 1867 and 1884, so that by the latter date two-thirds of adult males had the right to vote in parliamentary elections. Legislation was passed to introduce a secret ballot (1872) and to restrict corrupt practices (1883), as well as to redraw constituency boundaries on a more uniform basis (1885). Local government was also made progressively more representative, with the establishment of elected county councils in 1888–9 and parish and district councils in 1894. These changes reduced, though they did not eliminate, the scope for aristocratic influence to affect the outcome of elections and gave the middle and working classes a much more direct role in the political process, even if the non-payment of Members of Parliament meant that the immediate effect on the composition of the House of Commons was comparatively limited.[4]

The main corollary of this gradual democratisation of the political system, though, was the development of a more competitive type of 'mass' politics, in which parties appealed for votes on the basis of differing programmes and prospectuses, their efforts being reinforced by more sophisticated organisation in the constituencies and the backing of a highly partisan popular press.[5] Inevitably a greater degree of polarisation occurred, as leaders like Gladstone and Disraeli sought to give their parties a distinctive electoral identity and to consolidate their support among particular social, religious or ethnic groups. As a result, the broad political consensus which had sustained a prolonged period of Whig–Liberal government in the 1850s and 1860s began to break down, and by 1874 had been replaced by a more evenly balanced two-party system in which the Liberal and Conservative parties alternated in power. Of course considerable common ground continued to exist, and the differences between the parties should not be magnified disproportionately, but the divergence was real enough and introduced a new element of instability into the political world. It was a divergence, too, which interacted with the conflicts of class and nationality that were opening up in late-Victorian society.[6] The Liberal party, especially after the departure from its ranks of the aristocratic Whigs in the 1880s, came to represent mainly the radical, Nonconformist provincial middle classes, allied to the forces of organised Labour and Celtic particularism. The Conservatives, by contrast, were very much the party of the English, Anglican establishment, rallying their supporters with loyalist appeals to the defence of the constitution, the Empire and the status quo. By the turn of the century economic and social policies were playing a more prominent part in the polarisation process, particularly once Joseph Chamberlain and sections of Conservative opinion had embraced the cause of protective tariffs in place of the Free Trade regime which had been accepted by both parties since the 1850s.[7] Naturally, on this as on other matters, there were divisions within parties as well as between them, and the destabilising effect of party rivalries was checked to some extent by the fact that the Conservatives enjoyed a long tenure of power following the Liberal split over Irish Home Rule in 1886. But like the other causes of domestic controversy that were part of the Victorian legacy, political partisanship was to be a significant factor in the palpably rising tension of the years immediately prior to the First World War.

The ways in which that tension manifested itself are at the heart of the 'Edwardian crisis' which forms the subject of this book. After 1901 party political divisions became more acute. The Conservatives found their hold on power slipping away after the end of the South African War and the retirement of their long-serving Prime Minister, Lord Salisbury, in 1902. Growing unpopularity with the electorate and internal disagreements over Tariff Reform precipitated a rapid decline which led to the resignation of the government of Salisbury's successor, Balfour, in December 1905 and to a landslide defeat by the Liberals at the general election of January 1906. This dramatic electoral revolution was only the prelude to wilder times ahead. The Liberals retained office until after the outbreak of war in 1914, but from its inception their administration was beset by problems arising from continuing party rivalry and a rising tide of extra-parliamentary unrest. Liberal attempts to implement an ambitious programme of fiscal and social reform antagonised the Conservatives and met opposition from powerful vested interests. The government's plans had to contend with the obstructive tactics of a Conservative-dominated House of Lords and the Lords' rejection of Lloyd George's 'People's Budget' in 1909 resulted in a prolonged constitutional crisis. During the course of that struggle, two further general elections in 1910 deprived the Liberals of their independent Commons majority, leaving them reliant on the votes of Irish Nationalist and Labour MPs and inaugurating an even more bitter spell of inter-party warfare between the government and its Conservative opponents. The Liberal cabinet's authority was simultaneously assailed by the threat from without: the campaigns of the militant suffragettes, widespread industrial disturbances and the escalation of conflict in Ireland prompted by the government's decision to press ahead with a Home Rule Bill in defiance of resistance from Protestant Ulster. Between 1911 and 1914 all of the destabilising trends of the late-Victorian period seemed to be coming to a head, and by the summer of 1914 there was talk of the whole United Kingdom being perilously close to either a revolution or a civil war.

Whether, taken together, this combination of events amounted to a full-blown 'crisis' in British history is the question which will be considered in the following chapters. The answer depends not only on the seriousness of the problems Britain was facing but also on the way in which those problems were perceived by contemporaries and the skill with which they were addressed. From an historical point of view, it depends in addition on the definition of the term 'crisis' and the precision with which it is applied. The label is one with which historians have been so lavish that it risks becoming devalued through over-use. There are nevertheless circumstances in which its employment is perfectly legitimate. It can, for instance, refer to a specific event, or sequence of events, of critical and immediate importance: in politics, a 'crisis' leading to a change of government, the collapse of a regime, or a revolution. Alternatively, the crisis may be a climactic phase in a more gradual process of change, not necessarily producing a sharp discontinuity, such as a revolution, but funnelling or redirecting historical forces in a way which is evident in retrospect if not always at the time of its occurrence. In this interpretation, crises can be staging posts on a path of evolutionary development – 'pressure points' at which societies confront underlying problems or undertake fundamental reform – rather than preludes to violent or revolutionary change. A more extended typology could be advanced, using models from economics, sociology or political science, in which longer periods of change were themselves 'crises' in the history of a particular society. For Britain, the massive readjustments brought about by the industrial revolution of 1750–1850 might be a good example.[8]

To say at this stage which, if any, of these definitions best fits the situation in Edwardian Britain would be to prejudge the results of the present enquiry. In Dangerfield's classic account, the disorders of the pre-war years could all be traced to a core mood of rebelliousness, a semi-conscious revolt against the security, respectability and constraints of the Victorian era. He saw the Edwardian crisis as part of a rejection of the moderate, consensual, middle-class liberalism of the nineteenth century – not necessarily the ideas identified with the Liberal party alone (although Dangerfield was condescendingly critical of the Edwardian Liberal governments), but a more broadly-diffused liberalism that had become entwined with the Victorian self-image; a liberalism based on Free Trade, gradual but steady moral and material progress and the settlement of differences by rational, reasoned debate. This is almost certainly too simplistic a view. Nevertheless, Britain at the beginning of the twentieth century was facing the twin challenge of democratisation and modernisation. Across many aspects of national life the wisdoms of an earlier age were having to be reappraised and problems which had been building up over a long period – in foreign relations, economic and social organisation, party politics and the system of government – were demanding attention. To that extent, Dangerfield was right in seeing the conflicts of the Edwardian age as a clash between the old and the new. As will be seen, the role of the state (particularly in relation to questions of poverty and social reform), the remodelling of the constitutional and institutional fabric, the accommodation and integration of potentially disruptive influences within a new social and political dispensation, were all major issues at the heart of the Edwardian dilemma. One of the causes of the troubles of these years may well have been that the existing ruling elites were attempting to reorientate themselves in respect to new ideas, and to contain or control the democratic impulses that were at work, while still fighting party battles over more traditional areas of contention. The only general conclusion that can be arrived at with any certainty is that if Britain was undergoing, or moving towards, a crisis between 1901 and 1914, that crisis was many-faceted. It is therefore to a closer examination of those individual facets that attention must now be turned.

1

THE SOCIAL CRISIS

Poverty, Social Reform and the State

The war in South Africa between Britain and the Boers had
barely reached its half-way point when Queen Victoria died. By
the time it ended, in May 1902, its cost, in lives and money, had
reached over 40,000 British dead and wounded and an expenditure of more than £200 million, the latter resulting in the
imposition of an extra 7d in the pound on income tax. The war
was important, beyond the confines of South Africa, for the way
in which it hastened a reassessment of Britain's foreign and
imperial policies, leading to a greater emphasis on consolidating
the Empire rather than expanding it and accelerating a search for
foreign allies which bore fruit in the Anglo-Japanese alliance in
1902 and the ententes to settle colonial differences with France
and Russia in 1904 and 1907. It had an important impact on
attitudes and developments in Britain too. In its early stages
it divided the Liberal party and enabled the Unionists to win
a further period of office at the 'khaki' election of 1900, although their inability to bring the conflict to a swift conclusion
subsequently lost them support. More substantively, the misman-
agement of the war – rather like the earlier example of the
Crimea – had revealed, or drawn closer attention to, serious
defects in the administrative structures of the country and in the
nation's economic and social fabric. Much of the Edwardian
period was taken up with attempts to remedy these defects, by
redrawing the boundaries of responsibility between the state and
the individual and dealing with the problems of poverty and

ill-health which many believed might threaten Britain's future as a great power. Because it was perceived as the focal point of an incipient social crisis, a consideration of the problem of poverty, and of contemporary responses to it, forms an appropriate point of departure for a study of the Edwardian crisis in its broader setting.

The Problem of Poverty

Edwardian society was a society of contrasts, in which conspicuous consumption and a rising level of national wealth coexisted with widespread material hardship. Its glaring inequalities were illustrated by the statistics contained in a book entitled *Riches and Poverty*, published in 1905 and written by L. G. Chiozza Money, a social reformer and member of the Fabian Society who became Liberal MP for North Paddington at the general election of 1906. Money divided the 43 million inhabitants of the United Kingdom into three classes: 1¼ million who could be counted 'rich' (sharing between them an aggregate annual income of £585 million), 3¾ million who were described as 'comfortable' (with a total income of £245 million per annum) and the 38 million 'poor', whose share of the national income (£880 million a year) was only marginally greater than the amounts enjoyed by the considerably less numerous members of the other two classes.[1] When all forms of wealth were taken into account the contrast was even more stark, 'about one-seventieth part of the population owns far more than one-half of the entire accumulated wealth, public and private, of the United Kingdom'.[2]

Money's picture of Edwardian Britain was neither sociologically exact nor statistically unimpeachable (for example, his definition of 'the poor' simply included all those who fell below the income tax threshold of £160 a year), but it did reflect a growing concern about the persistence of mass poverty amid the relative plenty of a modern industrial society and about the social, economic and political implications of a continuing, and possibly increasing, maldistribution of wealth. This was in tune with a change in outlook which had begun to take root as early as the 1880s. Before that, although the existence of poverty had been acknowledged, it had been considered almost as part of the natural order of things. It was seen as resulting from defects of individual character rather than from faults in the economic system – a form of judgement on those who were idle, drunken or morally corrupt, or who otherwise did not conform to the standards of industriousness and thrift demanded by the Victorian work ethic. Insofar as there was a distinction to be made between the 'deserving' and the 'undeserving' poor, the needs of the former (the sick, the elderly) could be met by the operation of Christian charity, through the work of bodies such as the Charity Organisation Society, or by the mechanisms of the Poor Law. Economic growth was in any case expected to produce a rising material standard of living from which all those who were willing and able to work would automatically benefit.

In the 1880s, some of these assumptions began to be questioned. Britain's more chequered economic performance suggested that greater prosperity arising from industrial growth could no longer be taken wholly for granted. At the same time, revelations about the scale of poverty cast doubt on the belief that individual failings were its sole cause and provided evidence that some kinds of poverty at least were the product of structural imbalances in the economic system. The publication in Britain in 1881 of the influential *Progress and Poverty* by the American radical, Henry George, was the starting point for a sustained political and economic debate. Public interest was aroused by sensationalist accounts of the plight of the urban poor, for example those contained in Andrew Mearns' *The Bitter Cry of Outcast London* (1883) and taken up by the *Pall Mall Gazette*. The activities of socialist groups such as the Social Democratic Federation and the Fabian Society (both founded in 1884), and the publicity attracted by events like the riots of the London unemployed in February 1886 or the London dock strike of 1889, further heightened awareness of the difficulties experienced by the labouring classes, as did the findings of the Royal Commission on the Depression in Trade and Industry which reported in 1886. The mood of social discovery which characterised the decade was perhaps best summed up by William Booth, the founder of the

Salvation Army, in the title of his book, *In Darkest England and the Way Out* (1890). This was one of a number of works in which middle-class explorers ventured into the abyss of the poverty-ridden city slums to recreate the atmosphere of the 'Condition of England' debate which had been carried on by the social novelists, especially Disraeli, Dickens, Charles Kingsley and Mrs Gaskell, in the 1830s and 1840s.[3]

The revelations of the 1880s were reinforced by more sober statistical analysis. Charles Booth's multi-volume *The Life and Labour of the People of London*, which appeared between 1889 and 1903, set new standards for empirical social investigation. The conclusion of this painstaking survey of conditions in London's East End was that up to 30 per cent of the population were living in a state of poverty, below a 'poverty line' which meant that their income, or that of their families, was insufficient to meet basic needs of food, rent and clothing. Booth demonstrated that the plight of those in the lowest socio-economic groups could not realistically be attributed to personal inadequacies alone and that it stemmed far more from the low level of wages, the uncertainty or irregularity of employment, and from the ravages of sickness, infirmity and old age.

Booth's findings were confirmed, and indeed amplified, by the researches of the Quaker social reformer Seebohm Rowntree, whose enquiry into conditions in the working-class areas of York was published as *Poverty, A Study of Town Life* in 1901. Rowntree found that 28 per cent of the York population were living in varying degrees of poverty, either in what he called 'primary poverty' – where a family's total income fell below the 21 shillings a week needed to maintain 'merely physical efficiency' – or in 'secondary poverty', where spending, 'either useful or wasteful', took their residual income below the poverty line.[4] Having spelt out with appalling clarity the extent of the hardship that this entailed, he further elucidated the dynamic nature of the problem by expounding the concept of the 'poverty cycle', showing that most members of the working classes would be in poverty at some period in their lives, especially in childhood, in the early years of married life when having children dependent on parental income, and in old age. From this he concluded that, 'The proportion of the community who at one period of their lives suffer from poverty to the point of physical privation is therefore much greater, and the injurious effects of such a condition are much more widespread than would appear from a consideration of the numbers who can be shown to be below the poverty line at any given moment'.[5]

Although the methodology used by Booth and Rowntree has been criticised for possibly exaggerating the scale of poverty, their studies were too well documented to be easily ignored. They undermined any lingering complacency which might have been sustained by evidence of rising wage levels for some groups of workers or by the reduction of the numbers of those in receipt of poor relief in England and Wales from one million (5.7 per cent of the population) in 1850 to 792,000 (2.7 per cent of the population) in 1900.[6] The fact was that, despite vast increases in national wealth and in average per capita income, and improvements in the general standard of living, there remained a substantial underclass of the unskilled and casually employed who were denied the benefits of growing prosperity. In times of depression and high unemployment (the coining of the latter term was itself a feature of the more economically-conscious 1880s) their numbers could be swelled by those from more skilled occupations. Whether this amounted to a 'crisis' – other than in the minds and consciences of middle-class social reformers – is more difficult to decide. Fears of widespread social disorder were not generally realised. There were some outbreaks of violence, the riots of the unemployed in the mid-1880s being a case in point. These stirred anxieties among the propertied classes about the threat of popular insurrection, and incidentally encouraged the middle classes in London to make generous contributions to the Lord Mayor's Mansion House Fund for the relief of distress. Some socialist agitators openly talked the language of a violent class war. But for the most part the poor remained largely impervious to the promptings of occasional firebrands and were too engrossed in the business of sustaining body and soul to do more than suffer in silence. Trade unions and other labour organisations were committed to mainly peaceful activity, and in any case were most active among the better-off sections of the working class. Even disputes involving less skilled workers, such as the London dock strike of 1889, passed off without serious incident. For most of the period, the stratified nature of working-class life, and the cyclical experience of poverty for many workers, with good days following bad, militated against the development of revolutionary consciousness, while the operation of middle-class charity, of the Poor Law, and the communal self-help of the working classes themselves ensured that social cohesion was never completely eroded and that a measure of stability persisted even in the hardest of hard times.

However, if the scale of poverty did not necessarily create an immediate crisis in terms of public order, it did offer a warning of a crisis of a different kind. This in turn had two separate but related components, both of which were connected to the question of Britain's faltering supremacy as a world power. First, on the industrial front, the persistence of mass poverty alongside huge increases in national income raised doubts about the effectiveness of individualist economics as a means of distributing as opposed to creating wealth. Not only that, but there were those who were beginning to argue that the existence of a low-waged, povertied underclass might itself be having an adverse effect on Britain's chances of future prosperity; that, far from the poor acting as an essential reservoir of cheap, unskilled labour, they acted rather as a drag on economic growth by not being able to fulfil their proper function as consumers. According to radical economists such as J. A. Hobson, this problem of underconsumption lay at the root of the economic difficulties Britain was experiencing at the end of the nineteenth century. A progressive redistribution of wealth to boost the incomes of the poor would not only be beneficial to them as families and individuals, it would also give a much-needed stimulus to the economy, from which the whole community would benefit.

Fears for the future of the economy went hand in hand with fears for Britain's national security. The spread of ideas of Social Darwinism in the late nineteenth century, coupled with the militarisation of continental powers and their policy of establishing mass conscript armies, emphasised the importance of maintaining a fit, healthy population capable of defending the country's interests if the need arose. Traditionally Britain had retained only a small, volunteer peacetime army, relying on the navy for the task of national defence. The South African War made it necessary to mobilise a mass army for the first time since the Napoleonic wars, with consequences which were far from encouraging for those with Britain's military future at heart. Large numbers of volunteers proved physically unfit for active service, mainly because of long-term deficiencies of diet and health care. So serious was the condition of the nation's human resources seen as being that the government set up an Inter-Departmental Committee on Physical Deterioration to investigate the health of the population. When the Committee reported in 1904 it rejected some of the more alarmist visions of degeneracy and racial decline, but it did make a long list of recommendations for government action, especially in the area of children's health, which stressed the need to tackle the problems of poverty if Britain's military capacity relative to other countries was not to be further eroded.

Taken together, these concerns led to the emergence by the early 1900s of a growing consensus in favour of positive action by the state to improve the working of the economy and carry out social reform. To be fair, the Victorian era had already seen a significant move away from the minimal state which had been the classical liberal ideal. Central and local government had intervened in matters such as housing and public health and in the regulation of conditions in factories and workshops. The issuing of the Chamberlain Circular in 1886, recommending that local authorities schedule public works at times when they could offer relief to the unemployed, represented an early attempt to respond to the needs of those out of work, albeit in a fairly modest way. Since 1870, the state had extended its responsibility for the provision of public education in what were perhaps the most far-reaching social measures of the nineteenth century. The administrative apparatus of the state had expanded to provide machinery for monitoring a wide range of social and economic developments – as, for example, in the setting up of a Labour Department at the Board of Trade to collect industrial statistics and advise on labour policy – and at local level municipal authorities in various parts of the country had taken over the running of utilities such as gas and water, in addition to their other duties.[7] Yet although this amounted to a great deal of *de facto* regulation (and the many ways in which the Poor Law, for instance, contributed to public welfare are only now beginning to be fully documented by historians), the arrangements of the Victorian period had come about in a piecemeal, patchwork way. They tended to emphasise the role of local rather than national bodies, and much of the legislation enacted by parliament in the social field was permissive instead of mandatory. The interventionist mood of the early twentieth century placed a much greater emphasis on the state as the prime agent of reform, with less scope for permissive legislation. It was more thoroughgoing, in that intervention was contemplated in areas which had hitherto been outside the remit of the law, such as the regulation of adult male hours of labour or the fixing of minimum wage levels. Finally, there was an important ideological change as well. Whereas, earlier, individualism had been the rule to which intervention was very much the exception, increasingly, from the 1890s, a more collectivist viewpoint began to be adopted, in which state regulation was seen as a natural and necessary means of ordering the life of a complex and interdependent human community.[8]

This is not to say that the interventionist consensus carried all before it. In both major parties, and in the labour movement, there were those who opposed any extension of the power of the state and who stayed loyal to the individualist creed. The Liberty and Property Defence League was founded in 1882 to give expression to their views.[9] Even among 'collectivists' there was far from being a complete identity of view as to what the purpose of intervention should be. Some were altruistically concerned for the welfare of the poor; others saw social reform as a means of appeasing working-class discontent or appealing to a mass electorate that, after 1885, was two-thirds working-class in character. Then again, there were those who stressed primarily the needs of the state itself, who saw interventionist policies as a means of promoting greater social efficiency and enhancing Britain's economic and military competitiveness, for which purpose a healthy, educated, technically-literate workforce was a *sine qua non*.

These categories overlapped and cut across party divisions, but there were discernibly different strands of collectivist thinking which corresponded roughly to socialist, Conservative and Liberal schools. The socialists – who were themselves a diverse amalgam, ranging from doctrinaire, Marxian, Social Democrats to gradualist Fabians to the more socialist-radical adherents of the Independent Labour Party – were committed to using the power of the state to effect genuine social change; in the short term, incremental benefits for the working classes and the poor, in the longer run a more fundamental reorientation of social and economic relations based on greater equality of wealth and the collective ownership of the means of production, distribution and exchange.[10] Of the socialist groups active in the late nineteenth century, the SDF and ILP were vocal propagandists for their cause, and the ILP achieved a small measure of electoral success, but it was the members of the Fabian Society, especially Sidney and Beatrice Webb, who had the most direct impact on public policy through their tactic of 'permeating' the main political parties with their ideas and by virtue of the leading role they played in developing the 'gas and water' socialism of the Progressive majority on the London County Council. The *Fabian Essays in Socialism*, published in 1889, offered one of the first coherent statements of the collectivist case and the Society maintained a steady stream of tracts, pamphlets and reports which made a major contribution to the contemporary debate on social reform.[11]

The Conservative attitude to intervention was similarly positive but differently motivated. There had always been a paternalist strand in Conservative politics which had led to support for social reforms, from the Tory Radicals of the 1830s to the policies of Disraeli's second ministry of 1874–80. Underlying this paternalism was a 'one nation' philosophy which saw it as the duty of the Conservative party to pursue policies which would maximise social cohesion and minimise disruption. In the 1880s and 1890s Tory paternalism was given a new twist by its association with the

Liberal Unionism of Joseph Chamberlain. Chamberlain left the Liberal party in 1886 because of his disagreement with Gladstone's policy of Irish Home Rule. He was anxious, however, to maintain his reputation as a radical social reformer which he had earned as Lord Mayor of Birmingham in the 1870s and as the author of the *Radical Programme* of 1885. Accordingly, while carving out a second career as an ardent imperialist (and as Colonial Secretary in the Salisbury cabinet after 1895), he continued to press for the adoption of interventionist social measures by Unionist governments. From there he constructed a platform which blended state action to tackle social problems at home with a policy of developing the empire overseas, a 'social imperialism' in which the link between the two policies was a scheme for Tariff Reform: the abandonment of Free Trade in favour of a system of preferential duties which would provide funds for social spending while promoting colonial trade and transforming the Empire into a virtually self-sufficient economic bloc.

Imperialism and social reform on the Chamberlainite model were attractive watchwords for turn-of-the-century Britain and they were capable of winning support from some sections of socialist opinion (particularly the Fabians) and (shorn of the controversial proposal for tariffs) from the so-called 'Imperialist' wing of the Liberal party, on which Lord Rosebery, the former Prime Minister, was the most prominent, if not the most politically reliable, figure. Indeed, there was much discussion, at the time of the South African War, of a realignment of parties which would create a 'centre' party with 'National Efficiency' as its rallying cry. Rosebery appeared to suggest as much in a speech at Chesterfield in 1901 (though his precise meaning was obscure) and his stand was welcomed in advance in a panegyric on 'Efficiency' written by Sidney Webb[12], which was published in the *Nineteenth Century* in September of that year. Webb and others sought to stimulate cross-party activity by forming the 'Co-Efficients' club in November 1902, attracting Unionist, Liberal and Fabian members, including leading Liberal Imperialists such as Edward Grey and R. B. Haldane.[13] Chamberlain was not a party to these manoeuvres, however, and it was his decision openly to raise the standard of Tariff Reform in 1903 which scotched any putative realignment before it had properly begun and forced party politics back into their more accustomed channels.

In the event, it was neither the socialist nor the Unionist brands of interventionism which had most impact on the governmental response to poverty in the Edwardian period. For all their attempts to influence policy, the socialists were not able to gain office and their hands remained at one remove from the levers of power. The Unionists were in government for most of the twenty years after 1886 (the Liberal interlude of 1892–5 excepted), but, although they introduced some significant reforms in areas such as education, housing, factory conditions and workmen's compensation, they did not follow a consistently Chamberlainite path. By 1905 their time was running out. Chamberlain's espousal of Tariff Reform had split the Unionist cabinet and reunited the Liberals, hitherto divided over imperialism, in defence of Free Trade. When the Unionist government resigned in December 1905 to allow Campbell-Bannerman to form a minority Liberal administration the way was opened for a general election at which the Liberals won a decisive victory. Thus it was the Liberal party which inherited responsibility for dealing with the problem of poverty and averting the social crisis which some contemporaries feared was imminent.

The Liberal Reforms

The election of 1906, which returned 399 Liberal MPs to Westminster and gave Campbell-Bannerman's government a majority of 128 over all other parties combined, was fought only to a limited extent on the question of social reform.[14] Liberal candidates had mentioned in their speeches and election addresses the need to introduce reforms, as had Conservative candidates and those of the Labour Representation Committee.[15] But the overall result of the election was more of a referendum on ten years of latterly unpopular Unionist rule than a victory for specific Liberal policies. The Liberals did not come to power with a clearly-defined social programme, at least not one that went beyond commitments to educational and temperance reform to satisfy their Nonconformist supporters. Campbell-Bannerman had been very reluctant to give any definite electoral pledges on items of social legislation, for example on measures to combat rising unemployment.[16] Nevertheless, although it could not have been foreseen at their outset, the Liberal ministries which held office between 1906 and 1914 were to be responsible for one of the most concentrated bursts of social-reforming activity ever undertaken by any British government. Some historians would even argue that it was the Edwardian Liberals who 'laid the foundations' of the modern welfare state, making explicit the parallel between the governments of Campbell-Bannerman and Asquith and the Attlee administrations of 1945–51 with which they in many respects invite comparison. Why, then, did the Liberals take up the burden of reform in this way and how significant were their achievements?

The Liberal reforms were partly the product of the growing interventionist consensus. Although Gladstonian Liberals had been wedded in principle to limiting the role of the state, in practice Liberal governments had always been prepared to introduce interventionist measures in cases of proven need. From the late 1880s there had been a conscious move, especially among younger Liberals, towards a more collectivist 'new Liberalism'. The label had been used by the MP L. A. Atherley-Jones as the title for an article in the *Nineteenth Century* in August 1889 in which he had called for the party to pay more attention to improving the material condition of the working classes. In the 1890s, Liberal thinkers, the most prominent of whom were J. A. Hobson and L. T. Hobhouse, had developed a coherent theory of state intervention, employing biological analogies to demonstrate the organic interdependence of the different sections of society and portraying the state as the embodiment of the democratic will of the community.[17] Groups like the Rainbow Circle – a Liberal-socialist discussion group whose members published the short-lived *Progressive Review* – contributed to the practical task of working out priorities for state action. By the early 1900s, even if the New Liberals were not necessarily in the ascendant in Liberal politics, their influence was being felt at all levels of the party and they were well-placed to shape the policies of an incoming Liberal government. They were supported by sections of the Liberal press, including the *Nation* (edited by the former Fabian, H. W. Massingham) and C. P. Scott's *Manchester Guardian*. They had spokesmen in the parliamentary party, particularly among newly-elected MPs such as Herbert Samuel (himself the author of an explanatory treatise on the New Liberalism) and C. F. G. Masterman.[18] There were even ministers in the cabinet – Asquith, Lloyd George and, from 1908, Winston Churchill among them – who were either sympathetic adherents or, in the cases of Churchill and Lloyd George, open advocates of New Liberal ideas.

Ministers, though, were influenced by more than purely ideological considerations. The Liberal government elected in 1906 faced certain party-political imperatives which could not safely be ignored. One was the possibility that unless the Liberals were able to demonstrate conclusively that Free Trade and state-sponsored social legislation were not incompatible there might be an increase in the popularity of Tariff Reform and the Unionists, soundly beaten in 1906, would be presented with an early opportunity to repair their electoral fortunes. A more immediate threat was posed to the Liberals by the newly-formed Labour party. The 29 independent Labour MPs returned in 1906 represented Labour's first real breakthrough in parliamentary terms. It was true that Labour owed its gains mainly to the working of an electoral pact with the Liberals, but this did not prevent the party from challenging the government at by-elections and taking an independent line in the Commons. The Liberals lost two seats to Labour and socialist candidates at by-elections in 1907 and Liberal leaders were consequently only too well aware of the price they risked paying if they alienated Labour altogether by neglecting the work of social reform.

Other, more general, factors also came into play. One of the features of Victorian Britain had been the steady expansion of government activity and the consequent development of an 'administrative tradition' of reform which brought about incremental enlargements of the interventionist role of the state regardless of the party complexion of the ministry of the day. Civil servants and Whitehall experts were to have an important behind-the-scenes function in shaping the Liberal government's welfare programme. Nor were the turn-of-the-century concerns about 'national efficiency' absent from ministerial thinking. Lloyd George was only one of the Liberal ministers to be impressed, when he visited that country in 1908, by the competitive advantages which Germany seemed to enjoy by virtue of the advanced social welfare system established in the late nineteenth century. Churchill was another member of the Asquith cabinet who wrote privately of the need to 'thrust a big slice of Bismarckianism over the whole underside of our industrial system'.[19]

The differing pressures and motivations at work on the Liberal government were well illustrated by the social reforms introduced in the first two years of its period in office. In 1906 a Workmen's Compensation Act gave additional rights to workers injured in the course of their employment. This was an extension of earlier legislation, the Employers' Liability Act of 1880 and the Workmen's Compensation Act of 1897, the former introduced by a Liberal, the latter by a Conservative government. It was also part of an attempt to conciliate Labour opinion. A similar conciliatory motive can be seen in the passage of the Mines Eight Hours Act in 1908, the gratification of a long-standing demand for an eight-hour day on the part of the Miners' Federation, which had been campaigning for the measure since the late 1880s. Other reforms, notably those affecting children, revealed a different set of considerations. True, the School Meals Act of 1906, which empowered local authorities to pay for the feeding of school children from the rates, was originally tabled as a Private Member's Bill by a Labour MP, but it reflected the concerns over the health of the population which were part of the debate over national efficiency in the early 1900s and followed the recommendations of the Report on Physical Deterioration of 1904. The establishment of a School Medical Service in 1907 showed the same concern, as did some of the provisions of the Children's Act (the so-called 'Children's Charter') of 1908, although in the case of the former it should be noted that the main impetus behind the Act came not from ministers but from civil servants at the Board of Education, especially the Board's secretary, R. L. Morant.

A more decisive ministerial input was apparent in what was the most important of the social reforms introduced in the first phase of the Liberal government's life, namely the Old Age Pensions Act of 1908. Opinion had been gathering for some time in favour of a pension scheme. Booth and Rowntree had demonstrated that old age was one of the principal causes of poverty. Statistics in 1906 proved that whereas only three per thousand of the population aged between 15 and 25 were in receipt of poor relief, the figure for those aged 65–75 was 163 per thousand, and for those over 75, 276 per thousand.[20] Although the Royal Commission on the Aged Poor had failed to recommend state pensions in 1895, its position had been reversed by a parliamentary select committee in 1899, and Joseph Chamberlain had committed the Unionist party to a pension scheme, only to see the necessary funds swallowed up by the cost of the South African War. Pensions were a major issue at the election of 1906, however (even if social reform in general was not), and Asquith, the Liberal Chancellor of the Exchequer, promised that the new government would introduce proposals as soon as financial conditions permitted. Provision was duly made in the 1907 budget and in 1908 the Pensions Act was finally introduced, its parliamentary progress being entrusted to Lloyd George, who replaced Asquith at the Treasury on the latter's becoming Prime Minister. A weekly pension of five shillings was to be paid to all those over the age of 70 whose annual income was under £26, with smaller sums (on a sliding scale down to one shilling) going to those with incomes between £26 and £31 per annum. A contributory scheme was rejected, pensions being funded directly from general taxation, with no loss of citizen's rights on the part of the recipient, thus avoiding the social stigma that still surrounded much of the operation of the Poor Law.

The successful enactment of old age pensions, coinciding with Asquith's reversion to the premiership (following Campbell-Bannerman's resignation on grounds of ill-health), is usually seen as marking a change in the tempo of Liberal legislation. This is only partly true. The Liberals had attempted to introduce other reforms in 1906–8 – in education, land-holding, licensing – but these had been blocked by the House of Lords.[21] What the introduction of pensions really represented was a shift of emphasis rather than a change of tempo, a redirection rather than a rediscovery of reforming zeal. Asquith and Lloyd George were key figures in this process. So too was Winston Churchill, who, after only four years in parliament, had broken with the Unionist party in 1904 in protest against plans for Tariff Reform, joined the Liberals and served as under-secretary of state for the colonies before being promoted to succeed Lloyd George as President of the Board of Trade in 1908. Churchill had thrown himself with the enthusiasm of a convert into the development of the Liberal party's social programme and was one of the party leadership's most articulate exponents of the ideas of the New Liberalism, exemplified by his famous letter to the *Nation* in March 1908 in which he outlined his concept of the 'Minimum Standard' of social provision, 'below which competition cannot be allowed, but above which it may continue healthy and free, to vivify and fertilize the world'.[22]

Churchill was given an early opportunity in his new post to tackle two of the issues he had singled out in his *Nation* letter, low wages and the problems of unemployment and the labour market. The first was addressed by the passage of the 1909 Trade Boards Act, which set up committees of workers and employers, under independent chairmanship, in a number of 'sweated industries' such as tailoring, lace-making and chain-making to determine minimum wage rates for the industries concerned.[23] Again this was a response to a long campaign of agitation, led, among others, by the Liberal MP Sir Charles Dilke, to secure better conditions for poorly-paid, mainly women, workers. It was significant for being the first time that the government had intervened directly to influence the level of wages, a legislative precedent which was drawn upon in 1912 when the government introduced a Minimum Wage Act for the coal mines. The other measure with which Churchill was concerned in 1909 was an Act for setting up Labour Exchanges, where employers could recruit workers and the unemployed could register in the hope of securing employment. The scheme, the details of which owed much to William Beveridge, then a civil servant at the Board of Trade, was neither universal nor compulsory, but it was an important attempt to rationalise the labour market and to help the unemployed. It showed that the government was sensitive to the need to take action in the face of rising unemployment (although in fact the levels of unemployment, which rose sharply in 1908–9, were falling again by 1910), even if ministers were not prepared to offer guarantees of the 'Right to Work' which were being demanded by the Labour party.[24]

Important though they were, however, Churchill's reforms were overshadowed by the other major measure of 1909, Lloyd George's 'People's Budget'. Lloyd George, as Chancellor, was faced with the task of funding not only an expanding range of social commitments (pensions alone cost £8 million in their first year of operation) but also an expensive programme of naval rearmament to meet the threat posed by Germany. His strategy, approved by the Prime Minister, Asquith, was characteristically bold. In addition to raising a variety of indirect taxes on articles such as spirits, tobacco and petrol, he proposed the introduction of a new, progressive, system of income tax. There was to be a sliding scale of taxation, ranging from ninepence to 1s and 2d in the pound depending on the total taxable income, plus an extra 'supertax' of sixpence in the pound on incomes over £3,000 for those whose total income was in excess of £5,000 a year. More controversial even than this was a plan to tax the unearned increment from land, by devices such as a tax on land sales, a capital levy on unused land and taxes on mining royalties. As will be seen, these proposals aroused considerable political clamour, and it was not until 1910 that the bulk of Lloyd George's budget became law. But, in a sense, the 1909 budget was the hinge upon which the social reform programme of the New Liberalism turned. It established the principle of using the budget as a means of raising finance for new areas of state spending, and of redistributing wealth from the better to the less well-off. It provided the funding engine without which further attempts to combat the problems of poverty could not have been contemplated.

As it was, the People's Budget was the prelude to arguably the most ambitious of the Liberal government's welfare reforms, the National Insurance Act of 1911. Part I of the Act, which was the brainchild of Lloyd George and his advisers, established a contributory scheme of health insurance for workers who, in return for a payment of fourpence per week (matched by three-pence from their employers and twopence from the state), would receive ten shillings per week if unable to work because of sickness, plus medical treatment. The Act had to be implemented against initial opposition from the medical profession and from trade unions and friendly societies which already offered private schemes of medical insurance, but it was a further attempt to alleviate the causes of poverty identified by earlier social surveys and to reduce losses to industry arising from workers' illness. Part II of the 1911 Act, originally conceived during Churchill's tenure at the Board of Trade although not introduced until he had been moved to other cabinet posts, dealt with the effects of unemployment by offering a similar contributory insurance scheme for workers in industries such as building, engineering and shipbuilding which had a recurring problem of cyclical unemployment. Payments from the insurance fund were small (seven shillings per week) and temporary, but offered an improvement on previous lack of provision. Lloyd George's 1909 budget had also ear-marked funds for a national Development Plan, involving afforestation schemes and other public works, which held out the prospect of useful work for the unemployed, going beyond the local initiatives sponsored by the Balfour government's Unemployed Workmen Act of 1905. Nor was this the final shot in Lloyd George's locker. By the autumn of 1913 he was ready to embark on a further campaign of land reform to ensure im-proved living conditions, including a minimum wage, for agricul-tural labourers, and rating reform in the towns to open the way for improvements in urban housing, although both plans ran into trouble in 1914 and were postponed by the outbreak of war.[25]

The reforms of 1906–14 were a considerable legislative achieve-ment. They established new levels of state responsibility – for the welfare of the old, the young, the sick and the unemployed – and new principles of public finance. Though in one sense the measures represented a series of piecemeal improvisations and practical compromises, they had enough coherence of form and purpose to be considered as part of a single programme. They were a tangible embodiment of the interventionist consensus which had been growing in strength since the 1880s and a conscientious attempt to deal with some of the problems revealed by the social surveys at the end of Victoria's reign. If they did not result immediately in the creation of a 'welfare state' of the comprehensive kind established in the 1940s, they were certainly a decisive step away from the Poor Law mentality of the nineteenth century.

Politically, the measures demonstrated the capacity of the Liberal party to adapt itself to the demands of twentieth-century social politics without abandoning any of its underlying aims and beliefs. Free Trade remained the cornerstone of its economic policies. Interventionist measures had been introduced, but the state was only stepping in to do what individuals had been unable to do for themselves. Intervention to supplement individual initiative rather than replace it altogether was perfectly compatible with traditional Gladstonian principles of government, while the limited redistribution of wealth through taxation and social reform could easily be justified by a redefinition of Liberalism to accommodate the realisation, as Churchill put it, that 'political freedom, however precious, is utterly incomplete without a measure at least of social and economic independence'.[26] This was the message that Hobhouse, Hobson and others had been spreading since the 1890s, together with an insistence that social reforms would benefit the whole community, not just those in receipt of 'welfare', because of the greater general wellbeing and prosperity that would result. Thus the Liberalism of 1906–14 was different in detail from that of 20 or 30 years earlier, but its essential goals of individual liberty and social harmony remained the same. Lloyd George's Land Campaign of 1913–14 was an indication that the momentum of reform was far from exhausted. As the election of 1915 approached, the question was whether the reforms had won sufficient popular support to avert the threat of an impending social crisis and secure for the Liberals a further term of office in which to carry out the next stage of their plans.

A Social Crisis?

In order to make a judgement as to whether Edwardian society was indeed moving towards some kind of crisis in the years before 1914 it is necessary to place the growth of governmental welfarism in a wider context. The reforms introduced by the Liberal ministries were intended to reduce social tensions by attacking the problem of poverty, improving the efficiency of the labour market and redressing some of the deep-rooted imbalances of wealth and opportunity inherited from the Victorian era. How successful were the reforms in achieving their objectives and what conclusions can be reached about their impact in relation to the social trends at work in Britain on the eve of the First World War?

The impact of the Liberal reforms is difficult to gauge because they were by no means fully operational by the time war broke out. The health and unemployment insurance schemes, for example, were not fully launched until 1913 and their effectiveness cannot therefore be properly judged. Workers may have noticed immediate benefits from the availability of medical treatment and sick pay (though initially treatment did not extend to all members of the worker's family), but unemployment was in any case low in the immediate pre-war years and the main feature of the insurance fund was a steadily-accruing surplus which was not called upon to finance large-scale payments. It cannot be known with any certainty whether the scheme could have coped unaided with a serious depression in any of the major industries which it covered.[27] In other respects, though, more positive conclusions can be reached about the results of the reform programme. Old age pensions were immediately popular and there was a bigger than anticipated take-up. By 1914, 970,000 people were receiving pensions, at an annual cost to the Treasury of over £12 million. There was a reduction in the number of elderly people claiming poor relief, and the total number of paupers in England and Wales fell from 916,377 (2.6 per cent of the population) in 1910 to 748,000 (2.0 per cent) in 1914.[28] At the other end of the age scale, there were signs that improvements in child health and maternity provision (especially the improved training for midwives following the 1902 Midwives Act and the maternity benefits available under the National Insurance Act of 1911) were having some effect, with a noticeable fall in infant mortality rates, from 163 per thousand in 1899 to 95 per thousand in 1912. Better provision for the young and old, together with greater security for the sick and unemployed, had thus at least to some extent been achieved and the Liberals could justifiably claim that they had gone some way towards addressing each of the principal causes of poverty identified by Booth, Rowntree and others in the late nineteenth century.

That said, the Liberal reforms were at best only a small step along what was bound to be a long and difficult road. Despite measures such as the Trade Boards Act of 1909 and the miners' Minimum Wage Act of 1912, wages for many groups of workers remained stubbornly low. A. L. Bowley calculated that in 1911 32 per cent of all adult males earned less than 25 shillings a week.[29] Agricultural labourers, as the Liberal party's enquiry into rural poverty discovered, were a particularly low-paid group, in some cases earning as little as ten to fourteen shillings a week. Lloyd George's land campaign might have done something to remedy the situation, but its proposals had not been implemented before 1914. Similarly, there were still large numbers of workers (indeed a large majority, including millions of women workers) who were not covered by the unemployment insurance provisions. It would have been unrealistic to have expected the government's policies to have done more than scratch the surface of the poverty problem in the time available to them, and the surveys carried out in the later years of Edwardian Britain, such as Mrs Pember Reeves' classic study, *Round About A Pound A Week* (1913), show this to have been very much the case. Poverty and hardship remained deeply engrained facts of working-class life, on which government action had as yet had no more than a marginal effect.

On the other hand, both the extent of poverty and the ability of government to alleviate it must be kept in perspective, and in considering whether things were getting better or worse a useful distinction can be made between long-term and short-term trends. Put crudely, even if 30 per cent of the population were in 'poverty' (as opposed to the more extreme measure of pauperism), 70 per cent were not. The figures for those in primary, or absolute, poverty were proportionately smaller, about 10–12 per cent depending on economic conditions, which meant that up to 90 per cent of the population had sufficient income to maintain what Rowntree described as 'physical efficiency'. In this and other ways it could be argued that conditions for the mass of the population were improving decisively when compared with those of the mid-Victorian and late-Victorian periods. Long-term improvements in the quality of housing provide a case in point. Although one estimate put the number of people in 'over-crowded' (though not necessarily insanitary) accommodation at about three million in 1913, this represented fewer than one in ten of the population, a smaller figure than would have been recorded 30 or 50 years earlier, and one which measures like the Town Planning Act of 1909 and the rating reforms proposed in the 1914 budget were designed to reduce still further by facilitating slum clearance and stimulating local authority building schemes.[30]

In a sense, long-term advances like this were at the heart of the short-term political problem. The general increase in the standard of living in the late nineteenth century, at least for those in regular employment, had generated rising expectations about the level of future comfort, expectations which were fuelled by the more consumer-orientated retail culture of the 1890s and 1900s. Not only had this led to more subtle calculations of 'relative' as opposed to absolute poverty; it had also created an assumption of continuing improvement for individuals and their families of the kind that the Victorians had entertained for the economy as a whole. In the Edwardian period, however, these expectations were frustrated as far as many wage-earners were concerned by the onset of a prolonged bout of price inflation. Whereas from the 1860s to the mid-1890s falling prices had enabled workers to enjoy an increase in real income even if the money value of their wages was falling, from the late 1890s this trend was reversed. Wages continued to rise by an average of about one per cent per annum, but their real value was undercut by a faster rise in prices which threatened working-class living standards. It has been estimated that the cost of living rose by about 23 per cent between 1896 and 1913, with the rate of increase climbing in the later part of the period to about 2.3 per cent a year in each of the years 1909–13.[31] As prices were outstripping wages, this resulted in an effective decrease in real wages for many workers, although of course there were occupational and regional variations to the pattern and ways in which earnings could be supplemented or increased by overtime, promotion and job mobility.

The discontent arising from thwarted expectations and tightened belts was probably a more potent force in the political arena than that produced by absolute poverty, if only because the wage-earners whose ambitions were most at risk were more likely to be organised for industrial or political action.[32] By the same token, their grievances were less likely to be susceptible to a direct political remedy. There was little the government could do to influence the general level of wages or to control price inflation. Under a Free Trade regime, and given the absence of any tradition of economic management, market forces had to be relied on to reduce the pressure on working-class incomes as falling unemployment increased the demand for labour. Much was made of the importance of Free Trade in keeping food prices as low as possible. Some measures, as has been seen, were introduced to protect more vulnerable groups and to lubricate the operation of the labour market. The government's industrial policies also gave maximum freedom to the trade unions to strengthen the position of their members through collective bargaining, but more extreme interference with the working of the economy was considered neither feasible nor desirable.[33]

It is perhaps surprising that the adverse economic trends did not produce more reflexive calls for state action. The government was criticised in some quarters for not doing more in the battle against poverty. For instance, the 1909 Minority Report of the

Royal Commission on the Poor Laws (drafted by the Webbs, Beatrice having been a Commission member) called, among other things, for the break-up of the existing Poor Law, the creation of a Ministry of Labour and a massive extension of welfare services under the aegis of local authorities.[34] Tariff Reformers argued that the adoption of protection would aid economic recovery and boost employment. But the demands for intervention from the working classes and their spokesmen were much more selective. Some groups of workers, notably the miners, had used their political muscle (and/or industrial action) to bring about state intervention, as in the Mines Eight Hours Act of 1908 and the Minimum Wage Act of 1912.[35] Since the 1880s there had been a succession of campaigns to secure better governmental provision for the unemployed, from the demonstrations organised by the SDF in 1886–7 to the Labour party's 'Right to Work' campaign in the 1900s. Yet, as Henry Pelling and others have pointed out, these specific calls for intervention were more than balanced by working-class suspicion of, and even hostility towards, the state and its works.[36] This was partly because of the engrained individualism of sections of the working class, especially the artisans and skilled workers, who cherished Victorian ideas of independence and self-help. (The success of the Co-operative movement, which had 2.8 million members by 1913, was a testimony to the capacity of the working classes to organise collectively for their own benefit, without state aid.) There was also resistance to what could be seen as the coercive aspect of interventionism, either because it threatened working-class freedom or because it represented an extension of middle-class social control. The Poor Laws had always been unpopular because of the stigma attached to pauperism and the ideology of deterrence which they embodied. State education was received with hostility in some quarters, both because it was seen as a form of social conditioning and because it prevented children from working to supplement family incomes. The insurance schemes introduced by the Liberal government were similarly unpopular, at least initially, because of their compulsory character. Neither the government's extensive propaganda effort, nor Lloyd George's assurance that beneficiaries would receive 'ninepence for fourpence', could entirely counteract the belief that the measures were a form of disguised taxation from which most workers would get little return.[37]

It would probably be going too far to suggest that the working class was united in its opposition to state-sponsored social legislation, but there was enough scepticism among working-class voters for the introduction of such measures to be less than a panacea for electoral success. Meanwhile, the government had to be careful not to antagonise other members of the community, particularly those whom Money had characterised as the 'comfortable' middle classes, who were required to help finance the reforms by paying higher taxes. The middle classes had been expanding and diversifying throughout the second half of the nineteenth century and the process continued into the twentieth, the growth being especially pronounced among the 'suburban' middle classes, clerks, office-workers, junior managers and professionals. The better-off among these groups had incomes which put them well above the income tax threshold (and the rest would aspire to this position or, crucially, might be marginal tax payers), while the bulk of the working classes, the main targets of social reform, were likely to fall below it. At a time when the level of public spending was twice what it had been 20 years earlier (£272 million in 1910 as against £133 million in 1890) and the proportion of revenue raised by direct taxation had increased from about 44 per cent in the 1880s to 60 per cent by 1914, the redistributive aspects of Liberal welfare policy were clearly apparent.[38] Despite the argument of welfare publicists and politicians that all classes benefited, directly or indirectly, from reforms (because of the consequent improvements in the nation's health and efficiency), it was only to be expected that there would be some form of middle-class backlash, and that organisations like the Middle Classes Defence League would spring into existence to protect middle-class interests against the depredations of a spendthrift government.

Does this mean, as some historians have contended, that these years saw an approaching 'crisis of class society', with growing solidarity within classes and increasing antagonism between them as their interests and outlooks came into more direct conflict?[39]

The idea of a separation of classes into two potentially hostile camps was not new. In the 1840s, in his novel *Sybil*, Disraeli had drawn attention to the deepening gulf between 'the two nations', the rich and the poor. Marx and Engels had made the same point, and stressed its revolutionary implications, in *The Communist Manifesto*, published in 1848. Although by the late nineteenth century revisionist Socialists in Europe were moving away from the dogmatism of early Marxist beliefs, in material terms the contrast between wealth and poverty had been perpetuated into the late Victorian and Edwardian periods and seemed, in some respects, to be getting wider. In his book, *The Condition of England* (1909), C. F. G. Masterman wrote that 'even national distinctions seem less estranging than the fissure between the summit and the base of society'.[40] Other commentators were fearful of what Lord Rosebery referred to as the 'cleavage of classes' that was occurring in Britain, a development which threatened to destroy the spirit of class collaboration which had supposedly been the foundation of social stability in the mid-Victorian era.

Certainly important changes were taking place which may have made class conflict, or a conflict of interests between classes, more likely. The process of urbanisation continued, with over three-quarters of the population living in towns by 1911 and, in the larger cities and most other towns, a clear distinction existed between middle-class and working-class districts – a division further reflected in the political structure by the creation of single-member, and often therefore single-class, constituencies following the Redistribution Act of 1885. The middle classes were more numerous and better organised than in the nineteenth century, accounting for nearly a quarter of the total population, and, as the debate over taxation showed, those at the lower end of the middle-class income scale were keen to preserve the advantages of wealth and status which separated them from the working class majority.[41] Here, too, there were anxieties generated by the wider concern over national 'degeneracy'. The population of Edwardian Britain was still rising (from 37 million in 1901 to 40. 9 million in 1911), but the birth rate was falling. There were fears, though, that the fall was more marked among the middle classes than in the population as a whole (because of

their more widespread recourse to birth control) and that consequently they, and the more 'respectable' skilled workers who
followed their lead, risked being 'swamped' by the poorer,
'degenerate' classes. The other side of the coin was the working-
class perception, partially confirmed by statistical evidence, that
middle- and upper-class incomes were rising more rapidly than
those of the labouring masses (a belief encouraged by the
conspicuous spending of wealthier Edwardians on items such as
motor cars) and also that upward mobility into the middle class
was becoming more difficult. The spread of socialist ideas, the
upsurge of labour agitation and the rise of the Labour party,
together with the general atmosphere of questioning social concern which characterised Edwardian life brought the differences
between the classes more sharply into focus and suggested an
opposition of interests which the leaders of Victorian society had
always been at pains to deny.

Yet this heightened awareness of class interests did not necessarily presage a 'crisis', nor did it seem that there was any real
danger of a serious breakdown in social relations, despite alarmist
talk in some quarters. In many respects British society in the early
twentieth century was remarkably free from the kind of tur-
bulence that disfigured less stable countries such as Italy or
Tsarist Russia. There was comparatively little social violence,
crime rates were low and there seemed an instinctive respect for
the institutions of authority, from the monarchy down. Just as in
the crisis of adaptation in the early nineteenth century the
country had evolved a framework for managing change, so in the
opening years of the twentieth century that framework held firm.
There were powerful factors making for stability in spite of the
fast pace of change and temporary economic uncertainties.
Family life remained strong, the 'respectability' of the Victorian
middle classes spreading through most of society (except perhaps
at the very top and the very bottom of the social scale). Institutional religion may have passed its peak, but it too remained a
stabilising factor, while the arrival of universal elementary education also assisted the maintenance of social discipline. Alongside
the mechanisms of social control provided by the schools and the
churches, there were diversions for the potentially frustrated

working classes in the various types of leisure activity that were becoming increasingly common; music halls, spectator sport (particularly Association Football), seaside holidays, the cinema. There may have been, indeed there was, a separation of classes in terms of patterns of life, labour and experience, but this was almost an agreed divergence rather than a cause of antagonism or active grievance. The scope for outright confrontation was in any case lessened by the differentiation within classes, which weakened their solidarity, and by other factors such as denominational, regional and patriotic loyalties which brought classes together, as well as by the fact that, even allowing for the economic problems of the period, there was still an underlying faith in the possibilities of improvement, for individual and nation alike. In that sense, class harmony remained a stronger feeling than class war.[42]

It was this feeling of community, and communal endeavour, that the politicians of the time were striving to reinforce by the various strategies of integration which they adopted. Chamberlain attempted to combine popular imperialism with the promise of economic prosperity through Tariff Reform. The 'National Efficiency' movement was intended to promote strength abroad and social and economic improvement at home. So, too, the New Liberalism and the welfare reforms of the Liberal ministries sought to draw upon a basic unity of interest to raise the condition of the people and prevent the estrangement of classes which they believed might otherwise occur. To say that the reformers succeeded is to imply that had they not acted as they did some sort of cataclysm might have resulted, and this is by no means self-evidently the case. Indeed, in the short term the impact of higher taxation and the hostility aroused by increased state intervention may actually have exacerbated rather than assuaged class tensions, to say nothing of weakening the popularity of the government. Yet if there were no immediately tangible benefits in improved social cohesion, what is important in the longer run is that there had been a public recognition of the seriousness of the problems of poverty in Edwardian society and that those problems were being addressed, however tentatively, through the normal political process. As in the Victorian age, Edwardian Britain was showing itself capable of managing its affairs without recourse to anything more revolutionary than Royal Commissions and Acts of Parliament. Much of course remained to be done, particularly for the poorest sections of society, and there was always the danger that the size of the task would dwarf the resources or the resolve of the government. But at least between 1901 and 1914 the possibility of progress had been reaffirmed and the infrastructure of social support significantly strengthened. The Liberal reforms may not in themselves have prevented a social crisis, but they did perhaps make it less likely that one would occur.

2

THE CONSTITUTIONAL CRISIS, 1909–11

The Liberal government's attempt to find a solution to the problem of poverty through fiscal reform brought to a head a long-maturing conflict between the Liberal party and the House of Lords. When the Lords rejected Lloyd George's 'People's Budget' in November 1909, they ushered in a period of fierce political controversy which included two hard-fought general elections in 1910 and culminated in the struggle over the terms of the Parliament Act of 1911. In the course of this controversy, the futures of the government, the House of Lords, and even of the monarchy, were all, at various times, placed in jeopardy. Even the resolution of the crisis by the passage of the Parliament Act did not end altogether the political and constitutional turmoil, which continued to influence public affairs until the outbreak of war in 1914. This chapter will examine the origins of the constitutional crisis, describe the course which it took and discuss its outcome. In assessing its significance, an attempt will be made to decide whether, as Dangerfield believed, the crisis was symptomatic of growing extremism and loss of control in public life, or whether, for all its undoubted ferocity, it represented an ultimate victory for the parliamentary system of government and the values of democratic debate.

The Liberals and the Lords

The conflict between the Liberals and the House of Lords had long antecedents. Its history can be traced back well into the nineteenth century, if not earlier. The Glorious Revolution of 1688 and the Revolution Settlement of 1689 had accorded parliament a permanent place in the government of the country, and, in the eighteenth century, Whig constitutional theorists had celebrated the mechanism of 'checks and balances' which regulated the tripartite relations of Crown, Lords and Commons. Yet, notwithstanding occasional clashes between Crown and parliament (as, for example, in the early years of the reign of George III), what had really been established by these changes was a system of aristocratic government, with the great landed families controlling not merely the House of Lords but, through influence, patronage and pocket boroughs, much of the membership of the House of Commons as well. In the 1780s and 1790s, and again from the last years of the Napoleonic Wars, this system was challenged from without, as the campaign for parliamentary reform gathered strength. But, although in the 'Reform Crisis' of 1830–32 the House of Lords was compelled, under threat of a creation of new peers, to accept the first Reform Act, extending the franchise and abolishing the most rotten of the rotten boroughs, the early Victorian political system remained basically aristocratic in structure.[1] The House of Lords retained wide formal powers, including its legislative veto; the informal power of the aristocracy – as reflected in the membership of cabinets and in other ways which manifested their position as a natural governing class – was alike considerable. The reforming impetus of radicalism, and even spectacular successes such as the repeal of the Corn Laws in 1846, could assail this dominance but could not overturn it. Indeed, the political stability on which the mid-Victorians prided themselves stemmed in no small measure from the success with which the aristocratic leaders of the political world were able to resist pressure from more democratic forces, or at least channel it for their own purposes.

There were some disputes between Lords and Commons in the mid-nineteenth century – the rejection by the Lords of Gladstone's Paper Duties Bill in 1860 being perhaps the best known example[2] – but such instances were infrequent, partly because members of both Houses shared similar social backgrounds and political ideas, partly because the balance of parties in the House of Lords was broadly the same as that in the House of Commons, reflecting the strong position of the Whig–Liberal–Peelite coalitions which held office in the Palmerston years.[3] In the later nineteenth century, however, the situation underwent a dramatic alteration in two respects. First, the franchise reforms and the other democratising changes of the post-1867 period revived the inherent tensions between 'popular' and 'aristocratic' approaches to politics, reinforcing the moral authority of the House of Commons while making it less aristocratic in character. Aristocratic influence over the composition of the Commons declined, moreover, at the same time as the position of the traditional aristocracy was beginning to be undermined in other ways by economic and social trends, particularly a fall in landed incomes from the late 1870s. A second and not unrelated development, therefore, was that in the more polarised political world of late-Victorian Britain the House of Lords shifted markedly to the right in terms of its party allegiance, becoming pronouncedly more Conservative and showing a greater predisposition to defend the interests of its members by resisting radical measures proposed by the Gladstonian Liberals. In the early 1870s, the Lords opposed the introduction of the secret ballot for parliamentary elections and the abolition of the purchase of commissions in the armed forces. During Gladstone's second ministry of 1880–85 the Conservatives in the House of Lords refused to allow the Franchise Bill of 1884 to become law unless it was accompanied by a parallel measure for the redistribution of seats.

The events of 1885–6 increased the anti-Liberal bias of the Lords by depriving the Liberal party of the support of most of the Whig peers. Already unhappy with the thrust of Gladstonian policy towards Ireland, especially with the 1881 Land Act which they saw as a prelude to a more general assault on landed property, a majority of the Whigs backed Lord Hartington and Joseph Chamberlain in their opposition to Gladstone's first Irish Home Rule Bill of 1886. They broke with Gladstone to form their own Liberal Unionist party, supporting the Salisbury government of 1886–92 and joining the Conservatives to form a Unionist coalition in 1895. The consequences of this transfer of loyalties were made abundantly clear by the experience of the Liberal ministries of 1892–5. In 1893, the Liberals' second Home Rule Bill was rejected by the Lords by the overwhelming majority of 419 votes to 41, despite having been given a second reading by the House of Commons. Other Liberal reforms were also obstructed or, like the Employers' Liability Bill of the same year, so badly amended by the Lords that they had to be withdrawn. The Liberals, for their part, were by this time committed, under the terms of the Newcastle Programme of 1891, to the 'mending or ending' of the House of Lords, since it was plain that unless the Upper House was deprived of its veto, or in some other way reformed (if not abolished altogether), the work of an elected Liberal majority in the Commons could always be set at nought by an unelected Conservative majority in the Lords. Both Gladstone and his successor Lord Rosebery favoured Lords reform, but Gladstone's colleagues were unwilling to fight an election on the issue of the veto in 1893 and Rosebery's government had fallen from power before he could offer practical schemes to give effect to his ideas.

The quiescence of the Lords between 1895 and 1905, when a Unionist government was in office, emphasised that the conflict between Lords and Commons was a party-political as much as a constitutional one, even if the Lords were always scrupulous to ground their opposition to Liberal measures in constitutional form. Nor was the possibility of confrontation substantially lessened by the landslide nature of the Liberal election victory in 1906. Admittedly the Liberals could claim a much stronger popular mandate than in the 1890s. They were no longer dependent on the Irish Nationalist MPs as they had been in 1892–5, but had in their own right an absolute majority of seats in the Commons, as well as more votes in the country than the Conservative and Liberal Unionist parties combined. The Unionists had been decisively rejected at the polls. Yet, in another way, the results of the election were less decisive than they appeared. In the House of Lords, the new government's position was fragile in the extreme. Only 88 of the 602 peers formally accepted the Liberal whip, as against 355 Conservatives and 124 Liberal Unionists.[4] When the Conservative leader, Balfour, declared in a speech at Nottingham on 15 January 1906 that 'the great Unionist Party should still control, whether in power or whether in opposition, the destinies of this great Empire', his words were no empty boast.[5] It soon became clear that the Lords were as likely to use their powers to frustrate the efforts of Liberal legislators in the new parliament as they had been in previous years, regardless of the risk of provoking a crisis in the relations between the two Houses and between the opposition and the government.

The strategy which the Unionist leaders adopted was nevertheless carefully contrived and selective in its application of the Lords' powers. Balfour and Lansdowne, the Unionist leader in the Lords, reserved the stiffest opposition for those measures which, it could be argued, were only of sectional concern and which they felt did not command majority support among the voters. They were also keen not to antagonise Labour opinion, or that of the working class voters generally. So, despite some criticism of its provisions, the Trades Disputes Bill introduced to reverse the effects of the Taff Vale Judgement was allowed to pass.[6] The 1906 Education Bill, on the other hand, which the Liberals had made the centrepiece of their legislative programme for the first session of the new parliament, was so amended in the Lords as to be rendered useless to its purpose. Politically this was intensely damaging to the government. Nonconformist resistance to the 1902 Education Act (which, by abolishing School Boards and placing education in all districts under the county and county borough councils had resulted in rate subsidies for Anglican schools offering denominational teaching) had been one of the main factors behind the Liberal triumph at the general election. The failure of the 1906 Bill, designed as it was to restrict denominational teaching and place Church schools in single-school areas more firmly under impartial control, was a major blow to Nonconformist hopes. Since the Nonconformists were, at this time, the backbone of the Liberal party, but at the same time a minority among the electorate at large, the destruction of the Bill by the Lords was a shrewd manoeuvre by the opposition, calculated to cause maximum embarrassment to the government in its dealings with its own supporters without arousing a general outcry against the action of the Lords on the part of ordinary voters.

The Liberal response to the loss of the Education Bill was defiant but ineffectual. The cabinet decided against an immediate dissolution, preferring to wait for a more favourable issue on which to challenge the Lords.[7] Campbell-Bannerman did introduce a series of resolutions in the Commons in favour of restricting the Lords' veto in June 1907, but although the Commons approved their sentiment by 432 votes to 147 no attempt was made to give it statutory effect. In the meantime, the government suffered further reverses. A Plural Voting Bill was defeated in 1906. In 1907, two Scottish Land Bills were so badly amended by the Lords that they had to be withdrawn. In 1908, a Licensing Bill, intended to appeal to the Temperance lobby by restricting the number of public houses, was vetoed by Unionist peers protecting the interests of their party's allies, the brewers. It is true that these measures were only part of the Liberal government's programme and that it had compensating achievements to its credit: old age pensions, the children's legislation, the Mines Eight Hours Act, Lloyd George's reforms at the Board of Trade. But in a number of important areas – and on subjects, crucially, about which the Liberal party's traditional supporters cared most deeply – the government's record in its first two years of office was rendered barren by the obstructive actions of the House of Lords.

This, then, was the background to the introduction of the 'People's Budget' in 1909. It was not the case that the government framed the budget specifically to court its rejection by the House of Lords. There was no precedent for such a rejection and ministers did not believe that the Lords would dare to flout constitutional convention by challenging the Commons' traditional supremacy in matters of finance. This view had received recent confirmation in the Lords' handling of the Old Age Pensions Bill in 1908. There had been some Unionist opposition to its proposals, but, because it was interpreted as being a money Bill, the Unionist leaders in the Lords forebore from amending it. But, even if ministerial expectations were that the budget would be allowed to pass, this in no way lessened its political significance. It was vital in 1909–10 for the government to raise additional revenue to pay for pensions and naval rearmament, and the new Chancellor, Lloyd George, chose to do this in such a way as to derive maximum party advantage by undoing some of the damage done by the Lords' rejection of earlier measures. His increased taxes on spirits, for example, while perfectly justifiable as a revenue-raising ploy, were also an attempt to achieve the objectives of the defunct Licensing Bill by other means. His proposals for a more progressive taxation of incomes (including a supertax) and for land valuation and land taxes were a subtle blending of the 'Old' Liberalism and the New, calculated to appeal to most sections of the party's followers. The Liberals were moving away from some of the accepted canons of Gladstonian finance, in order, as Lloyd George put it, to wage war on 'poverty and squalidness'. At the same time they were moving forward on the path of land reform, which had been central to all schemes of radical reconstruction since the 1880s and was widely supported even by the Gladstonians in the party. If the budget was carried, the chances were that it would boost the morale of the government's supporters in the Commons, rekindle enthusiasm in the constituencies and provide a springboard for further social reforms such as health and unemployment insurance to which Lloyd George and other New Liberals were committed.

Seen in this light, the budget appears to have been more a way of circumventing the Lords' veto than of forcing its use. But this, in turn, made it a more serious threat to the opposition and to the Unionist leaders. By 1908–9 the Unionist parties were showing signs of recovery from their catastrophic defeat of 1906. In 1908 they made seven by-election gains from the Liberals (six seats being won by Conservative candidates and one by a Liberal Unionist), and they won a further seat at Glasgow Central in March 1909, making a total of ten gains since the general election. Electoral trends, and the destruction of major items of Liberal legislation in the House of Lords, had done much to restore the confidence of the Unionists and the credibility of their leaders. More than that, the onset of economic depression and rising unemployment was bound to reduce the popularity of the government still further and to strengthen the case for Tariff Reform, or at least so its supporters believed. The budget, however, forced Balfour and his lieutenants to reconsider the situation. If passed, the budget would not only strike at the interests of Unionist supporters such as the brewers and the landlords. It would also provide the government with potentially unlimited sources of extra revenue, so substantially weakening the short-term case for Tariff Reform and depriving the Unionists of what was their most distinctive electoral card. With the prospect of economic recovery on the horizon by the latter part of 1909, and with the weapon of the Lords' veto blunted by the budget, the Unionist revival might well be nipped in the bud and the party's enforced sojourn in opposition indefinitely prolonged.

In view of the severity of the struggle to come and the magnitude of the stakes involved, it was perhaps surprising that the initial Unionist reaction to the budget was so muted. When it was introduced to the Commons by Lloyd George on 29 April 1909, in a speech lasting four-and-a-half hours, the first opposition spokesman, Austen Chamberlain, made only a comparatively limited attack. Once they had had time to study the detail of the budget more fully, and to consider its political implications, the mood of the opposition changed. Balfour and his colleagues decided to launch an all-out assault on the budget and its provisions in the House of Commons and to fight the Finance Bill giving effect to the budget resolutions clause by clause. Anti-budget meetings were held in the City of London and a Budget Protest League was formed to take the campaign to the country. Unionist spokesmen also challenged the constitutionality of the budget, claiming that its provisions went beyond the accepted bounds of a money Bill and that it was for that reason not necessarily immune from amendment by the House of Lords, even that the Lords might be justified in rejecting it altogether.

Faced with stiffening resistance, the Liberals were not slow, nor were they especially unwilling, to take up the gauntlet which the Unionists had thrown down. A Budget League, presided over by Churchill, was formed to counter Unionist anti-budget propaganda and to take the fight to the constituencies. Inevitably, though, as the campaign got into gear, it was the Chancellor of the

Exchequer who was its star turn. Lloyd George was, in 1909, at the height of his powers. A parliamentarian of nearly 20 years' standing, an acknowledged master of debate and a spellbinding platform orator, he had served his apprenticeship in the cabinet as a reforming President of the Board of Trade.[8] His appointment as Chancellor in 1908 made him the most important man in the government next to the Prime Minister and opened the way for him to embark on a programme of social reform of which the 1909 budget was the necessary foundation. This in itself would have been enough to oblige him to take the lead in its defence, even had his fighting instincts not been aroused by the prospect of taking on the massed ranks of landowners and peers gathered under the Unionist banner. Yet Lloyd George's approach was not openly confrontational, at least not in the early stages of the crisis. In the early summer he confined his speeches to the House of Commons where he was, wherever possible, conciliatory towards his opponents. As the temperature of the conflict in the country rose, however, and as the possibility of a rejection of the budget by the Lords increased, he entered the thick of the extra-parliamentary fray. His speech at Limehouse in East London on 30 July was a robust vindication of the budget, delivered to a largely working-class audience and couched in language which the King considered inflammatory enough to warrant a protest to the Prime Minister. Undeterred, Lloyd George stuck to his guns and at Newcastle in October switched his fire directly on to the members of the House of Lords itself. Corruscating the Lords as 'five hundred men . . . chosen accidentally from among the unemployed', he portrayed the Unionist opponents of his budget as enemies of the constitution. 'Let them realise what they are doing,' he warned. 'They are forcing a revolution, and they will get it.'[9]

Constitutionally, the issue may not have been as clear-cut as Lloyd George implied. The fact that the Lords had not previously vetoed a budget did not mean that its veto was inoperative (indeed, convention decreed that the Lords could reject money Bills but not amend them), and the Finance Bill of 1909 was an unusually large measure, including some items which were dubiously enough lodged in a money Bill to justify their rejection. In any case, at the time of Lloyd George's second speech the Bill had not even reached the Lords, which led some to conclude that he was being deliberately provocative, even that he had wanted a confrontation with the Lords all along. Be that as it may, it seems unlikely that the Newcastle speech, or similar utterances by Churchill, had much effect one way or the other. The Unionists, as has been shown, had their own imperative reasons for defeating the budget, and, although there were misgivings in some quarters, they were prepared to use their parliamentary position to achieve that end. It is probable that by early October the decision to use the Lords' veto had already been taken in principle by the Unionist leaders. Lloyd George's speech may have hardened their resolve, but it did not materially alter the case in which they found themselves.

The Finance Bill finally passed its last stages in the House of Commons on 4 November 1909 by 379 votes to 149, following an unprecedented total of 70 days of parliamentary debate and no fewer than 554 divisions.[10] It then went to the House of Lords where Lord Lansdowne successfully moved its rejection on 30 November by 350 votes to 75. In the Lower House on 2 December Asquith carried a motion declaring that the Lords' action was 'a breach of the constitution and a usurpation of the rights of the Commons'. He sought and obtained a dissolution from the King and the focus of the budget battle shifted from parliament to the country, with a general election to be held in January 1910.

The Peers and the People

In rejecting the budget, the Unionists' strategy had been to force the government to call a general election at which they could put forward their idea of tariffs as an alternative to the Liberal plans for fiscal reform. And, indeed, the budget, and the choice between Free Trade and Protection, was the central issue of the long election campaign, which began when parliament was prorogued on 3 December 1909 and continued until close of polling in the last constituencies on 10 February 1910 – at ten weeks, the longest election campaign in British history.[11] Behind the budget, though, there lurked the bigger constitutional question: the future of the House of Lords and the Lords' veto. The 1907 resolutions were still the basis of government policy, and Asquith made it clear in his keynote speech at the Albert Hall on 10 December that the Liberals were not prepared to submit to renewed obstruction from the Lords in a new parliament, declaring to his supporters that he and his colleagues would not take office 'unless we can secure the safeguards which experience shows us to be necessary for the legislative utility and honour of the party of progress.'[12] Asquith also repledged his party to the measures of licensing, education and land reform which had been blocked since 1906, as well as to Welsh Disestablishment and social legislation for the working classes. These themes were taken up by the other principal campaign speakers on the Liberal side, Churchill and Lloyd George, and in party propaganda in the constituencies, with the battle for the budget being subsumed in the language of a more heroic campaign for constitutional reform and social improvement. The Liberals were thus reaffirming their traditional role as the champions of popular, representative government against rule by the aristocracy, at the same time promising tangible economic and other measures to their supporters, while the Unionists were left trying to defend the actions of the House of Lords, with only the dubious appeal of tariffs as a potentially popular rallying cry. The latter were hampered, too, by Balfour's absence from the early part of the campaign through illness, and by the fact that, with Joseph Chamberlain an invalid recluse following his earlier stroke, they had no other major figures to compete with the Liberal platform stars.

In the event, neither of the major parties could be wholly satisfied with the outcome of their labours. The Unionists' fortunes picked up in the second half of the campaign, once Balfour had returned to assert his presence, and in all they gained about a 100 seats, cementing a partial recovery after the debacle of 1906. Compared with the previous general election, their share of the vote had risen (from 43. 4 per cent to 46. 8 per cent) and the total number of votes they polled increased from 2. 4 million in 1906 to 3. 1 million in 1910.[13] Since the Liberal poll had also increased slightly (though their percentage share had fallen), this suggested that many Unionist voters who had abstained in 1906 had been won back to the fold. The Unionists could also congratulate themselves on having obtained a majority of seats in the English constituencies (233 to the Liberals' 188). But in the overall context of the election, this was small comfort. The Liberals had lost the massive independent majority which they had won in 1906, but they still had solid backing in Scotland and Wales, and even in their reduced circumstances managed to achieve slightly-better-than-parity in terms of seats with the Unionists (274 to 272). In addition, they could count on the support of the 40 Labour and most of the 82 Irish Nationalist MPs in the new parliament, for while the latter had opposed some of the budget proposals (mainly the whisky duty) they were prepared to accept the budget as the price to pay for the removal of the Lords' veto and the clearing of the last remaining obstacle (as they thought) from the path of Home Rule. So, although the Liberals were undoubtedly disappointed with the final election result, in view of what they had felt to be a successful start to their campaign, they were at least still the government. The Unionists had gambled for high stakes, only to find that, while they were not entirely out of the game, the dice had refused to roll decisively in their favour.

Yet although the Liberals had been returned to office, they found themselves in something of a quandary. The quandary was partly of the Prime Minister's own making. He and other ministers had given the impression during the election campaign that if the Liberals were victorious they would proceed immediately to limit the Lords' right of veto. Since it was unlikely that the Lords would meekly acquiesce in the curtailment of their powers, the possibility clearly existed of a deadlock arising between the two Houses of Parliament, with the intervention of the King the only means of resolving the situation, if necessary by the employment of the royal prerogative to create sufficient additional Liberal peers for the government to have a majority for its legislation in the Lords. This much was obvious. Furthermore, both Asquith and Lloyd George had implied in their speeches that they would not accept office unless they were assured that the issue of the Lords could be dealt with within the lifetime of a single parliament, which gave their followers to understand that the party leaders had received guarantees from the King that the prerogative of mass creation would be placed at their disposal should its use be considered necessary.

This was emphatically not so. Not only had the King (who privately disapproved of the Liberal government's policy) given no such guarantees; his private secretary, Knollys, had informed Asquith before the election that the King would not even consider the use of the prerogative until a second general election had been held on the specific question of the Lords' veto.[14] Much to the frustration of their supporters, therefore, Asquith and his cabinet could not immediately 'settle' the question of the Lords. Instead they were forced to temporise while they decided what to do. The possibility of reforming the composition of the Lords rather than removing its veto was considered, with Grey and Haldane being in favour of this course. In the meantime the budget was reintroduced and passed the Lords without a division in April. Only on 18 March – more than a month after the election – did Asquith, in a speech at Oxford Town Hall, finally set out the government's position in relation to the Lords, a policy embodied in resolutions which were presented to the Commons on 21 March. A Parliament Bill based on these resolutions, containing a preamble in favour of reform but also providing for the substitution of powers of delay for those of veto, was published. Asquith announced that if the Bill was defeated he would seek an immediate dissolution, and he let it be known that if necessary he would recommend the use of the prerogative to secure its eventual passage.

Following this display of renewed determination on the part of the government, the scene was set for a summer of feverish campaigning, culminating in a second general election. There was the prospect, too, of a clash of wills between the King and his ministers. Indeed, the Crown was being drawn more deeply into the arena of party politics in the early months of 1910 than at any time within living memory, possibly since William IV's dismissal of the Melbourne government in 1834. Would the King refuse to give Asquith guarantees about the creation of peers?

Might he refuse a dissolution of parliament? If the government resigned without a dissolution, because of the King's disfavour, would the opposition be prepared to take office? These were the questions which were being seriously canvassed in April 1910. In respect of the last, a meeting had even taken place at Lambeth Palace on 29 April, at which Balfour had indicated to Knollys, in the presence of the Archbishop of Canterbury, that he would be willing, under certain circumstances, to take over as Prime Minister to prevent the embarrassment of his sovereign by the Liberal government. These were deep waters, more redolent of the closet government of the eighteenth century than the democratic politics of the twentieth. As Asquith later recorded, the country was 'nearing the verge of a crisis without example in our constitutional history',[15] its events soon to be made all the more portentous to impressionable minds by the reappearance, in Wellsian fashion, of Halley's Comet in the skies of Europe.

What Edward VII's actions would have been from this juncture will remain forever unfathomable to historians. On 6 May, on his return from a spring visit to Biarritz, and after a short illness, King Edward died. He was succeeded by his son, who became King George V. The new King was respected for his uprightness of character and his personal integrity, but politically he was an unknown quantity and there were doubts about the possible consequences of his lack of experience. However, both the fact of his accession and his subsequent conduct were materially to affect the outcome of the crisis.[16]

In the hiatus of mourning which accompanied the end of Edward's brief reign, the politicians stepped back from the brink. Asquith proposed that discussions should be held between the party leaders to see if an agreed solution to their differences could be found. Balfour, on behalf of the opposition, accepted the invitation and a series of meetings took place as part of a Constitutional Conference. There were in all 12 meetings in June and July, followed by further meetings in October and November, after the summer recess. On the Liberal side the participants were Asquith and Lloyd George, together with Crewe, the Liberal leader in the House of Lords, and Augustine Birrell, the Chief Secretary for Ireland. For the Unionists, Balfour was joined by Lansdowne, Austen Chamberlain and the Earl of Cawdor. No Labour or Nationalist leaders were invited to attend.

The discussions covered all aspects of the constitutional problem: the relations between the two Houses of Parliament; how disagreements between them might be resolved; whether the House of Lords could be reformed to reflect more fairly the balance of parties in the Commons.[17] Both sides showed some interest in achieving a compromise, or at least in investigating alternative routes out of the impasse. On the treatment of financial measures, the Unionists were willing to accept the proposals in the government's Parliament Bill for making a formal distinction between money bills (which would not be subject to a veto) and other types of legislation. Where disputes arose on non-financial issues the idea of these being resolved through some kind of joint sitting of the two Houses was considered. Yet throughout the talks there was one fundamental stumbling block to a settlement which no amount of ingenuity could evade. It is true that some Liberals, like Grey, gave reform of the composition of the House of Lords priority over the abolition of the veto. In so doing they were motivated in part by the realisation that once the veto had been removed the Liberal government would be honour-bound to devote large swathes of parliamentary time to measures such as Irish Home Rule and Welsh Disestablishment which were of dubious electoral appeal. Nevertheless, following the January election, Asquith and Lloyd George had effectively made a deal with Redmond, the Irish Nationalist leader, in which the removal of the veto was to be the *quid pro quo* for Nationalist support for the budget, which otherwise the Irish would have opposed. The Liberals had thus mortgaged the future of their government in a way which inseparably linked a reduction in the powers of the House of Lords to the question of Irish Home Rule. Precisely because of its Irish implications, however, the Unionists were adamant that, on controversial questions like Home Rule – what they described as 'organic' legislation, affecting the basic structures of the constitution – some form of veto should remain. At the very least, the Lords should retain the right to delay the enactment of such measures pending either a referendum or a general election.

Whatever their personal views on Home Rule, this was a proposal which, given the constraints of parliamentary arithmetic, and their public assurances to their supporters on the veto question, the Liberal negotiators were unable to accept, and it was on this rock that the Constitutional Conference ultimately foundered.[18]

The only way in which the Conference could have succeeded was if the two front benches had been prepared to come together to produce not simply a joint plan for dealing with the reform of the House of Lords, but an agreed solution of the Irish question as well, perhaps along the quasi-federal lines that were already being suggested in some quarters. The possibility of bypassing the Nationalists in this way was canvassed most directly by Lloyd George, who, during the parliamentary recess in August 1910, produced a confidential memorandum advocating a formal coalition of the Liberal and Unionist parties to provide a stable parliamentary base for dealing with urgent national problems.[19] He discussed the memorandum with a number of leading politicians in both parties, including Churchill and F. E. Smith (who were known to be sympathetic to the idea of cross-party cooperation), and raised the issue with Balfour and Asquith. His motives, and indeed the significance of the whole episode, have recently attracted considerable attention from historians and have become a matter for much debate. Some writers have argued that the coalition scheme reveals Lloyd George's essential hostility to conventional party politics and his preference for a 'centrist' government of national efficiency, a preference which eventually flourished in the coalitions he led from 1916 to 1922 and which, even in 1910, found an answering echo among Unionists such as Smith, Milner and Austen Chamberlain. It is equally possible to see the proposal as a short-term expedient to meet a particular situation (and to facilitate the introduction of reforms like National Insurance) rather than as part of a more deeply-laid plan. Either way, the fact that a coalition could be seriously considered shows the gravity with which some politicians viewed the gulf that was opening up between the parties, even if the idea of cooperation had to be abandoned because party feelings were running too high and because the official leaders on both sides felt that their rank-and-file supporters would refuse to endorse it.[20]

With the coalition plan still-born, and the Constitutional Conference deadlocked, the Liberal government had to return to its Parliament Bill and the assault on the veto. Once again the attitude of the King, this time George V rather than Edward VII, became crucial. The cabinet were agreed on the need to obtain guarantees about the creation of peers before recommending a dissolution, and they placed their advice in a memorandum which Asquith presented to the King on 16 November. The King was unwilling to give 'contingent' guarantees before the Lords had pronounced its verdict on the Parliament Bill and in advance of a general election. He was in any case unsympathetic to the proposed legislation (perhaps even more so than his father had been) and he had been misled by an earlier audience with Asquith on 11 November into supposing that no guarantees were to be asked for. He was furthermore receiving conflicting advice from his two private secretaries, Stamfordham and Knollys. The former argued that it was unconstitutional for the King to give Asquith the guarantees he demanded, and that in doing so he would be taking sides in the party struggle against the Unionists. Knollys, on the other hand, argued that to refuse Asquith's request, thereby precipitating a ministerial resignation, would be even worse for the King's impartiality. Knollys also tendered the vital information (the veracity of which was subsequently challenged)[21] that Balfour would refuse to form a minority government if the Liberals resigned, which meant that the King would be forced to accept the advice of the Liberals sooner or later, whatever happened. Faced with this situation the King gave way, although, as he confided to his diary, 'I disliked having to do this very much, but agreed that this was the only alternative to the Cabinet resigning.'[22]

The constitutional merits of these various arguments are endlessly debatable.[23] On one reading, the contingent guarantees were unnecessary, since if the Liberals won an election on the issue of the Lords' veto the King would have been obliged to accept the electorate's express wish, or otherwise risk provoking an even more serious crisis, with the position of the monarchy itself coming under scrutiny. But although the pre-election guarantees were constitutionally redundant, and much resented by the

King, it was politically important for Asquith to have the assurance that there could be no repetition of the uncertainty which had arisen after the first election of 1910, with the conflict between Lords and Commons being drawn out still further. Given that judgement, and for as long as Asquith was the King's prime minister, George was constitutionally bound to accept the government's advice, whatever his own feelings. For the King to have forced Asquith to resign, and then to have appointed Balfour in his place (supposing Balfour to have been willing to take office), would have triggered a constitutional storm and placed the monarchy in the front line of the party-political battle. When the King accepted Knollys' advice rather than Stamfordham's, and gave Asquith his assurance that 'in the event of the Government being returned with a majority at the General Election I should use my Prerogative to make Peers if asked for',[24] he was almost certainly taking the wisest course, both from the country's point of view and his own. As the assurances were to be kept secret during the election, the role of the King was prevented from becoming a platform issue.

Once the King's reluctant consent had been obtained, the government was able to go to the country for the second time in less than a year. Parliament was dissolved on 28 November and polling was completed before Christmas. Inevitably there was an element of *déjà vu*, with arguments being recycled from the earlier contest. But the campaign was short enough to prevent staleness, and the question of the Lords' veto was more prominently before the public than on the previous occasion in the shape of the Liberals' Parliament Bill.[25] The opposition was caught off-guard by Balfour's offer (made, without consulting his colleagues, in response to a challenge from Lloyd George) to put Tariff Reform to a referendum if the Liberals agreed to do the same with Home Rule. Nor could they work up much enthusiasm from the electorate, or even among their own supporters, for the various plans for reforming the House of Lords which Unionist peers and others, including Lord Rosebery, had suggested at different times earlier in the year. There was little expectation in the Unionist camp that victory could be theirs, given the perpetuation of the

Liberal–Labour–Nationalist alliance, and in this at least they were not disappointed. The results showed that there had been some exchange of seats between the parties, but the outcome of the December election was more or less the same as that of January/February. The Liberals returned three fewer MPs than in the previous contest, but Labour and the Nationalists gained two seats each, so that there was actually a slight increase in the majority available to the governing alliance. Both of the major parties recorded fewer votes than in the earlier election (though the Liberals increased their percentage of the poll from 43.5 to 44.2), but the lower turnout in the second election (81. 6 per cent compared with 86. 8 per cent) was due mainly to an increased number of unopposed returns, added to the fact that the December election was being fought on an old register and that the weather during polling was generally poor. The voters may have been tiring of the politicians' inability to agree, but they played their part to the full all the same, and the Liberals were returned to office with a chance to bring their conflict with the House of Lords to a successful conclusion.

The Crisis and its Significance

The Parliament Bill which the government reintroduced in the new parliament and which was given its first reading in the Commons on 22 February 1911 by 351 votes to 227 contained three main provisions. It stipulated that the House of Lords should be unable either to amend or reject money Bills as certified by the Speaker of the House of Commons. It deprived the Lords of their right of veto over all other categories of legislation, leaving them instead only with a two-year delaying power, so that any measure which passed substantially un-changed through the House of Commons in three successive sessions of parliament would automatically become law, subject to the royal assent. Finally, in order to balance this reduction in the powers of the Upper House and to make parliament as a whole more accountable to the electorate, the maximum period between general elections was to be reduced from seven years to five. These proposals were approved in principle by the House of Commons in the second reading debate which took place between 27 February and 2 March, the vote for the Bill being 368 to 243.

Asquith and his colleagues may have hoped that this, effectively, would be the end of the opposition to their measure and that after the election the Lords would give way over the Parliament Bill as they had over the budget in the previous year, thereby removing the need for further conflict and eventually a mass creation of new peers. Many Unionists still believed that the government was bluffing, however, in its threat to coerce the Lords, or that, even if the government wished it, the King would be unwilling to use the prerogative to make large numbers of additional Liberal peers. They decided therefore to continue their resistance to the removal of the veto, both by attempting to block the Liberal Bill and by the ostensibly more constructive strategy of bringing forward their own proposals for settling disputes between the two Houses and reforming the composition of the House of Lords. In March, Lord Balfour of Burleigh introduced in the Lords a Reference to the People Bill, the purpose of which was to provide for a referendum in cases of measures on which there was disagreement between the Lords and the Commons. In May, Lord Lansdowne brought forward a Bill which proposed a radical restructuring of the House of Lords, reducing its total membership to 350, of whom 100 would be members elected by the hereditary peers from those among their number who had held governmental or Crown office, 120 would be elected by regional electoral colleges of Members of Parliament and 100 appointed by the government of the day in proportion to party strengths in the House of Commons, the balance being made up by a small number of Law Lords and Lords Spiritual.[26]

The attempt to reform the membership of the House of Lords in this way was severely criticised by many Unionists, and as a strategy for defeating the Parliament Bill its credibility was undermined by an announcement by the government that their Bill would apply equally to a reformed or an unreformed House of Lords. The Unionists had consequently to shift their full attention on to the Parliament Bill itself. The Bill received its third reading in the Commons on 15 May (362 votes to 241) and a second reading in the Lords on 23 May. But the Unionists in the Lords had allowed the Bill a second reading only with the intention of amending it in committee, which they duly did. In what the Liberal Lord Morley described as 'tearing up the Bill', the Unionist peers substituted their own proposals for those of the government. Their amendments provided for a joint committee of both Houses, rather than the Speaker of the Commons, to adjudicate on the status of money Bills. They also, once again, returned to their favoured device of a referendum, to be available in the case of legislation affecting the Monarchy or the Protestant succession, the establishment of 'National Parliaments or Councils' in the constituent parts of the United Kingdom, and in the case of other measures considered by the joint committee to be of 'great gravity on which the opinion of the country had not been fully ascertained'.[27]

The carrying of these amendments in the Lords (after a temporary lull in the controversy to allow the King's coronation to take place in June 1911) set the scene for the final act of the drama. The Liberals were not prepared to accept the introduction of the referendum as a mechanism for settling disputes between the two Houses, having already identified it at the constitutional conference of the previous year as a device for obstructing Home Rule and other Liberal measures which were not popular with the electorate as a whole. In any case, ministers were determined to assert their own authority, and that of the Commons, by acting on the mandate they had received in December for removing the Lords' veto. They thus warned the King (in a minute written, whether deliberately or not, on Bastille Day, 14 July) that once the Lords' amendments were rejected *en bloc* by the Commons the contingency provided for in his pre-election undertaking would have arisen and he would be advised by the cabinet to use his prerogative to create sufficient Liberal peers to secure the passage of the unamended Bill through the House of Lords. The King expressed himself reluctant to use his power until the last possible moment, and urged that the Lords should have the chance to respond to the Commons' rejection of its amendments before the prerogative was invoked – necessitating a further delay in the Bill's progress if the Lords remained intransigent – but otherwise, with whatever misgivings, he agreed to honour his pledge.

The King's decision brought the full pressure of the crisis on to the Unionists. Already, in an attempt to weaken Unionist resistance, Asquith had informed Balfour privately of the substance of the royal guarantees, and Lloyd George confirmed their existence in a meeting with Balfour and Lansdowne on 18 July. Asquith formally notified Balfour of the government's intentions in a letter on 20 July. The choice facing the Unionists was thus clear. They could continue their opposition to the Parliament Bill, and risk the 'swamping' of the House of Lords with new Liberal peers, or, alternatively, they could cut their losses and accept defeat on the veto in return for the preservation, at least in the short term, of the Lords' aristocratic character and its overwhelming Unionist majority. When the Unionist 'shadow cabinet' met on 21 July opinion was divided. The two leaders of the party, Balfour and Lansdowne, favoured the latter policy of compromise, and in this they were supported by Lord Curzon (formerly one of the staunchest opponents of the Parliament Bill), Lords Middleton, Londonderry, Derby and Ashbourne, and by leading Commons figures such as Bonar Law, Walter Long, Alfred Lyttleton and Henry Chaplin. Those who favoured outright resistance included Lords Selborne and Halsbury, Austen Chamberlain, F. E. Smith, George Wyndham and the Irish Unionist leader, Edward Carson.

This division – between the so-called 'hedgers' who favoured compromise and the 'ditchers' who were for resistance to the government regardless of the consequences – gained in significance in late July and early August as the crucial votes on the Parliament Bill approached. The 'hedgers' had the weight of the official Unionist leadership behind them, although both Balfour and Lansdowne were criticised for failing to give a firmer lead than they did. Balfour's lack of grasp was exemplified by his inability or unwillingness to restrain the rowdier members of his party on 24 July when Asquith was shouted down while trying to make a statement to the Commons. The 'ditchers', or 'diehards', on the other hand, had the benefit of enthusiasm and organisation, and were given a new lease of life as the crisis neared its climax by being able to dispense with the need to pay lip-service to the official support of the party for the idea of Lords reform, which they mostly opposed. It has been shown, too, that it would be wrong to equate the diehards with politically-unsophisticated 'backwoodsmen' whose opposition to Liberal policy was based on blind or reactionary emotionalism. Recent studies have demonstrated that the diehards represented a distinct and coherent tendency in Unionist politics, with their own political agenda, and with leaders like Lords Halsbury and Willoughby de Broke, not to mention figures such as Austen Chamberlain in the Commons, who, in different circumstances, might have presented a more than credible alternative to the Balfourite camp.[28] Indeed, it could be argued that in some respects their preferred policies – defence of the Union and the constitutional status quo, support for Tariff Reform, the upholding of property rights and distrust of the democratic tenor of Liberal radicalism – were those of the mainstream rather than of a minority in Unionist ranks.

That said, the diehard strategy was a desperate one, with little prospect of ultimate success. They had no chance of forcing a general election by defeating the government. All that they could realistically do was to deny the Liberals a majority for the Parliament Bill in the hope that the King would refuse to create peers, or that any such creation would be limited in scale. To this end, the Unionists moved motions in both Houses on 7 August declaring that the King's pledge to Asquith had been obtained by 'unconstitutional' means and was therefore void. But this was merely opposition for form's sake: the vital question by that time was whether, if the Unionist 'hedgers' abstained, the 'ditchers' could mobilise sufficient strength in the Lords to block the Bill. The issue was resolved in the second week of August, as the temperature in London reached record levels (it was one of the hottest summers of the century) and the political establishment metaphorically held its breath. On 8 August the Commons predictably rejected the Lords' amendments, though some small concessions were made by the government. On the following day a two-day debate began in the Lords. Perhaps the decisive moment came when Lord Morley, speaking on behalf of the government, let it be known that, in the event of the Bill failing to achieve a majority at the end of the debate, 'the King would assent "to a creation of peers sufficient in number to guard against any possible combination of the different Parties in Opposition by which the Parliament Bill might again be exposed a second time to defeat".'[29] This statement ended any lingering doubts about the King's intentions or those of the government. It also made it certain that any creation of peers would be large enough fundamentally to alter the character and composition of the Upper House. Morley's words did little to affect the resolve of the 'ditchers', but sufficient of the 'hedgers', including Lord Curzon, were determined to prevent what they saw as the catastrophe of a mass creation that they decided to vote with the government rather than abstain. Their decision, taken after much heart-searching and in the face of conflicting pressures from conscience and friends, just tipped the result in the Bill's favour. When the final vote was taken on 10 August, 131 peers voted for the Parliament Bill, 114 against, but it was the 37 Unionists who voted with the government whose victory it was, to the 'great relief' of the King, who in the privacy of his diary recorded his gratitude at being spared 'any further humiliation by a creation of peers'.[30]

The last-minute crumbling of Unionist resistance, and the fact that the government was not pushed to the extremity of recommending a creation of peers, might easily lead the historian to underestimate the real severity of the constitutional crisis. Similarly, the undemonstrativeness in 1911 of a public opinion apparently more concerned with other events − the Agadir crisis, industrial troubles on the railways, the King's coronation − might well lead to the conclusion that the crisis lacked a wider resonance. Yet this would be only partly true. The events of 1911 certainly lacked the direct public engagement, say, of the Reform crisis of 1830–32, when crowds rioted in the streets and burnt down buildings. The temper of the times was different in 1911, and excitement did not reach quite that fever pitch. But the participation rate in the elections of 1910 was high, and the political classes at least were watching developments at Westminster with a keen interest. Nor should the inherent seriousness of the crisis itself be underrated. Whatever the validity of the cries, from either side, of 'The constitution in danger', the clash between the Commons and Lords was arguably the most important since 1831-2, with profound implications for the future conduct of government in Britain, and matters of vital concern to both the main political parties were at stake. In a sense, the viability of parliamentary and party government on the British model had been placed on trial. So, too, the role of the monarchy in politics was more of an issue in 1909-11 than it had been for most of Victoria's reign. Edward VII, and more particularly George V, were drawn almost fatally close to expressions of partisanship, with potentially destructive consequences for the impartiality of the Crown, which had been such an important ingredient in the success of party government in the nineteenth century.

Set against these concerns, the way in which the crisis was resolved, and its eventual outcome, can be made to seem a triumph for the adaptability and inherent soundness of Britain's constitutional arrangements. To adopt the evolutionary perspective that was fashionable among the late-Victorians, what happened in 1909-11 can be seen as a progressive continuation of the rise of the Commons - a process begun with the origins of parliament itself in medieval times, continued through the seventeenth and eighteenth centuries in struggles against the King and consolidated by the electoral reforms of 1832, 1867 and 1884-5. The Parliament Act vindicated the claim of the Commons to undisputed authority in matters of finance and entrenched that authority in statute. The provisions of the Act, and the removal of the Lords' absolute veto, were a victory for the principles of representative over those of aristocratic government, while still not depriving the constitution of all of the 'checks and balances' which had been integral to its successful working since the Glorious Revolution. The fact that the dispute between Lords and Commons could be settled peacefully, and by due constitutional process, was a testimony to the underlying strength of the country's basic political structures. The durability of the 1911 settlement showed the success with which the Edwardians had surmounted the problem of the relations between the two Houses of Parliament, thereby completing the work of constitutional reform which their Victorian predecessors had begun.[31]

This is not altogether a false view, but it is a one-sided one. The durability of the 1911 settlement and the absence of long-term conflict between Lords and Commons owed more to the Conservative dominance of politics in the inter-war period than it did to the shape of the settlement itself. In the short term, the Parliament Act did little to prevent clashes between a Liberal government and the House of Lords. There remained considerable scope for conflict even in matters of finance, where the Parliament Act did not allow social legislation to be incorporated in the annual Finance Bill. It is ironic that under the post-1911 definition, the 1909 budget would not have been classifiable as a money Bill, thus giving the Unionists a kind of posthumous moral victory for their earlier resistance.[32] The Unionists had more substantial victories to celebrate as well. The Lords lost their right of veto, but under the 1911 Act they retained very considerable power to delay legislation and obstruct a government's legislative programme. Moreover, by concentrating on the issue of the veto at the expense of more fundamental reform, the Liberals had left the composition of the Lords unchanged, so perpetuating its permanently Unionist majority. The simultaneous reduction in the maximum life of a parliament from seven years to five, while providing greater accountability and bringing nearer the old Chartist ideal of annual parliaments, gave the Lords further incentives for obstruction, in that from the mid-point in a parliament they could rely upon the coming of a general election before controversial measures could be passed into law against their objections. In that sense, the Parliament Act did as much to conserve as to curtail aristocratic power – something of which some Liberals were only too well aware and which provided a platform for a continuing aristocratic revolt against the Liberal government between 1911 and 1914.[33]

If the outcome of the crisis was mixed in constitutional terms, the same was true of its impact on party politics. At the end of 1911, the Liberals' position was in some respects more favourable than it had been at the beginning of 1909. They had successfully carried the People's Budget and the Parliament Act, as well as placing the National Insurance Act and other social reforms on the statute book. The morale of the party had been bolstered by these victories and by the struggle against the House of Lords. Against that, the party's electoral and parliamentary position was weaker. The first election of 1910 had cost the Liberals their independent Commons majority; the second confirmed that the Unionists had re-established their dominance in the English constituencies (solid since the 1880s and only temporarily shaken in 1906), forcing the Liberals back on their heartlands in Scotland, Wales and the industrial districts. In parliament, the Liberal government was dependent after January 1910 on the Irish Nationalist and Labour MPs. A breach with the Nationalists or a rift in the progressive alliance with Labour could threaten the survival of a Liberal government, perhaps even make its return to office impossible. The Nationalists in particular exacted a high price for their support, namely the introduction of a new Home Rule Bill which made another bout of constitutional strife inevitable and took up valuable time which could have been devoted to potentially more popular domestic reforms.[34] If not entirely empty, therefore, the Liberal victory was certainly flawed, and there were plentiful problems ahead for the party and the government.[35]

Yet if the Liberals had problems, the plight of the Unionists was worse. In the wake of their 1906 defeat they had embarked on a deliberate strategy of using their vast majority in the House of Lords to frustrate the Liberals in the fulfilment of their election programme. When Lloyd George brought forward his 1909 budget, this too fell victim to the Lords' veto, as the Unionists strove to prevent the success of the government's Free Trade policies and to force an election which might give them a chance of returning to power. In this, Balfour was supported by an aristocracy fearful for their privileges and by a Unionist party eager for a fight. But the grand strategy had not worked. The Unionists regained some lost electoral ground in England; they forced the government into a second general election in December 1910; they salvaged a still-defensible position for their peers from the summer debates over the Parliament Bill in 1911.

Beyond that, however, they had little to show. The 1909 budget and the Parliament Act became law. The Liberals had struck a powerful blow for Free Trade and against Tariff Reform. Above all, the Unionists had lost three successive general elections and, unless the Liberal–Nationalist–Labour alliance broke up, seemed condemned to remain a minority in the Commons for some time to come, with the even more mortifying prospect of having to watch Liberal reforms like Home Rule and Welsh Disestablishment being steamrollered through a now veto-less House of Lords. The failure of the Balfour–Lansdowne strategy inevitably opened up deep fissures within the Unionist party, in which former diehards were joined by others critical of Balfour's leadership. Even while Balfour was recovering from the tribulations of the Parliament Bill crisis in the comfortable convalescence of a continental spa, a 'Balfour Must Go' campaign was gathering support. In November 1911 Balfour resigned as Unionist leader, to be replaced by Andrew Bonar Law, a compromise candidate who it was felt could best reunite the different wings of the party and whose personal qualities at least suggested a more vigorous and forceful style of leadership than that of his predecessor.[36]

The constitutional crisis left both parties facing a difficult future. What did it reveal about the state of the party system itself? The rhetoric of radical Liberals and Unionist diehards certainly invested the party battles of 1909–11 with a high level of ferocity, suggesting that the gulf between the parties was wider than at any time since the 1860s and that the underlying consensus which was essential to the British model of party government was becoming dangerously eroded. Yet even at the height of the crisis a complete estrangement was prevented and the social amenities were observed. Asquith and Balfour both attended a fancy dress ball given by Lord Winterton and F. E. Smith at Claridge's on the night after the Parliament Bill received its second reading in the House of Lords in May 1911. Winston Churchill, significantly both a leading radical and a pro-coalitionist, took the initiative in forming the 'Other Club' at which Liberal and Unionist politicians could meet privately for dinner-table discussion while the party dogfight raged around them – and indeed while they, in their other selves, contributed to it.

More substantially, the Constitutional Conference of 1910 and Lloyd George's proposal for a national coalition showed that political leaders were aware of the dangers of allowing partisanship to develop unchecked and that they retained a capacity for the rational debate of party differences.[37] For reasons already described, this attempt to reach an agreement failed, but there was nevertheless a degree of restraint in the behaviour of party leaders throughout the crisis which was at odds with the facade presented to their followers and to the public at large. The Unionists were prepared to play a partisan game with their Lords majority, but in August 1911 pragmatic counsels prevailed over the outright defiance of the diehards and ditchers. Equally, there is a suspicion that the Liberal leaders, for all the furore over 'peers versus people' in 1910, were reluctant to push the attack on the Lords to its limit, for fear of destabilising the delicate mechanisms of the governing system.[38] In short, both sides knew how far their opponents were likely to go and adjusted their own behaviour accordingly, with the result that the crisis of 1909–11, serious though it was, ended in a form of negotiated settlement rather than in an outright victory for one side or the other which would have been foreign to the spirit of the British constitution.

However, this is only apparent in hindsight. At the time, there was always inherent in the public atmosphere of the crisis the chance that things would get out of hand. Indeed, in a sense they did. In the larger political drama of Edwardian Britain the constitutional crisis was really only a prelude, some might have said a sideshow, to the more elemental conflict over Irish Home Rule. The events of 1909–11 had altered the configuration of parliamentary politics in the Nationalists' favour; on the Unionist side they had left frustration and discontent. Even as the Parliament Act passed into law, the passions were rising, and it was impossible to ignore the gathering clouds of the storms that were still to come.

3

SUFFRAGISM AND FEMINISM

The conflict between the Liberal party and the House of Lords was only one of the problems bequeathed by the Victorians which intensified in the early twentieth century. At least three others have been identified by historians, from Halevy and Dangerfield onwards, as reaching a climax in the Edwardian/Georgian years after 1910: the problems of women's rights, organised Labour and the struggle for Irish Home Rule. According to Dangerfield, the three movements shared common features which challenged the middle-class liberalism of Victorian England and threatened the existence of the Liberal government in 1914. The question of the interrelationship of the movements will be considered in due course. This chapter will be concerned specifically with the changing position of women in late-Victorian and Edwardian Britain, with the emergence of a women's movement and the campaign for 'Votes for Women' in the Edwardian period, and the nature and extent of the challenge which suffragism and feminism presented to the prevailing attitudes and habits of the men and women of the day.

Women in Late-Victorian and Edwardian Britain

The explosion of interest that has occurred in all aspects of women's history in recent years has led to a deeper understanding of gender issues in Victorian Britain and has made it possible to place the study of campaigns for women's rights in a more fully realised social and historical context. In some respects, however, this has made it more difficult to generalise about the position of women in Victorian society. It is clear that the majority of women faced similar life experiences: marriage, childbirth, motherhood, running a home – the manifold duties of the 'domestic sphere' to which society sought to confine them. It is equally clear that they lived under a regime of legal and civil disabilities which reinforced the discriminatory structure of the existing social order. Yet the character and quality of the lives which individual women lived were obviously powerfully shaped by their own personal circumstances, and by a further factor that was at least as important as that of gender, and arguably more so, namely that of the social class to which they belonged. It is the interaction of these two determinants of gender and class, and the way in which they impacted upon individual lives, which must be at the heart of any attempt to describe the conditions from which the women's movement of the late nineteenth century emerged and the multiplicity of forms which that movement took.

Differences of class affected all aspects of a woman's existence: childhood, education, prospects for marriage and home life, opportunities for employment and leisure. For the women of the upper classes – that 'top ten thousand' which embraced the ranks of the aristocracy, the landed interest and the plutocratic cream of the upper middle class – life was lived in a world that was at once leisured and restrictive. This was the world of 'Society' very much with a capital 'S', a comparatively closed world of country houses, coming-out balls and the measured festivities of the London season, of high fashion and fine living as depicted in the pages of the Court circular and the society magazines. Young women born into this class could expect a private education, often from private tutors or governesses, concentrating on the politer arts and social accomplishments such as French, music, dancing and deportment. They would be likely to make a good marriage (or have it made for them) with a member of their own class, whereupon they would enter into the lifestyle of the lady of leisure, eventually emulating the experience of their mothers before them as the mistress of a large establishment of servants and the pliant consort of their husbands, the rigours of child-bearing and motherhood alleviated by the support of nannies, maids and the best available medical treatment. Outside employment, still less an independent career, was neither an economic necessity nor a practical possibility, the main outlet for personal activity being a perpetual round of social calls, regulated by etiquette, or some form of charitable work, an occupation which enabled the 'lady bountiful' to combine social condescension with Christian humility in a manner sufficiently proper to salve the conscience of the Victorian public soul.

Middle-class women could expect a pattern of life that shared some similarities with that of their upper-class sisters, albeit on a less grand scale. After some education at home or in private schooling, marriage and motherhood was the most likely destiny. Domestic life would be comfortable, but was increasingly suburban rather than spacious in the aristocratic sense. Middle-class society was more likely to be provincial than metropolitan, and, particularly outside London, circumscribed by the boundaries of local, professional or denominational communities to which husbands or fathers belonged. The middle classes were also highly stratified, so that at the lower levels the wife and mother would be more directly involved in the day-to-day domestic management of the home – and possibly in some of the actual work – than women living in higher echelons of society with a more plentiful supply of servants.

Perhaps a more distinctive difference between the middle-class and the upper-class experience, though, was the existence of more widespread opportunities outside the home, at least for young, unmarried women. In the early nineteenth century the governess had become an archetypal, even stereotypical, figure, in literature as well as reality. In the second half of the century, increasing numbers of young women were drawn into expanding professions such as nursing and teaching. There were 172,000 women school teachers by 1901; by 1914 75 per cent of all elementary school teachers were women. Middle-class girls were also finding employment as clerks, typists, telephonists and shop assistants as technological and commercial change transformed the labour market. There were, of course, occupations which remained stubbornly resistant to female penetration, especially the older professions or the higher levels of a traditionally male preserve such as the civil service. Only 212 out of 22,000 doctors in Britain were women in 1901. Even in teaching, where women were numerically in the majority, salary levels were lower by about 25 per cent than those of their male counterparts. Another major difference was that women were much less likely than men to continue in employment after marriage; indeed, some occupations expressly forbade it. This was something which threatened to breed dissatisfaction, since the trend towards smaller families was most marked among the professional middle classes and middle-class women were spending less time than their predecessors in child-bearing and child-rearing, making it more likely that they would seek to pursue interests, if not careers, outside the home. Demographic trends were working in favour of a more flexible attitude towards women's employment in another way too, in that from the 1850s there was an increasing preponderance of women in the population, making marriage for all women by no means a certainty. Although over 80 per cent of women did marry at some time in their lives, there were by 1911 over 1. 1 million 'surplus' women in the population, either as spinsters or widows. Among the middle classes, the identification of the problem of 'redundant' women helped, together with other social changes, to make the idea of a working or 'career' woman more acceptable by the early twentieth century.[1]

For working-class women the debate over whether it was acceptable to work was somewhat academic. Most unmarried women took work of some kind, factory work, the clothing trade and domestic service being the most common occupations. When they married (as most did) they might be under pressure to give up full-time employment outside the home, but in most cases they would still be expected to make some contribution to the family budget – for example by taking in laundry or sewing, child-minding or possibly part-time cleaning – in addition to fulfilling their 'proper' domestic role of shopping, cooking, washing and all the other household tasks associated with looking after a husband and a growing family.[2] A significant minority of women (13–14 per cent in Edwardian Britain)[3] continued to work full-time after marriage. Work, though, was not always easy to find, and opportunities were becoming more restricted in some ways as the century progressed. The great expansion of the textile industry, which had provided employment for working women in the early nineteenth century, was slowing down by the 1870s and 1880s. Legislation introduced to protect female workers from exploitation had also made women a less attractive economic bargain for employers. In addition, working-class women encountered the same kinds of prejudice and discrimination which frustrated the ambitions of career-minded middle-class women. They found that they were offered only the lower-paid, less skilled work. The average wage of young women in the non-textile industries in 1906 was 12s 11d – far from a living wage.4 The range of occupations for working-class women was narrow, a third of all women employed in 1906 being engaged in domestic service. Many unmarried women, and some others, were pushed to the margins of sweatshop work or prostitution. Those in more mainstream industrial occupations had great difficulty in securing promotion and little success in improving their conditions through collective action. This was partly because of hostility on the part of employers or male workers, the latter fearing competition from women workers and concerned mainly with boosting their own earnings to the level of a family wage, so that their wives did not have to work. The women themselves had little time or energy for trade union activity, or else were in occupations which were difficult for trade unions to penetrate. There were some exceptions – such as the successful Match Girls' strike in London in 1888 – and a Women's Trade Union League was formed in 1891 (from the earlier Women's Protective and Provident League), but these initiatives depended heavily on middle-class organisers and were not the prelude to any large-scale breakthrough as far as the unionisation of women workers was concerned. In 1901 only 2. 9 per cent of women workers were trade union members, compared with 17.2 per cent of men, the Lancashire cotton industry providing the only substantial concentration of women's trade union activity.[5]

It can thus be seen that the lives of women were profoundly shaped by the social class of which they were part. Yet it is equally true that for all women in the Victorian period, be they duchesses or textile workers, the idea of a society divided into 'separate spheres', male and female, public and private, was all-pervasive. Women were deemed to be biologically and intellectually inferior: not only physically weaker than men, but more emotional and potentially unstable. Notions of respectability, as well as many of the teachings of the Church, dictated that a woman's place was in the home, the 'angel of the hearth', enjoying a subordinate and dependent role while fulfilling her pre-ordained functions of motherhood and domesticity. This essentially middle-class ideology of family respectability was accepted by many members of the working classes as well, so that the pinnacle of satisfaction for the male head of a working-class family was to be able to boast that his wife did no work (other than housework!) and that his own earnings were sufficient for the family's needs. Many women, it must be said, appear to have subscribed to the same view, and it was the pinch of necessity rather than any more clearly articulated dissatisfaction which undermined the idyll for the majority of working-class families in the late-Victorian and Edwardian eras.

All the same, changes were occurring in the late nineteenth century which affected the position of women in society and their own perceptions of their social role. One such change was the broadening of the range of educational opportunities that were available for young women. In the 20 years following the Education Act of 1870 elementary education became, by stages, universal, free and compulsory, for girls as well as boys. School authorities may still have imposed some segregation both in the physical organisation of schools and the teaching of classes, with a greater emphasis in girls' schooling on fitness for home-making and domestic tasks, but at least all pupils received rudimentary instruction in literacy, while the presence of large numbers of women teachers provided some kind of non-domestic role model for ambitious pupils. Moreover, above the level of the Church and Board schools – which catered mainly for working-class and lower-middle-class children – there were more and more private schools which provided young women from wealthier backgrounds with the chance to enjoy an academic education every bit as rigorous as that undertaken by their male contemporaries. The foundation of institutions such as the North London Collegiate Day School for Girls in 1850, and Cheltenham Ladies College in 1854, showed a new seriousness about the provision of education for girls. Women's colleges were established at Oxford and Cambridge (although only London University was at first prepared to admit women students to take degrees). The setting up of training colleges for women teachers, and the admission of some women students to medical training, also extended the possibilities of a higher education, even if, outside teaching, women still found the road to professional advancement blocked by formal restrictions and prejudice. By the 1890s it was coming to be more widely accepted that in most areas, if not all, women were intellectually the equals of men, and the growing ranks of educated women formed an increasingly self-confident pressure group behind demands for further change.

Another area in which change occurred was that of legal rights. As early as 1792, Mary Wollstonecraft had written a *Vindication of the Rights of Women*, claiming legal and civic equality for her sex, but the movement for emancipation made few significant advances before the middle of the nineteenth century. The crucial breakthrough which women needed to make was that of persuading the law to view them as individuals in their own right. Because, in English law, legal status was accorded largely on the basis of the ownership of property, hitherto only unmarried women (or widows) who were property owners had anything approaching equality of legal rights. Not only were married women deemed to surrender any income or property which they possessed to their husbands as part of the contract of marriage, they also, in the eyes of the law, became themselves virtually the property of their husbands, denied a separate legal existence and the rights and freedoms that followed from it.[6] This was a situation which women in the nineteenth century campaigned to alter, and with some success. A series of Married Women's Property Acts, beginning with the Act of 1870, was passed, giving all women the right to retain a separate income after marriage and to possess and administer their own property. Acts of 1882 and 1884 went further in defining the rights of married women as legally-recognised individuals, ending the situation whereby in law they could be treated simply as 'chattels' of their husbands.[7] Other changes in the law further strengthened the rights of women as wives and mothers. Already in 1839 the Custody of Infants Act had given mothers of 'unblemished character' access to their children in the event of separation or divorce. The Guardianship of Infants Act of 1886 made it legal for a widow to act as the 'sole guardian' of her children, ending the practice whereby only male guardianship was recognised by law. An Act of 1884 gave a divorced woman the legal right to 'maintenance' from her former husband.

These reforms were part of a more far-reaching examination of the institution of marriage and of issues of sexual morality which took place in late-Victorian Britain. In 1857 the Matrimonial Causes Act had, for the first time, set up civil courts for divorce proceedings. This made divorce more widely available,[8] at least for those with the money to pay legal fees, although the number of divorces remained comparatively small and a social stigma still attached to those involved. From a woman's point of view, however, the 1857 Act served merely to confirm the 'double standard' that operated in Victorian society, because, while a husband could gain a divorce upon proof of his wife's adultery, a wife seeking divorce would have to prove her husband guilty of a further 'cruelty' in addition. The causes were eventually brought into line, but the need for many years of campaigning to achieve this goal emphasised the precariously subordinate position in which women found themselves. Until 1884, a wife who refused to live with her husband in their marital home was still liable to imprisonment by the courts. The newspapers in the 1880s published exposés of the incidence of 'wife-beating' and physical cruelty within marriage. Attention was focused, too, on the 'white slavery' of prostitution, partly as a by-product of the campaign for the repeal of the Contagious Diseases Acts, which provided for the medical inspection of prostitutes and were seen not only as giving official sanction to what was widely considered as a social evil but also as a blatant measure of discrimination against women whose paying customers were free from any censure or opprobium. The moral values of a society which permitted the exploitation of women for male sexual gratification while hypocritically espousing the ideal of the purity of womanhood were thus brought under increasing scrutiny, and the more open discussion of all aspects of relations between the sexes (including hitherto taboo subjects such as birth control) was one of the features of the nineteenth century's closing years.

So, also, were women drawn into a more active involvement in the political arena. Upper-class women had always performed a quasi-political role – as the wives or mistresses of public men, as the holders of Court appointments, or as hostesses at the endless round of dinners, receptions and country-house gatherings which formed the social context of party-political life in the mid-Victorian period.[9] Working-class women had an equally traditional, but more direct, experience of political activity, from involvement in food and price riots in the late eighteenth century to participation in the Chartist movement in the 1830s and 1840s.[10] Perhaps even more significant, though, was the way in which middle-class women were participating in politics to a growing extent from the middle of the nineteenth century onwards – writers and commentators like Harriet Martineau, campaigners like Josephine Butler (who led the struggle against the Contagious Diseases Acts), and reformers and social investigators like Beatrice Potter, who forsook a comfortable middle-class existence to join Charles Booth's survey of conditions in London's East End and (as Beatrice Webb) became one of the leading figures in the Fabian Society.[11] Between 1850 and 1900 large numbers of women emerged in this way as political figures in their own right, with wide experience of writing, public speaking, lobbying and committee work which enabled them to carve a niche for themselves in what was still very much a male-dominated public sphere.

In a parallel development, as the new world of mass politics took shape after 1867, the political parties became more anxious to enlist female support, not yet as voters but as social organisers and volunteer workers in the constituencies. It was the Conservative party which pioneered the integration of women into constituency work on a large scale. Martin Pugh has demonstrated that the party's Primrose League, formed as a vehicle for mobilising latent popular conservatism in the 1880s, included a high proportion of women among its members, possibly totalling 'hundreds of thousands'.[12] Surviving habitation (branch) records suggest that in some localities more than half the members may have been women and that, furthermore, although at its upper levels the League divided into 'Knights' and 'Dames', for ordinary members no distinction of sex was made and women were not only able to take up positions of leadership but were encouraged to do so. It should be noted, however, that while the League organised social functions and played a full part in canvassing and electioneering it had no role in the formulation of Conservative party policy and remained formally separate from the official party machine, which was still a male preserve. The Liberals operated a similar segregation of roles. A Women's Liberal Federation was formed in 1887. The Federation supported the party's candidates at elections, held its own discussions on matters of policy and received intermittent attention from the party's leaders, but the party apparatus as a whole was comparatively untouched by feminine influence. Indeed, of the main political movements in Britain in the late nineteenth century, only the socialists admitted women on terms of equality with men and allowed them to play a more or less unfettered part in organisation, policy making and campaigning.

The one very significant exception to the qualified acceptance of women into the political sphere (in the sense that female participation encountered less resistance) was in the realm of local government, where women were given more formal rights as the century progressed. In 1869, the Municipal Franchise Act gave women ratepayers the right to vote in municipal elections. In 1870 the same rights were granted in respect of the School Boards created under the Forster Education Act; women were, additionally, made eligible to become members of the Boards, and, in 1875, of the Boards of Poor Law Guardians. This was followed in 1894 by equality of treatment for women under the Parish Councils Act of that year and, in 1907, by the passage of the Qualification of Women Act, which codified all the previous changes and extended the right to vote and to stand for election to the County Councils, bringing them into line with the authorities covered by previous legislation. By that time, it has been estimated that between 10 and 12 per cent of local electors were women. Women candidates were also coming forward and being elected in increasing numbers. In her pioneering, and possibly definitive, study of this process, Patricia Hollis has identified about 270 women members of School Boards in 1900, over 1,000 women serving as Poor Law Guardians, and nearly 200 women district councillors.[13] Despite the abolition of School Boards under the terms of the 1902 Education Act, the contribution of women to the local political process – as candidates, voters and elected representatives – continued to grow throughout the Edwardian period, with over 2,000 women holding elected office in England and Wales on the outbreak of war in 1914.[14]

Nevertheless, important though these changes were, they were not in themselves enough to effect a dramatic alteration in the lives of the majority of women. At the turn of the century, as Victoria's reign drew to a close, women were still a long way from achieving equality with men in public life, whether in politics, education or professions and careers. The doctrine of 'separate spheres' was still powerful and pervasive, and within the marital home women were for the most part economically dependent on their husbands, even if no longer legally as subordinate as in the past. This is not to say that they were necessarily unhappy or discontented, but, for some women at least, particularly those of the younger generation, the need for further change was a strongly-felt imperative. In the Edwardian era the desire for change was to reveal itself in a variety of ways – in a challenge to social convention, in the search for new and more varied forms of employment, in campaigns for improvements in education, working conditions and social welfare. Above all, it found an outlet in the demand which became, for many, the defining slogan of the women's movement in the 1900s: the demand for 'Votes for Women'.

Suffragists and Suffragettes

The campaign for female suffrage is conventionally dated from the 1860s, at the time of the debate over the Second Reform

Bill.[15] A petition in favour of women's suffrage was presented unsuccessfully to the House of Commons in June 1866. In May 1867, John Stuart Mill, the Liberal MP for Westminster, a supporter of the 1866 petition, and author of the emancipationist *The Subjection of Women*, proposed an amendment to Disraeli's Reform Bill to substitute 'person' for 'man' in the wording of the measure. The attempt failed, but the interest it and the earlier petitions had aroused stimulated further efforts by suffrage activists. In 1867 Lydia Becker formed the Manchester Women's Suffrage Committee; similar societies were established in Bristol, Edinburgh and London. Through the 1870s and 1880s they maintained a steady level of propaganda, lobbying, arguing and persuading to win converts to their cause. In practical terms, however, their labours brought little immediate reward. There was still considerable opposition to the idea of female enfranchisement, from women as well as men, based on the ideology of separate spheres. Politics lay clearly within the public sphere; women, it was believed, either lacked the intellect or temperament to take decisions affecting public affairs, or else their feminine innocence would be corrupted by the sordid touch of political life and it was better that they should be protected from such by the stronger and more worldly male.[16] Of course, there was a great deal of self-serving and masculine hypocrisy in such ideas, but they were widely held none the less. It could also be argued by its opponents that the demand for the suffrage was not sufficiently general to justify reform, since even those most active in the movement for women's rights did not necessarily see the vote as an overriding priority, some indeed feeling that the issue was a distraction from more immediately important educational and social reforms.[17]

By the beginning of the Edwardian period, though, there were signs that a change was occurring. The case for excluding women from the franchise was being undermined by the social, legal and political trends outlined in the previous section. There were increasing numbers of unmarried women whose interests were not protected by any kind of 'virtual representation' through fathers or husbands. As women acquired greater legal rights as property owners so too they had a stronger claim on an electoral system which equated the ownership of property with fitness to vote, while the progress of male enfranchisement (to the point, after 1884, where roughly two-thirds of all men had the vote) highlighted the way in which the existing arrangements were uniquely discriminatory where women were concerned. Add to these factors the undeniable truth that in a variety of fields women were showing themselves the equals of men in intellect and responsibility, and that they were playing an ever more important part in local government and in political debate at both local and national level, and their permanent exclusion from the franchise seemed almost unthinkable, even if there was still room for disagreement over the terms and timing of any measure of suffrage reform.[18] The growing acceptance of the principle of female enfranchisement was illustrated in 1897 when a women's suffrage motion was passed by the House of Commons with a majority of 71 votes. In the same year the suffrage campaigners regrouped their forces outside parliament, most of the existing suffrage organisations coming together in the National Union of Women's Suffrage Societies under the presidency of Millicent Garrett Fawcett. Other bodies such as the Women's Liberal Federation and the Independent Labour Party were also committing themselves to the women's suffrage cause.

Another accession of strength to the suffrage movement was provided by the formation in Manchester in 1903 of the Women's Social and Political Union, led by Mrs Emmeline Pankhurst, widow of the radical socialist and veteran suffrage campaigner Dr Richard Pankhurst, and herself a supporter of the ILP and a prominent figure in local politics through her membership of Poor Law and School Boards. Perhaps unfairly, historiographical attention has concentrated overmuch on the WSPU and the Pankhursts, especially the mother and her daughters Christabel and Sylvia, who became noted campaigners in their own right.[19] There has also been a tendency to exaggerate the differences between the 'suffragists' (the supposedly moderate NUWSS) and the 'suffragettes' of the WSPU, or to assume that all the supporters of the latter were imbued with the extreme militancy which surfaced in the immediate pre-war years. In fact, the NUWSS remained the larger and more typical organisation throughout the Edwardian period, with 480 branches and 53,000 members by 1914.[20] Equally, the WSPU was never a purely militant body. In its first two years it pursued a conventional pattern of pressure group activity, working particularly closely with the ILP and the nascent Labour party (or Labour Representation Committee as it then was). Keir Hardie, Labour MP for Merthyr from 1900, was one of the Pankhursts' closest and most loyal allies. Even in later years, when militancy was at its height, the WSPU never completely abandoned more peaceful methods of campaigning and propaganda, cooperating on occasion with other suffrage organisations and with pro-suffrage members of other political groupings to further their aims.

That said, differences undoubtedly did exist between the WSPU and the other suffrage organisations which were, in some senses, its rivals. Initially there were differences of political orientation, the WSPU inclining towards the Labour and socialist parties, the NUWSS being largely a pro-Liberal organisation. These differences were reflected in differences of membership and constituency. Although all of the main suffrage groups were largely middle class in their composition, the WSPU, through the work of figures like the former mill-girl Annie Kenney and, later, Sylvia Pankhurst, made more strenuous – if not necessarily successful – efforts to recruit working-class support.[21] The age-profile of NUWSS members was higher, as befitted a federation of established bodies, and those members were more likely to be married women. The WSPU, by contrast, appealed to younger, unmarried women, perhaps with more of a taste for adventure and rebellion.[22] This last fact was probably related to the forceful leadership which the Pankhursts and the WSPU provided, and to the employment of those tactics of direct action which, for contemporaries and historians alike, became the defining characteristic of the WSPU as a campaigning movement.

The militant campaign began in the autumn of 1905, as the Balfour government tottered to its fall and a general election approached. In October, Christabel Pankhurst and Annie Kenney were arrested for obstruction and assaulting a police officer outside the Free Trade Hall in Manchester, whence they had been ejected, having tried without success to persuade Sir

Edward Grey to say whether an incoming Liberal government would give votes to women. Their arrest and brief imprisonment attracted considerable attention and signalled the start of a more widespread use of militancy once the general election was under way.[23] When Campbell-Bannerman failed to mention women's suffrage in his keynote election speech at the Albert Hall on 21 December, Annie Kenney and Teresa Billington brandished pro-suffrage banners and were promptly thrown out of the building. During the election, the WSPU leaders campaigned in support of their Labour allies, notably Keir Hardie in Merthyr, but in Manchester suffragette hecklers systematically disrupted the meetings of the young Winston Churchill, a recent Unionist convert to the Liberal party, who became one of the WSPU's principal targets. Churchill, although personally sympathetic to female suffrage, refused, in characteristically robust language, to be 'henpecked' by the militants and numerous confrontations between himself and the WSPU ensued.

Such episodes were of only marginal significance in the overall context of the general election campaign and did little to alter the views of politicians thus assailed. But the return of a Liberal government with a large majority did offer renewed hope to the pro-suffrage lobby. The Liberal party had championed the cause of broadening the franchise since the days of Gladstone. It was committed to the introduction of a number of specific electoral reforms, including the abolition of plural voting and the reform of the registration system. Liberal MPs were rightly believed to be more likely to support women's suffrage, and to be more amenable to pressure in the constituencies, than were their Conservative opponents. Despite these encouraging signs, however, it quickly became apparent that the prospects of real progress were slim. After ten years out of office, the Liberals had more pressing priorities than women's suffrage. Nor was this the only obstacle to action. When Campbell-Bannerman met a suffrage deputation at the Foreign Office in May 1906 he told them that although he personally was in favour of women being given the vote, opinion in the cabinet was divided, and therefore he could not commit the government to supporting early legislation. The most that could be done was to rectify anomalies in the local government franchise, which was duly accomplished with the introduction of the Qualification of Women Act in 1907.[24] As for the rules concerning parliamentary elections, it was left to private Members to bring forward their own measures in the House of Commons to try to force the government's hand.

Once the government's intentions were clear, both the 'militant' and 'non-militant' campaigns outside parliament were intensified. The NUWSS redoubled its efforts to lobby MPs and to exert pressure through the constituencies. But it was the WSPU which again grabbed most of the headlines. In September 1906 they opened their new London headquarters at 4 Clement's Inn. A new newspaper, *Votes For Women*, was launched, and by the autumn of 1907 a recruitment drive had resulted in the formation of seventy branches in London and the provinces. The total membership of the WSPU was still well below that of the older societies (which were also expanding rapidly at this time), but what the Pankhursts and their followers lacked in numbers they made up for in showmanship and campaigning zeal. Mass lobbies of parliament led to the arrest of a number of suffragettes who tried to force their way into the House of Commons. Publicity stunts, such as the Downing Street demonstration of 17 January 1908, when two suffragettes chained themselves to the railings outside the Prime Minister's residence and one leading WSPU member, Mrs Drummond, actually gained admittance to 10 Downing Street, proliferated. In February 1908, to coincide with a debate on a Women's Suffrage Bill being introduced by the Liberal MP for Kensington, H. Y. Stanger, suffragettes concealed in furniture vans tried to storm the Houses of Parliament. The WSPU also sought to influence the electoral process by campaigning in by-elections against government candidates. At Newton Abbot in January 1908 Mrs Pankhurst was violently attacked by a hostile crowd when a Liberal seat had been lost following suffragette intervention.[25]

Militant tactics did not win universal approbation, and there were some defections from the WSPU in consequence of their use. Nor did militancy bring about an early change in the position of the government. Asquith, who succeeded Campbell-Bannerman as Prime Minister in 1908, was a confirmed anti-suffragist. Even had he not been, it is difficult to see how the impasse could have been broken. The Liberals were already embroiled in their conflict with the House of Lords and were not in a position to bring forward a major suffrage measure (except, perhaps, as part of a policy of 'filling the cup' as a prelude to Lords' reform). Equally, there was opposition to the idea of supporting a limited measure of female enfranchisement which might benefit the Conservatives by giving votes to propertied women alone. Even those Liberals who were not opposed to the suffrage for other reasons were reluctant to be seen to be giving way before the militant challenge. The result of this was that the government remained intransigent and the militancy intensified. In May 1908 Stanger's Bill received a second reading in the Commons by a majority of 179 votes, but Asquith refused to give it government backing, thereby virtually killing its chances of making further progress. Suffragette protesters responded by smashing the windows of 10 Downing Street and making further attempts to storm parliament, one of which, at the opening of parliament in October 1908, led to the arrest of Mrs Pankhurst and to her being sentenced to three months' imprisonment. In 1909 there were further violent outbreaks: on 29 June, 108 suffragettes were arrested for stone-throwing in London in protest against Asquith's refusal to meet a suffrage deputation. As the political temperature was raised by the confrontation over the People's Budget, Lloyd George's meetings at Limehouse and Newcastle, and Asquith's at the Bingley Hall in Birmingham, were disrupted by demonstrators. Imprisoned suffragettes adopted the tactic of hunger-striking to reinforce their demand for 'political' status, and their treatment by forcible feeding produced emotional clashes in the House of Commons and in the press.[26]

The years 1908–9 saw a dramatic increase of pro- and anti-suffrage activity alike. In addition to the militant outbreaks, peaceful marches, meetings and demonstrations were held. 'Women's Sunday' in June 1908 brought together large crowds of suffrage supporters (one estimate suggested as many as 500,000) to listen to speakers in Hyde Park. In May 1909 a 'Women's Exhibition' drew attention to the achievements of women in order to emphasise the injustice of their exclusion from the franchise. Gradually this peaceful propaganda had its effect and politicians began to search for a compromise which would satisfy the immediate demands of the suffrage campaign and prevent a further escalation of militancy. After the January 1910 general election, a cross-party Conciliation Committee brought forward a Conciliation Bill, designed to admit women house-holders to the existing property-based franchise. One of the sponsors of the Bill was Lord Lytton, whose sister, Lady Constance Lytton, had suffered damage to her health as a consequence of being imprisoned while disguised as a working-class suffragette, Jane Warton. Lytton and his committee clearly felt that the time had come to put an end to militancy by a bold gesture, even if the government would not take the initiative. The attempt at com-promise was encouraged by the WSPU declaration of a truce pending the Bill's consideration by parliament, and by the general desire to resolve outstanding constitutional differences following the death of Edward VII. The Bill, introduced in the name of the Labour MP, David Shackleton, received an unop-posed first reading. After its second reading debate on 11/12 July 1910 it was approved by the substantial margin of 109 votes.

However, this proved to be no more than a token success. The vote disguised the fact that a number of serious parliamentary obstacles still had to be overcome. First, the success of the Conciliation Committee had stimulated a more effective organ-isation of the anti-suffrage forces, the anti-suffrage camp including prominent Conservatives such as Lord Curzon and some mem-bers of the Liberal government, among them Charles Hobhouse and 'Loulou' Harcourt. In the later stages of the Bill's progress, in addition to seeking to win over those MPs who were as yet uncommitted, its opponents could also play on the divisions of opinion which existed on the part of those Members who had supported the second reading. These included those who were prepared to vote for the principle of suffrage but who wanted a more limited enfranchisement than the Bill proposed, as well as those who felt that the Bill did not go far enough in a democratic direction.[27] Allied to this last group were figures like Lloyd George, who announced during the second reading debate that he was unable to support the measure because of the anti-Liberal bias it would be likely to give the electorate.[28] All of these cross-currents made the future of the Bill highly problematic, the situation being further complicated by the likelihood of an early general election brought about by the government's attempts to reform the House of Lords. When Asquith – who was personally convinced that the enfranchisement of women would herald a national disaster – refused to guarantee that the Bill could complete its passage before an election was called, the chances of resolving the suffrage question in 1910 were doomed. Predictably the WSPU thereupon abrogated its truce, the first fruits of their decision being the clashes between police and demonstrators outside parliament on 18 November which went down in the annals of the movement as 'Black Friday' because of the violent methods which the police used to restrain the protesters.

The Conciliation Bill controversy was renewed in 1911 when the measure was reintroduced by Sir George Kemp. On the face of it, support for the Bill had strengthened, the voting being 255 to 88 in favour, with a majority among those voting from each of the four main parties in the Commons.[29] But the figures were rendered academic by the government's continuing refusal to back the proposals, and by Asquith's announcement that the government was preparing its own Franchise Bill for the 1912 session which would take precedence over private legislation. The intentions of the Liberal government at this juncture have been subjected to close scrutiny. The Bill brought forward by the government in 1912 was a Manhood Suffrage Bill which made no reference to votes for women. The suspicion was raised, therefore, that the government was using this measure as a tactic to block female suffrage and that Asquith's contention that the Bill would be framed so as to allow women's suffrage amendments was merely a device to placate Liberal suffragists. These suspicions were given added weight because of the ruling by Speaker Lowther in January 1913, in response to a challenge from the Unionist leader, Bonar Law, that women's suffrage amendments to the Bill were inadmissible because they would fundamentally alter its character. On the other hand, Martin Pugh has shown that the pro-suffrage members of the cabinet, notably Grey and Lloyd George, worked actively to promote the amendments to enfranchise women, with Asquith's acquiescence.[30] It may charitably be concluded that the government was not being deliberately deceitful; that the device of relying on amendments to the Bill to introduce women's suffrage was in deference to the anti-suffrage views of some members of the cabinet and the parliamentary party and that to preserve the unity of the government it was felt best to let the House of Commons decide. Certainly the electoral prospects of the Liberal party were likely to be better served by votes for women being introduced as part of a move towards full adult suffrage than in the more limited form envisaged in the Conciliation Bills.

Whatever the truth of these speculations – and despite Asquith's admission in a private letter to Venetia Stanley that the Speaker's ruling came as 'a great relief'[31] – the debacle over the Suffrage Bill left the government in the worst of all possible worlds. Their measure had to be withdrawn, amid general embarrassment. Meanwhile they had alienated not only the militant suffragettes but also the more moderate suffrage societies. Hitherto the NUWSS had worked closely with the Liberal party and had drawn much of its support from the Women's Liberal Federation. By 1912 that alliance was at an end and the suffragists were looking instead to the Labour party as their principal parliamentary ally. The events surrounding the ill-fated legislative efforts of the Liberal administration merely served to strengthen the suffragist–Labour convergence.[32] At the other extreme, the militants of the WSPU had never been supporters of the government, but their hostility became more marked from 1911 onwards. Cabinet ministers and their property were subjected to physical attacks. This campaign of intimidation was accompanied by other forms of assault – window-breaking ('the argument of the broken pane'), arson (including the burning down of the Theatre Royal in Dublin), and attacks on museums, churches and art galleries. Imprisoned suffragettes continued to employ the hunger strike as a weapon to embarrass the government and attract public sympathy. In 1913 the government replied with the so-called 'Cat and Mouse' Act which gave the authorities the power to re-arrest hunger strikers released temporarily from prison on medical grounds, though this did little to solve either the practical or propaganda problems which the hunger strike tactics presented. In June 1913 the suffragettes acquired their most famous martyr with the death of Emily Wilding Davison from injuries received when she had been knocked down by the King's horse after running on to the racetrack during the Epsom Derby.

As 1914 succeeded 1913, a deadlock seemed to have been reached. Practically speaking, women's suffrage appeared as far off as ever. The government had antagonised many of its former supporters among the moderate suffragists and was no nearer to defeating the militants. On this reading, it was only the coming of the First World War which – by putting an end to militancy, bringing into existence a coalition government which could tackle franchise reform on a cross-party basis, and above all by giving women an opportunity through their war work to justify their claims to equality with men – opened the way to a settlement of the suffrage question. Yet, while it would have been rash to predict such a settlement in 1914, it can be argued that the raw material for a settlement existed even before the crisis of war transformed the domestic scene. There were some signs that the militant movement was beginning to run out of steam and that the Pankhursts (Christabel and her mother) were becoming more isolated within the suffrage movement. Most suffragists, in the NUWSS and elsewhere, were still working peacefully for a constitutional solution to the suffrage problem. A pro-suffrage majority probably existed in the House of Commons if only it could be mobilised and divorced from the exigencies of party politics.[33] Significantly, Asquith himself gave indications – in conversation with a deputation of East London suffragists in June 1914 – that his opposition to reform was lessening, and there is thus at least the possibility that the Liberal party might have gone into an election with 'Votes for Women' inscribed on its banner, and that a future Liberal government would have introduced a measure of women's suffrage with or without the further changes resulting from the First World War.[34] None of this, admittedly, is susceptible to proof, but it must be kept in mind when relating the controversy over female suffrage to the wider question of the

Edwardian crisis and in attempting to assess the scale and depth of the 'women's revolt' which may have been taking place in the Edwardian period.

A Women's Revolt?

George Dangerfield portrayed the militant campaign for votes for women as part of a more general 'women's rebellion' which was characteristic of the mood of rebellion which permeated Edwardian society as a whole. Recent writers have not necessarily endorsed his analysis in every respect. However, no examination of the validity of the concept of an Edwardian crisis would be complete without some attention being given to the two main questions which Dangerfield's account raises. First, how serious were the political problems presented by the suffrage issue? Second, what was the relationship between the suffrage debate and the changing position of women in Edwardian society, and to what extent could it be considered as part of a feminist assault on the existing social and political system?

Certainly it would be wrong to minimise the importance of the suffrage campaign, even in purely political terms. The suffrage societies showed themselves capable of attracting a mass membership and of mobilising large numbers of supporters – men and women – in rallies, demonstrations and propaganda activity. In this respect there was a direct line of continuity between the agitation of the Edwardian period and the movements for extending the franchise which had flourished in the nineteenth century – at the time of the Reform crisis of 1830–32, during the Chartist decades of the 1830s and 1840s, and in the years preceeding the passage of the Second Reform Act in 1867. It is true that in scope and strength the Edwardian suffrage movement could not compare with the extra-parliamentary campaigns of the Chartist era. It may even be, as some writers have suggested, that as Britain approached male democracy after 1885 the suffrage question lost some of its appeal as a touchstone of radical faith. But there was at least as strong a demand for reform in the 1900s as there had been in the 1860s, and a much greater popular clamour between 1905 and 1914 than there had been, for example, in 1884–5. Add to this the manner in which the Edwardian campaign focused attention firmly on the issue of women's rights, raising perhaps the most fundamental principle of electoral reform since the bulwarks of the aristocratic old order had first been breached in 1832, and the true political significance of the suffrage question in Edwardian Britain becomes clear.

The question of whether, and in what way, to reform the franchise posed problems for all of the main political parties. The Conservatives were the least troubled, although they wanted to stave off a thoroughgoing democratisation for as long as possible. Some Conservatives were ready to support a limited enfranchisement of women, but the party was not strongly committed on the issue (a majority of peers and MPs were probably at least latently anti-suffrage) and its members were for the most part quite willing to sit back and reap what benefits they could from Liberal strife. The position of the Labour party was apparently more straightforward, since the party was in favour of votes for women and its MPs voted solidly for most of the suffrage Bills introduced in the 1906 and 1910 parliaments. Beneath the superficial unity, however, there were disagreements between supporters of 'equal suffrage' (who were prepared to give women the vote on the same terms as men, even if this resulted in an increase in the number of middle-class, propertied voters) and those who insisted that female enfranchisement should come about only as part of a move towards full democracy as provided by 'adult' (that is, universal) suffrage legislation. The rejection of 'equal suffrage' by the 1907 Labour conference created divisions within the party, and keen suffragists like Keir Hardie were quick to declare that the conference resolution was not binding on MPs.[35] Arguments continued to rage in the party until they were in some measure resolved by the decision of the 1912 conference not to support any future electoral reform introduced by the government unless some provision for female suffrage was included.

The problems of Conservative and Labour politicians were comparatively minor ones when set against those with which the question of electoral reform confronted the Liberal party and the

Liberal government. In previous struggles over the franchise the Liberals had always been on the side of the reformers, just as now a majority of Liberal MPs supported the principle of the enfranchisement of women. The Liberal party was likely to benefit from the introduction of adult suffrage, and in the parliamentary situation as it was after the elections of 1910 even a marginally more pro-Liberal (or less anti-Liberal) bias in the electoral system could mean the difference between victory and defeat.[36] With no fewer than 12 seats being lost to the Conservatives between 1910 and 1914, and with a general election pending in 1915, the Liberals were anxious for any reinforcement they could get; they were equally anxious to prevent any erosion of loyalty and enthusiasm among their own supporters. Yet, as the events of 1912–13 and the fate of the Manhood Suffrage Bill had shown, the government was neither united enough to incorporate women's suffrage into its own reform Bill, nor could it contemplate the passing of a measure such as the Conciliation Bill which would enfranchise only wealthier women whose votes were likely to be cast for the Conservative party. As long as the deadlock lasted, the Liberals were denied the advantage of adult suffrage, while forfeiting the support of the suffrage lobby. Women's suffrage itself may not have been a certain vote-winner, as George Lansbury, the Labour MP, discovered when he resigned his seat to contest a by-election on the issue in his Bow and Bromley constituency in 1912 only to be beaten by a Conservative. But a Liberal government which could not satisfactorily resolve the suffrage question lost much of its radical credibility. Already the Liberals were the main target of the suffrage campaigners, especially those in the WSPU. So, too, by 1912–13 the Liberals were losing the support of the formerly pro-Liberal NUWSS and of women activists in the constituencies. The NUWSS actually took up a pro-Labour stance after 1912 and launched an Election Fighting Fund to support Labour candidates. In a tight election such as that of 1915 promised to be, such factors could be sufficient to tip the scales against the government and oust the Liberals from office.

A further dimension of difficulty was added to the problem by the use which certain sections of the suffrage movement –

principally the WSPU – made of so-called 'militant' tactics. The phenomenon of militancy has to be kept in perspective. Only a minority of suffragists actively supported the militant campaign. Even then, their 'militancy' – in the sense that such a term implies unrestrained, terrorist or quasi-revolutionary violence – was of a limited kind. The phrase 'civil disobedience' perhaps conveys a better definition of the movement in relation to other forms of popular protest. Nevertheless, militancy, and the arguments to which it gave rise, played a part in heightening the controversy over the suffrage issue. The militants themselves claimed that they were responsible for the great strides made by the suffrage campaign after 1905. Mrs Pankhurst, in her personal account of the movement, stated her belief that the WSPU's tactics 'made women's suffrage a matter of news it had never been before'.[37] She also argued that it was the single-mindedness of the suffragettes – their refusal to dissipate their energies in pursuit of reforms other than the vote, and their insistence on attacking all those who would not give top priority to suffrage reform – which opened the way to their eventual success. Yet hers was necessarily a one-sided and partisan view. Militant tactics aroused public interest, but they also aroused public opposition. Some of the emotionalism surrounding the suffrage debate was fuelled by the militant excesses. Militancy antagonised moderate suffrage supporters, who did not want to be associated with the extremists or to be seen to be making concessions to violence. Within the suffrage movement itself (even within the WSPU) there was criticism of the dictatorial and provocative methods used by the Pankhursts, a feeling that they were somehow degrading to the women's cause, especially as the militant campaign entered its most uncompromising phase following the end of the truce over the Conciliation Bill in 1910.[38]

The question of the impact of militancy is thus a complex one. The use of militant tactics may have alienated some politicians, particularly if they themselves were subjected to attacks; it may also have given the opponents of suffrage reform a stronger case for resisting suffragist demands. That being so, it could be argued that the employment of more conventional forms of pressure would have been more effective in unlocking the door to reform.

But this in turn may be a false conclusion. For one thing, it underestimates the extent to which the supposedly divergent 'moderate' and 'militant' campaigns were actually complementary strands of the same movement, the moderates undoubtedly benefiting in terms of increased support and a higher political profile from the publicity which the militants attracted. For another, it risks missing the point of the threat which the suffrage campaign in general, and the militant campaign in particular, posed to the Liberal government and the political system it represented. This was not, in any simple way, a threat to the authority of parliament or to the rule of law. Rather it was a challenge to the moral basis of the existing system and to the much-vaunted 'liberal' values which regulated its operation. The challenge, moreover, was one which arguably necessitated the use of some form of militancy or civil disobedience if it was to achieve its full force, because in no other way could the discriminatory nature of the nation's power structure be so graphically revealed. In attempting to deal with suffragette attacks the Liberal government was forced to resort to what were, by most definitions, 'illiberal' acts. The exclusion of women from public meetings was an infringement of the rights of freedom of speech. The use of the police against women demonstrators, the force-feeding of suffragette hunger strikers and the farcical expedient of the 'Cat and Mouse' Act brought the government into ridicule if not actual contempt, weakening its resolve and ceding the moral high-ground to its opponents. Even if the government was not in danger of being brought down, its image was tarnished and its reputation for liberalism (in the non-party sense) diminished. The militant campaigners may not, in the short run, have achieved their objective, but they were instrumental in highlighting the oppressive character of the political system to which they were opposed.

Beyond the narrow confines of the debate on militancy lies a more important question: that of the extent to which the gathering momentum of the suffrage campaign was part of a more deep-seated 'women's revolt'. Some observers affected to believe that the agitation for votes for women, at least in its militant form, was the product of a kind of psychological derangement –

a view expressed in an infamous letter to *The Times* by Sir Almroth Wright in 1912. The charges of irrationality did not have any real substance, since the demand for female enfranchisement was a perfectly rational one, but such accusations did deflect attention from the more serious feminism that was at the heart of the movement. The suffrage campaigners wanted the vote not just as a means of achieving a symbolic equality with men; they saw electoral reform as a necessary precondition for making the political system more open to women's ideas and more responsive to their needs. Christabel Pankhurst was one of those who emphasised the feminist implications of political change. In *The Great Scourge and How To End It* (1913), she made the link between male domination of politics and the spread of sexual disease, her remedy being summed up in the typically forthright slogan, 'Votes for Women and Chastity for Men'.[39] Other feminists, such as Teresa Billington-Greig (who left the WSPU in 1907 to found the rival Women's Freedom League), did not necessarily support either the Pankhursts' programme or their tactics, preferring instead to give precedence to education and moral force (in the Chartist sense). There was some concern, too, at the way in which the suffrage question seemed to have monopolised the energies of so many campaigners for women's rights. But in reality the suffrage campaign was no more than the most visible manifestation of an increasingly dynamic and self-confident feminist movement in Edwardian Britain – a fact which may help to account for the desperation with which opponents of female suffrage attempted to discredit its supporters by convicting them of 'mental disorder'.

The development of feminism was the intellectual accompaniment to the changes that had taken place in the position and outlook of women in the late nineteenth century, and was connected in particular with the emergence of the phenomenon of the 'New Woman' in the 1880s and 1890s. In some respects the New Woman was a literary and journalistic creation rather than an actual social type. She was first and foremost a rebel: she rejected Victorian conventions of dress, behaviour and morality. She was likely to be young, educated, probably unmarried, and almost certainly employed in a career or in some artistic or similar pursuit. She was also likely to be middle (or possibly upper) class – a product of the new schools founded after 1850, and perhaps of the universities, art colleges or medical schools. She would be outspoken and independent, and, by definition, a supporter of women's rights. In the popular mind she would be associated with strong views on sexual behaviour, exhibiting either a liberated attitude to sexual relations between men and women or a diametrically opposite enthusiasm for abstinence and celibacy.[40]

Needless to say, this was a stereotype to which few women of the period conformed. It did, however, contain more than a kernel of truth. Contemporaries were aware of the existence of a new generation of women for whom marriage was not necessarily the sole aim of life and who were, through education or employment, throwing off the shackles of a traditional home and upbringing – the sort of progress acutely described in H. G. Wells' novel *Ann Veronica*, published at the height of the first phase of suffragette militancy in 1909. Contemporary awareness similarly pointed to a clash between the ideas represented by the 'New Woman' and those of the society in which she lived. Nor was this clash simply a confrontation between the 'new' and the 'old'. As has been seen, in turn-of-the-century Britain a variety of social movements were active and there was a considerable and lively debate about the nature of the social organism and the principles of social organisation. In the early 1900s the 'National Efficiency' movement was perhaps the most important example of this trend. The ideas of the National Efficiency school emphasised the vital role which the health of children and the maintenance of population growth played in Britain's future: 'Motherhood and Empire' were seen as the twin pillars of national regeneration.[41] This insistence on the importance of women's traditional roles (even at a time when a surplus of females reduced the chances of a conventional family life) directly challenged the liberationist thinking of some sections of the feminist movement and the more varied aspirations of the rising generation. The resurgence of 'separate spheres' thinking in the context of the debate about imperial survival paralleled the growth of feminism, adding to the deeper conflict which underlay the suffrage struggles of the Edwardian era and the 'battle of the sexes' of popular perception.

How serious this clash of ideas was, and how far it represented a threat to social or political stability, is another matter. The vast majority of men and women lived in the centre of the contested territory rather than at either of its extremes. They married, raised families, made ends meet (or not) without taking much notice of the fads and fancies of intellectual or journalistic debate. They were more interested in day-to-day concerns than in schemes for restructuring society, regardless of whether the rebuilding was carried out in accordance with feminist ideas or the nostrums of the 'neo-traditionalist' lobby. Yet that is not to say that tensions did not exist. The ideas of the feminists and those of most of the power-brokers of Edwardian society were in conflict. The changes taking place in the Edwardian period itself made that conflict in places more obvious. The state moved decisively into a more interventionist role in family affairs. The introduction of the Midwives Act of 1902, of maternity allow-ances and child welfare legislation, led to marked improvements in the health of mothers and children, and as such could be welcomed by feminists and non-feminists alike. But it also placed the authority of the state more openly behind the 'motherhood' movement. At the very least there was a potential divergence of perspectives here which made the political battle for control of the state all the more important.

What does this mean for the concept of an Edwardian crisis? The question must be answered on a number of different levels. From a political point of view the most pressing problem was that of the suffrage. There is some evidence that the Liberal govern-ment was moving towards a solution of the problem in the summer of 1914 and that the militant campaign was losing momentum. It is true that militancy was continuing and that an agreed solution was still some way off, but at least the suffrage issue was something which was capable of being resolved within the normal processes of the parliamentary system. The deeper and more imponderable challenge, of which the suffrage cam-paign was only one aspect, was presented by the changes in society at large – the altered balance between the sexes, the spread of legal rights, education and employment opportunities for women, the growth of feminism and changed attitudes to sexual relations and family life. These developments intersected with politics – as in the discussions over the reform of the divorce laws – and they obviously had a political dimension. But they were also part and parcel of a more gradual process of adaptation which had been in train since the middle of the nineteenth century. An old order was passing away, but in most individual lives the changes would be incremental, perhaps almost imperceptible, rather than revolutionary. In society as a whole there were greater stresses, and there were likely to be periods of more acute conflict (as might occur in individual families). However, it is difficult to argue that the occasional conflicts consequent upon the adjustment of society to new ideas of itself constituted a crisis. It may be correct to say that the excitements of the suffrage agitation made the other areas of controversy seem greater than they were. There was a growing debate about the roles of men and women in Edwardian society, and some change was inevitable, but for the most part change was conceivable through compromise and accommodation. The settlement of the suffrage question might have presaged a further transformation of political life, though the experience of politics after 1918 suggests otherwise. But once such a settlement had removed the immediate atmosphere of crisis the normal patterns of social amelioration would probably have reasserted themselves. Suffragism and feminism contributed to the impression of an Edwardian crisis; they were not its root cause.

4

THE CHALLENGE OF LABOUR

While the struggle for 'Votes for Women' was at its height, another struggle was entering a potentially decisive phase. An organised Labour movement had been growing in strength since the middle of the nineteenth century. Socialist ideas began to spread in Britain in the 1880s and by the turn of the century a separate Labour party was in existence to challenge the parliamentary duopoly of the Liberals and Conservatives. In the Edwardian era the Labour challenge intensified. Twenty-nine Labour MPs were returned at the general election of 1906, 40 in January 1910. The trade union movement doubled in size between 1901 and 1914, from two million to four million members. The years 1910–14 were marked by the 'Great Labour Unrest', with national strikes in major industries, violence in industrial areas and the threat of Syndicalist-inspired 'Direct Action', causing some writers to discern a quasi-revolutionary disposition on the part of certain groups of workers which endangered the structures of parliamentary government and the system of liberal capitalism on which they were built. Even if the 'workers' revolt' was less revolutionary in its implications than this view would allow, the 'Labour Question' was one of the most serious aspects of the Edwardian crisis with which the Liberal government elected in 1906 had to deal.

The Rise of Labour

The 'challenge of Labour' which was a feature of the Edwardian period had gathered momentum only gradually. Before the middle of the nineteenth century the limitations of the Labour movement were more obvious than its strengths; indeed, to talk of a Labour movement at all is somewhat misleading. There were various trade union and labour organisations – for example among the miners – but attempts to draw all members of the working classes together into general, national trade unions such as Robert Owen's Grand National Consolidated had failed.[1] Those unions which did exist were mainly small and localised. They had no more than a grudgingly accorded, semi-legal status (following the repeal of the Combination Laws in 1824) and they were regarded with suspicion by employers, political economists and government ministers. There was no central body through which trade unionists could make their views known to parliament, nor did working men have any real political power to compel attention for their wants. The failure of Chartism had left them without the vote in parliamentary elections and the abolition of the property qualification for MPs remained little more than a gesture without an extension of the franchise. The authorities were sometimes prepared to make concessions to extra-parliamentary protest, but that was no substitute for the fuller participation that the Chartists had sought to achieve.

The situation began to change in the 1850s and 1860s. In the 1850s a small but well-organised trade union movement emerged, taking advantage of more stable economic conditions and a more favourable attitude on the part of employers and politicians. Permanent, national trade unions were formed by skilled workers such as the Engineers and Carpenters and Joiners. These 'new model' unions were accepted as partners in negotiation by employers impressed by the benefits of a more structured approach to labour relations and their leaders, men like Robert Applegarth, were regularly consulted by ministers in successive governments. The appointment of a Royal Commission on Trade Unions in 1867 and the subsequent passage of important pieces of legislation (the 1871 Trade Union Act, the 1875 Conspiracy and Protection of Property Act and the Employer and Workmen Act) gave the unions a clearer, better protected status in law, legalised peaceful picketing during industrial disputes and ended the practice whereby breach of contract by workers was considered as a criminal rather than a civil offence.[2] The influence of the unions on the national stage was enhanced by the founding of the Trades Union Congress in 1868 and its establishment of a Parliamentary Committee in 1871 to coordinate the lobbying of government, and by the granting of the vote to working men householders, many of them trade unionists, in the boroughs under the terms of the Second Reform Act of 1867. The first two trade union MPs, the miners Thomas Burt in Morpeth and Alexander Macdonald in Stafford, were elected to parliament at the general election of 1874.

The accommodation of an organised Labour movement in the framework of what Harold Perkin has described as the 'viable class society' of mid-Victorian Britain was facilitated by the generally non-violent, non-revolutionary nature of trade union activity and by the acceptance on the part of most trade unionists of the dominant liberal ideology of the period. They embraced the individualistic, self-help doctrines of the manufacturing middle classes, together with a belief in the shared economic interests of capital and labour. Politically they were enthusiasts for the reformist radicalism of Gladstone and Bright. The working classes played an important part in shaping the popular Liberalism of the 1860s and after 1868 'Lib–Labism' – the outlook of working men who upheld the rights of Labour but who otherwise supported the aims of a mainly middle-class Liberal party – became the central strand in the politics of the trade union movement.[3] The unions' allegiance to the Liberal party was shaken briefly by the 1871 Criminal Law Amendment Act (with which a Liberal government had delayed the legalisation of picketing) but it was quickly restored, bolstered by the sympathetic attitude of many Liberal employers and by the personal rapport which Gladstone was able to build up with working-class voters. By 1885, after a further extension of the franchise by a Liberal government, there were a total of eleven Lib–Lab MPs in the Commons to testify to the closeness of the Liberal–Labour alliance – a closeness emphasised when one of their number, Henry Broadhurst, secretary of the TUC's Parliamentary Committee, became the first working-class government minister by being appointed to a junior post at the Home Office in Gladstone's third ministry in 1886.

From the mid-1880s on, however, some of the tensions which had always been implicit in the relations between the Liberal party and Labour became more obvious, and between 1886 and 1906 the Liberal–Labour alliance was subjected to increasing strain. This was partly because 'labour questions' themselves became a more controversial item on the political agenda, with concern about the mass unemployment resulting from the depression in trade and industry and more vocal demands for intervention by the state in the management of the economy and the regulation of the labour market, for instance by limiting the length of the working day. These demands were associated with the growing popularity of socialist ideas. The formation of the Social Democratic Federation and of other socialist groups such as William Morris' Socialist League offered an alternative to the Liberal radicalism of earlier years and to the 'class collaborationist' model of politics embodied by the Lib–Labs. SDF members were active in orchestrating the demonstrations of the unemployed and in the work of Tom Mann's Eight Hours League, founded in 1886.[4] The socialists also played a prominent part in the affairs of the TUC, where they staged a series of outspoken attacks on Broadhurst and other members of the Lib–Lab 'old guard'.

These changes coincided with important changes in the character of the trade union movement itself. Before this, the unions were small organisations of mainly skilled workers. Attempts at mobilising unskilled workers such as the agricultural labourers had had only limited success and total union membership remained at less than a million, despite a substantial increase in the size of the industrial working population as a whole. In social and occupational terms the Lib–Lab unions of the third quarter of the nineteenth century were exclusive organisations, with few links to the wider industrial working class. Then, in the late 1880s, in the era of the so-called 'new unionism', the union movement enjoyed its first period of sustained expansion since the early 1870s. Between 1888 and 1892, in the favourable conditions created by a temporary economic boom, the number of trade unionists increased from 800,000 to 1.5 million. Admittedly much of the expansion occurred in the already well-established unions such as the Engineers, whose membership rose from 53,740 in 1888 to 71,221 in 1891. But, for the first time, there was also a successful extension of trade union organisation to less skilled groups like the dockers and gasworkers. In this process, individual socialists were closely involved and the unions displayed new levels of militancy and arguably a more coherent sense of class consciousness. The victorious gasworkers' strike led by Will Thorne in London in 1889 and the London dock strike masterminded by John Burns, Ben Tillett and Tom Mann in the summer of the same year were merely the most memorable examples of a wave of disputes involving many different groups of workers – men and women – from the seamen of North East England to the London match girls and the dockers and labourers of Plymouth and the South West.[5] As troubles mounted in 1889–90, one contemporary confided his fears that 'from present appearances we are on the eve of a very serious crisis between Capital and Labour in pretty well every trade in the Kingdom'.[6]

Industrial militancy gave a boost to the idea of independent Labour politics. This possibility had been made more realistic by the Reform and Redistribution Acts of 1884–5 which had doubled the size of the electorate to 5.6 million (about two-thirds of all adult males) and created at least 100 single-member constituencies in which working-class voters were the decisive voice.[7] The election of eleven Lib–Labs in 1885 was an indication of the potential support that was waiting to be tapped. However, the Lib–Lab successes had not been repeated at the election of 1886 (at which two Lib–Lab MPs lost their seats) and in the late 1880s Liberal caucuses were reluctant to make more constituencies available to working men candidates, either for reasons of class prejudice or because they preferred wealthier men who could pay their own expenses. The TUC formed a new Labour Electoral Association in 1886 to put more pressure on the Liberals, but with only limited effect. Meanwhile the first tentative steps towards independence were already being taken. The Scottish miners' leader, James Keir Hardie, stood as an independent candidate in the Mid-Lanark by-election of 1888, having been rejected by the local Liberals. He was defeated, coming bottom of the poll in a three-way contest, but the momentum of the campaign carried him on to found the Scottish Labour Party later in the year and his growing reputation, together with the support of Will Thorne's gasworkers, secured his return as MP for the London constituency of South West Ham in 1892. Two other independent Labour MPs – John Burns at Battersea and Havelock Wilson, the seamen's leader, at Middlesbrough – were also elected at the same time, although both subsequently gravitated to the Liberals. Nor were these entirely isolated victories. The industrial struggles of the period gave birth to a large number of independent Labour groups, on the pattern of the Bradford Labour Union formed in the wake of the Manningham Mills strike of 1890–91.[8] The propaganda of socialist writers and evangelists like Joseph Burgess, founder of the *Workmen's Times*, and Robert Blatchford, author of the influential tract *Merrie England* and editor of the *Clarion* newspaper, was helping to consolidate a power base for critics of the Lib–Lab strategy, which was being challenged within the TUC by Hardie, H. H. Champion and others of a rising generation of Labour leaders. In January 1893, these strands partially coalesced in the formation of a socialist-led Independent Labour Party, of which Keir Hardie, as its lone MP, became the leading figure.[9]

The Liberals did their best to respond to the new mood in the Labour world. Arnold Morley, the party's chief whip from 1886 to 1892, and Francis Schnadhorst, secretary of the Liberal Central Association, ensured that more than 20 Lib–Lab candidates were adopted prior to the 1892 election, even if over half of them were eventually defeated.[10] Liberal leaders, from Gladstone downwards, made favourable references to the trade unions in their speeches and were sympathetic to their demands, while younger MPs, including Asquith, R. B. Haldane and A. H. D. Acland, were working behind the scenes to give the Liberals a more advanced labour policy. The Gladstone and Rosebery governments of 1892–5 implemented a number of useful labour reforms, among them the 1895 Factory Act, the limitation of working hours on the railways and in government workshops, and the appointment of more working men magistrates.[11] But these measures were not enough completely to satisfy the government's own supporters, let alone their sterner critics. The Liberals failed to deliver on a range of key issues, from payment of MPs and an eight hour day for miners to the extension of the law on employers' liability.[12] Keir Hardie was especially scathing about government inaction in the face of rising unemployment, and made this the centrepiece of his attacks in the Commons. There was also criticism of the Liberals' handling of industrial disputes (notably when the despatch of troops by Asquith, the Home Secretary, to the Yorkshire coalfield during the coal strike of 1893 led to the shooting of two miners at Featherstone), while the continuing opposition of local Liberal Associations to the nomination of more Lib–Lab candidates tested the patience even of the pro-Liberal secretary of the LEA, T. R. Threlfall.[13] Gladstone's retirement from the premiership in 1894 removed an important focus of working-class attachment to the Liberal cause and although his successor, Lord Rosebery, had a record of interest in labour questions the disintegration of the government in 1894–5 and its overwhelming defeat at the 1895 election was a serious setback to Liberal attempts to establish themselves as the 'friends of Labour' in the rapidly changing industrial politics of the late Victorian period.

The extent to which the Liberals were losing working class and Labour support should not, of course, be exaggerated. Even after 1895, the bulk of the organised Labour movement was still pro-Liberal in orientation and socialism, of whatever stamp, had attracted no more than a minority following.[14] The ILP was making little headway against a political tide running heavily in the direction of Unionist imperialism. At the 1895 election, all of the ILP's 28 candidates – Keir Hardie included – were defeated, and its by-election sorties in the 1895 parliament were almost uniformly disappointing, Tom Mann's good showing at North Aberdeen in 1896 being a noteworthy exception. Attempts to restore the party's fortunes by negotiating a fusion with the SDF in 1897–8 predictably came to nothing and left the ILP with profound problems of finance, organisation and morale. In one vital respect, however, events were beginning to move in their favour. The late 1890s saw a steady worsening of the situation on the industrial front. A return to depression in 1892–5, following the boom of 1888–91, together with a more determined resistance to union claims on the part of the employers, had placed the trade unions on the defensive. The defeat of the powerful Amalgamated Society of Engineers in a lock-out in 1897–8 showed that the easy victories of the new unionist phase were a thing of the past.[15] As part of a concerted 'employers' counter-attack', non-union labour was being recruited for strike-breaking and more frequent use was being made of the courts to curtail union activity, as in the case of *Lyons v. Wilkins* where the court's judgment effectively rendered illegal the use of secondary picketing in the furtherance of a trade dispute. With the employers organising their own Parliamentary Council in 1898, and public opinion turning increasingly hostile, the unions were impressed with the need to secure fuller representation in parliament to provide political protection for their interests. This the Liberal party, in its weakened state, and because of its presumed pro-employer – or at best neutralist – stance in industrial relations, seemed unable or unwilling to provide.[16] The way was thus opened for the creation of a closer 'Labour alliance' between the trade union movement and the various independent Labour and socialist organisations.

It was in this atmosphere of concern for the unions' future that the Labour Representation Committee, the forerunner of the Labour party, came into being. A resolution was carried at the TUC's annual meeting in 1899 agreeing to a conference of trade union and socialist groups to consider ways of increasing Labour's representation in parliament. Not all unions sent delegates to the meeting in the following February which set up the LRC, and the early progress of that body was far from dramatic, only two MPs (Keir Hardie at Merthyr and Richard Bell, secretary of the Amalgamated Society of Railway Servants, at Derby) being returned under its auspices at the election of 1900. But with the final judgement of the House of Lords in the Taff Vale Case in 1901 the fortunes of the LRC improved. The Lords' decision against the ASRS, Bell's union, in favour of the Taff Vale Railway Company, requiring the union to pay heavy damages for losses incurred by the Company during a strike, sent a frisson of alarm through the entire trades union movement, laying union funds open to plunder by the courts and threatening to make strike action impossible for fear of reprisals. As a result, trade union affiliations to the LRC rose rapidly, only the Miners' Federation (which already had its own MPs) among the big unions remaining aloof. Under the judicious tactical guidance of its secretary, the ILP-er Ramsay MacDonald, the LRC scored a string of by-election victories – at Clitheroe in 1902, and Woolwich and Barnard Castle in 1903 – and made a major breakthrough at the general election of 1906, when its 29 MPs outnumbered the 24 Lib–Labs who were returned as official candidates of the Liberal party.

The significance of these developments has been much debated. It can be argued that the establishment of the LRC and the subsequent emergence of the Labour party – even though that party was not explicitly socialist in character – was a vital staging post in the ideological as well as the organisational disengagement of the Labour movement from the traditions of Lib–Labism and that it represented a decisive move towards a more class-based system of 'industrial' politics in which the Liberal and Labour parties were bound to compete ever more fiercely for working-class votes. Conversely, it is possible to minimise the extent of the change that had occurred and to stress the basis for continuing cooperation between two parties which, while nominally separate, were rooted in a common radical heritage. Despite the LRC's formal declaration of independence at its Newcastle conference in 1903, Liberal and Labour politicians were in agreement on most of the general political questions of the day. They were united in the early 1900s by their opposition to the Unionist government and, insofar as they offered distinctive programmes to the electorate, their differences could be seen as complementary rather than competitive in their appeal. This last point is supported by the successful working of the secret electoral pact made between the Liberal chief whip, Herbert Gladstone, and the LRC secretary, MacDonald, in 1903 and by the number of Labour victories that occurred in 1906 in areas such as Lancashire which had previously been dominated by the Conservatives but where, in the absence of Liberal opposition, Labour candidates were able to attract the support of Tory working-class voters whose loyalty the Liberals had been unable to tap.[17]

Whichever of these interpretations is nearer the truth, the 'Labour question' which confronted the Liberals as they took office in 1905–6 was a more complex one than they had faced in their previous term in government in 1892–5. In addition to Labour's electoral challenge, there were important tasks of industrial and labour reform to be tackled: the relief of unemployment, the regulation of wages, hours and conditions of labour, the promotion of 'national efficiency' through infrastructural investment and the reform of the labour market. There was also, in the wake of the Taff Vale Case, the vexed question of trade union law and the creation of a more stable framework for industrial relations. The industrial conflicts of the 1890s and the employers' counter-attack in the courts had undermined the mid-Victorian settlement of union rights negotiated in the 1870s and it remained to be seen whether an 'Edwardian settlement', redefining the legal relationship between unions, employers and the state, could be put in its place, to the general satisfaction of all concerned. The Liberal party was in one sense well fitted to make the attempt. It contained within its ranks representatives of both capital and labour. The interventionist ideology of the New Liberalism emphasised the disinterested classlessness of a Liberal state committed to the organic reconciliation of divergent interests. Individual Liberal politicians were known to be sympathetic to the workers and their concerns. Equally, though, these apparent advantages could be double-edged. As a party of government, the Liberals had to be able to resist as well as reward the pressure of sectional interests. In particular cases reform might have to be balanced by control, while for party purposes Liberal leaders would be driven to accentuate the differences between Liberalism and socialism, if not between Liberalism and Labourism. The Labour party, meanwhile, flushed with the success of its parliamentary breakthrough, would have the opportunity to stand forth, unmuzzled, as the voice of the organised working class, uninhibited by the responsibilities of power. The two parties may have fought the election of 1906 as allies, but that did not preclude clashes and confrontations in the years ahead.

Labour's Political Challenge

In assessing Labour's political challenge to the existing parties and the system they represented, two considerations have to be borne in mind: the extent to which the Labour party was establishing itself as an independent force, capable of expanding its electoral base, and the outlook and aims of socialist and Labour politicians. Were they consciously seeking to supersede the existing system, or merely to gain a foothold within it? These questions have a bearing on the broader interpretative debate about the rise of Labour to which reference has already been made. The 'inevitabilists' would argue that the Labour party was not only putting down firmer political roots but that it was carving out for itself a coherent electoral, organisational and ideological identity which meant that it was well placed to benefit from, and indeed to encourage, the development of a more acute sense of working-class consciousness in the later Edwardian period. Against this, the 'progressivist' case would be that Labour was still dependent for its representation in parliament largely on Liberal support; that there were few signs of an irresistible electoral advance by the Labour party before 1914; and that in areas such as social policy and industrial reform its thunder had been stolen by the New Liberalism of the Campbell-Bannerman and Asquith governments. By the time of the elections of 1910, and even more by 1914, so it has been claimed, the adoption of interventionist social policies had enabled the Liberals to make the transition from being a party of the middle class to a party which could attract working-class votes and act as the leading partner in a 'progressive' alliance in which Labour was cast firmly in a supporting and subordinate role.[18] The evidence adduced in support of these conflicting arguments needs to be examined with some care before any conclusions about the nature and seriousness of the Labour challenge to the structure of Edwardian politics, and to the

Liberal party and the Liberal government in particular, can be arrived at.

The early years of the 1906 parliament were successful for the new Labour party. Although 24 of its 29 seats won at the election had been gained in the absence of Liberal opposition, and Labour's position in the House of Commons depended to that extent on Liberal goodwill, the Labour MPs were determined to demonstrate their independence from the Liberal government and from the 24 Lib–Lab Members, refusing the Liberal whip and taking their seats on the opposition benches. They scored an important legislative victory when the Liberals accepted the substance of a Labour measure in preference to the government's own Trades Disputes Bill, reversing the effects of the Taff Vale Judgement. Labour MPs played a part in shaping other measures of social reform such as the 1906 School Meals Act and a new Workmen's Compensation law. Parliamentary successes were rewarded with electoral progress. Jarrow was gained from the Liberals at a by-election in 1907, Sheffield Attercliffe in 1909. In 1908 the Miners' Federation of Great Britain voted to affiliate to the Labour party, increasing its Commons strength to 45 MPs and virtually ending the tradition of Lib–Lab representation which stretched back to the 1870s. The Labour party's involvement in the 'Right to Work' campaign at a time of rising unemployment in 1907–8 gave Labour politicians a chance to capitalise on working-class disaffection and to distinguish themselves as a pressure group to the left of the Liberal government.[19]

Yet not all was plain sailing. The Labour party had problems of discipline, exemplified by the triumph of the 'independent socialist', Victor Grayson, at the Colne Valley by-election of 1907 without official Labour support. In parliament, Keir Hardie, the chairman of the Labour group from 1906 to 1908, was uncomfortable and ineffective in his unaccustomed role, though things improved when Arthur Henderson assumed the post in 1908. More seriously, the Labour party's cohesion was threatened by tensions between socialist ILP-ers and the trade union MPs, a problem exacerbated by the forced incorporation of a number of Lib–Lab miners' MPs in 1909 following the MFGB's decision to affiliate in the previous year. As if these difficulties were not enough, Labour received a further blow from the courts with the announcement of the 1909 Osborne Judgement. As a consequence of a case brought by the Liberal W. V. Osborne against his union, the Amalgamated Society of Railway Servants, it was ruled inadmissible for trade unions to use their general funds for political purposes, thereby threatening the basis of trade union representation in parliament and presenting the Labour party with an imminent financial crisis.[20]

The prospect of a financial crisis was accompanied by a crisis of confidence, as the radical reforms of the Liberal government raised the question of whether a Labour party was necessary at all. In 1908 the Liberals had introduced the long-awaited Mines Eight Hours Act. In 1909 they pioneered the establishment of labour exchanges. By then, the return of prosperity was reducing unemployment and the Trades Disputes Act had recreated a secure context for trade union action. In these circumstances there seemed to be little for the Labour party to do and parliamentary representation for the unions was no longer so urgent a necessity. Meanwhile the Liberals were moving their reform programme into a higher gear, partly to consolidate their hold on working-class support. The introduction of old age pensions in 1908 was followed by the People's Budget in 1909 and by the conflict with the House of Lords which led to the two general elections of 1910. Throughout this period the Labour party was hampered by the impact of the Osborne Judgement and by the more fundamental difficulty of sustaining a show of independence while supporting the Liberal government on most of the major issues of the day.

Labour's first objective, therefore, in the elections of 1910 was to safeguard its position and to keep a sizeable parliamentary party intact. This it did. Forty of its 78 candidates were elected in January 1910 (a net loss of five on its pre-dissolution strength) and its total poll was a respectable 505,857 (seven per cent of the national vote). In December, 42 of 56 candidates were returned (three of them unopposed) and the party's 371,802 votes represented 6.4 per cent of those cast. But these results, while creditable, disguised some causes for concern. By-election gains

like Jarrow and Colne Valley had returned to their former
Liberal allegiance (although of course Colne Valley had not been
an official Labour seat anyway). Even more worrying in the
longer term, the party had been unable to dispense with the
security of its electoral pact with the Liberals and to win
additional seats on its own account. It is true that two seats were
won against Liberal opposition, but these were exceptional. Most
Labour victories were in straight fights with the Unionists or in
two-member seats fought in alliance with a Liberal candidate. In
35 three-way contests in the two elections of 1910, Labour won
none, came second in only six and third in the remaining 29.[21]
Some of these were seats which Labour had not previously
contested, and the party's poor showing can be put down to local
factors and to the operation of a third-party 'squeeze'. It is worth
pointing out too that, despite their close identification nationally
with the Liberal government, Labour held on to a higher
proportion of their 1906 victories than did the Liberals.[22] Yet
even if this was due to the popularity of Labour candidates, the
achievement of 1910 was still no better than a qualified success
rather than a major advance.

Perhaps it would have been unrealistic to have expected more.
Labour was a relatively new party, able to contest only a limited
number of seats, in two closely spaced elections where the odds
were heavily stacked against it. In that sense, as its leaders
recognised, to have survived at all was something to celebrate.
Moreover, the results of the 1910 elections, which had deprived
the Liberals of their Commons majority, had given Labour the
opportunity of exerting increased leverage in parliament, although in practice it was difficult for Labour MPs to vote against
a Liberal government which was enacting reforms which Labour
candidates had supported at the polls, and as long as the Liberals
retained the backing of the Irish Nationalists they could not
actually be defeated.[23] Nevertheless, MacDonald, as the new
chairman of the parliamentary party, used his position of influence with some skill, securing the introduction of payment of
MPs in 1911 in return for supporting the government's National
Insurance Bill, and in 1913, against some Liberal opposition, the
passage of a Trade Union Act which undid the worst effects of

the Osborne Judgement by allowing trade unions to set up separate funds for political purposes. The establishment of these funds had to be approved in a ballot of the union's membership, and individual trade unionists had a legal right to opt out of paying the political levy, but the measure was important in strengthening the Labour party's financial base and providing the wherewithal for a more broadly-based electoral assault if and when conditions were favourable.

What was unclear was when those more favourable conditions might be expected to materialise. The Liberal reform programme was continuing, seemingly unabated, with the National Insurance Act in 1911 and the launching of Lloyd George's land campaign in 1912–13. There was resistance from local Liberal Associations to enlarging the scope for Labour candidates under the terms of the electoral pact, yet there were few signs that Labour was capable of making headway independently of Liberal support, suggesting that the 1910 results might constitute a plateau, or even a peak, in the party's fortunes. Such prognostications received apparent confirmation from some of the contests that occurred during the December 1910 parliament. At 14 by-elections in industrial seats between 1911 and 1914, Labour came bottom of the poll in each case, nowhere taking more than 30 per cent of the vote.[24] The party also lost four seats which, nominally at least, it was defending, two to the Liberals and two to the Conservatives. The circumstances of these contests were admittedly peculiar, and too much should not be read into the results. One was Bow and Bromley, where in 1912 George Lansbury quixotically resigned his seat to fight a by-election on the question of women's suffrage and was beaten by a Conservative. The other three defeats – Hanley, Chesterfield and North East Derbyshire – came in the Staffordshire and Derbyshire mining districts where the Labour party was up against a strong Lib–Lab tradition. None of the contests was typical. In North East Derbyshire in 1914 Liberal and Labour rivalry resulted in the seat going to a Unionist on a split poll. At Chesterfield in 1913 the victorious Liberal candidate was the Lib–Lab Barnet Kenyon, but he had previously been the Labour nominee, only to be disowned by the Labour party after accepting the official endorsement of the local Liberals, whereupon he had been challenged unsuccessfully by an independent socialist, John Scurr. The most interesting case was Hanley in 1912, where a Labour trade union candidate was defeated by the radical Liberal land reformer, R. L. Outhwaite, but again it would be unwise to extrapolate too extensively from an isolated result.[25] The only conclusion that can safely be drawn is that there were still some constituencies where Lib–Labism was more than a match for independent Labour, a conclusion reinforced by the fact that two sitting Labour MPs were actually expelled from the parliamentary party in 1914 because of their continuing pro- Liberal sympathies.

In any case, the by-election evidence needs to be interpreted as part of a broader strategic picture. The Labour party was not winning additional seats, and in places was having difficulty in holding its own in the face of a Liberal fight-back, but it was polling well enough to establish a foundation for future operations and, more importantly, to be able to deprive the Liberals of victory in closely fought three-cornered contests. In the context of the electoral pact this gave MacDonald and Henderson (MacDonald's successor as party secretary) a bargaining counter with the Liberals when it came to negotiating the allocation of constituencies prior to the next general election in 1914 or 1915. At the same time, even if the party was not making visible progress in parliamentary elections, in other respects its position was arguably improving more quickly. Affiliated membership was increasing rapidly. Trade union affiliations rose from 904,496 in 1906 to 1,572,000 in 1914, those of the socialist societies from 17,000 to 33,000. The number of affiliated trades councils and local Labour parties rose from 73 in 1905 to 177 in 1914. Labour representation on local authorities also increased, from 56 in 1907 to 184 in 1913.[26] There are, however, some reservations to be expressed about these trends. The percentage increase in trade union affiliations, for example, was less than that for the overall growth of union membership between 1906 and 1914.[27] Again, while most of the major unions voted to establish political funds under the 1913 Trade Union Act, there were in many instances (such as the Miners' Federation) substantial minorities against paying a levy to the Labour party, showing the far from unanimous hold which Labour had over the loyalty of individual trade union members, even at a time of mounting industrial unrest.[28] The advance of Labour representation in municipal elections was also patchy, and heavily influenced by local factors. All of this reinforced the raw data from by-elections to emphasise the uphill struggle that the Labour party was facing if it was to establish itself as a permanent feature of the Edwardian political system, let alone as a credible alternative to the Liberal government.

Even so, Labour could not be dismissed as a negligible factor in the political equation. Duncan Tanner is probably right to argue that MacDonald and the Labour leadership were not about to abandon the progressive alliance strategy on the eve of the First World War,[29] but, by the same token, it has to be accepted that they were not about to abandon their party's independent stance either, MacDonald's consideration of offers of coalition from the Liberals notwithstanding. Although Labour's progress was fitful and uneven, progress undoubtedly was being made and a separate Labour party was a reality, as was confirmed by the publication of a new party newspaper, the *Daily Citizen*, in 1913, as well as by the recruitment of more full-time officials and the enthusiasm for an expansion of electoral activity on the part of the rank-and-file. What is more, despite internal disputes over policy issues such as National Insurance and over the strategic question of future relations with the Liberals, the party was beginning to develop a more clearly defined political identity. Though still not explicitly socialist, the Labour party had positioned itself as a party committed to social and industrial reform, and, by 1912, as a supporter of radical causes like adult suffrage and Irish Home Rule. Keir Hardie and others were working to provide Labour with an anti-militarist foreign policy which would link it to the mainstream socialist movement of the Second International. MacDonald, in addition to his tireless efforts as party organiser and parliamentary chairman, was offering the party an evolutionary socialist ideology which transcended class conflict while adopting a subtly different perspective from that of the more middle-class New Liberalism.[30] In all these respects, Labour was building up a profile which distinguished it from the

Liberal and Conservative parties, grafting the attributes of a fully-fledged national party on to its original role as that basically of a trade union pressure group.

The question is, how much of a threat did this present to the existing political system and to the Liberal government in power in 1914? Even if the Labour party was capable of expansion – and that had yet to be conclusively proven – its growth before 1914 was limited.[31] If the Liberals won the election of 1915 a further period of cooperation between the two progressive parties seemed probable. In the event of a Conservative victory, strains in the progressive alliance were perhaps more likely to appear, as they had in the period of prolonged Liberal opposition between 1886 and 1906, but the battle for influence on the left would have been a war of attrition rather than a sudden coup, with the Liberals still holding many of the trump cards. In more general terms, while the future of the Liberal party as a party of government might conceivably be threatened by Labour's growth, it was not necessarily the case that the political system itself was in danger. The Labour party was certainly not revolutionary in character. Its socialism was muted, its strategy staunchly parliamentary, as its conference decisions repeatedly affirmed. The somewhat hyperbolic comment which Balfour had made in 1906, to the effect that the emergence of the Labour party was an echo of 'the same movement which has produced massacres in St Petersburg, riots in Vienna, and Socialist processions in Berlin', had not, it appeared, been borne out by events.[32]

But Balfour's observations were not altogether wide of the mark. The MacDonaldite Labour party did have its more extreme socialist wing, represented by the ILP. The latter, which set up more than 500 new branches between 1906 and 1909, issued a manifesto entitled *Let Us Reform The Labour Party* in 1910, endorsing some of the criticisms which had been made in Ben Tillett's 1908 pamphlet, *Is The Parliamentary Party A Failure?* Its authors did not reject parliamentary action, but they did want a more aggressive political line to be taken, with greater emphasis on socialist ideas and more strenuous attempts to link the parliamentary party with working-class movements in the country. Another strand of criticism came from Victor Grayson and his supporters. Grayson, who served briefly as MP for Colne Valley following his by-election victory in 1907, acted as a focus for discontent with the official Labour leadership, with whom he was permanently at odds. He lost his seat in January 1910, but played a part, with dissident ILP-ers and members of Hyndman's Social Democratic Party (the rechristened SDF), in forming the British Socialist Party in 1911.[33] The BSP flourished only for a short time in 1911–12, losing many of its 37,000 rapidly recruited supporters to the Syndicalists, and it never seriously challenged the position which the Labour party was building as the institutional embodiment of working-class politics. But its appearance indicated that there was socialist dissatisfaction with 'MacDonaldism' and that an alternative strategy was available which socialists could pursue if the Labour party failed to deliver the goods. In that sense, Balfour's analysis, which linked the rise of socialism in Britain with similar developments on the continent, was more perceptive than might at first be thought.

In any event, even if the Labour party was scrupulously committed to parliamentary methods, and its leaders publicly eschewed the language of class war, the emergence of an independent and predominantly working-class Labour party still had far-reaching political implications. The Victorian party system had evolved to accommodate two parties which, though they did represent certain class interests, were nevertheless coalitions of different social groups and could therefore claim with some legitimacy to be 'national' or 'classless' in character. A Labour party, particularly if it broke away from the protective umbrella of the progressive alliance with the Liberals, necessarily diverged from this ideal, at least until such time as it had replaced one or other of the existing parties and taken on many of their 'national' characteristics. The rise of the Labour party, consequently, did present a threat, or certainly a challenge, to the assumptions on which British politics had hitherto been based. Liberal, and to a lesser extent Conservative, politicians may have been speaking out of party self-interest when they deprecated the intrusion of a class-based party into their previously closed political world; but they were also articulating a genuine and not completely groundless fear that new elements of class bitterness were going to be injected into political life, with ultimately damaging consequences not only for their own parties but for the stability of the social and political system they represented. Add to this the fact that the Labour party was the political voice of the trade unions at a time when industrial strife was increasing and the state and the unions were having to renegotiate their relationship in an atmosphere of conflict, and it will be seen that Labour's rise as a more powerful political force was not something which ministers in the last Liberal government could view with total equanimity, irrespective of whether it was the future of their party or their country which was uppermost in their thoughts.

The Workers' Revolt

The 'Labour Unrest' of 1910–14, though it had its more specific causes, was part of a pattern of worsening industrial discontent which can be traced back to the 1880s. The strike waves of the new unionism had been succeeded by the more defensive disputes of the mid- and late 1890s. A temporary lull from the turn of the century until after the passage of the 1906 Trades Disputes Act[34] gave way to renewed unrest from 1908 on, culminating in a series of massive strikes in the coal, dock and transport industries in 1910–13 and the formation of the 'Triple Alliance' of transport workers, miners and railwaymen in 1914. For a time it seemed that a new spirit of ungovernability was abroad in the industrial districts and that Britain was on the verge of an industrial relations crisis from which socialist militants and other revolutionary elements might be able to benefit. The spectre of class war, of which the emergence of the Labour party as a parliamentary force was but a genteel shadow, came to haunt the country as violence flared on the picket lines and the juggernaut of industrial strife gathered apparently unstoppable momentum.

That, at least, is one version of what happened in the closing years of the Edwardian era. George Dangerfield, in his dramatic account of the 'workers' rebellion', stressed not merely the scale of unrest – which was, at its peak, considerable – but also the importance of a more uncompromising mood among the workers, a mood heightened by their awareness of social inequalities and by the growing purchase of the ideas of Syndicalism which encouraged 'Direct Action' by the workers for political as well as industrial ends. Other writers have questioned both the influence of Syndicalism and the depth of the industrial crisis. Once again it is necessary to re-examine the events of the period before a final judgement as to their seriousness can be made.

Certainly the problems of industry had been becoming more serious towards the end of the nineteenth century. As has been seen, the performance of the economy was faltering in the face of periodic depressions of trade and mounting foreign competition. Employers were striving to maintain the profitability of their enterprises at precisely the time when the rapid expansion of trade unions was confronting them with a better organised, more disciplined workforce seeking to improve its own position through collective bargaining and, if necessary, strike action. This was not automatically a recipe for open conflict. In the 1860s and 1870s many employers had recognised the advantages of dealing with organised rather than unorganised labour. They shared with the leaders of the trade unions a belief that the success of their industries depended on cooperation between employers and workers, and agreed procedures for settling wages and conditions evolved as a consequence. On the coalfields, for example, the 'sliding scale' committees fixed the level of wages in relation to the price of coal; in other industries local conciliation committees of masters and men, sometimes under independent chairmanship, were set up to fulfil a similar function. By the 1890s, however, the system of essentially localised bargaining was coming under strain. The scale of industrial organisation was becoming national, or at least regional, rather than local. Adverse economic conditions introduced a more confrontational spirit into negotiations. Possibly Labour's consciousness of its own increasing power made its representatives less willing to give way in the face of employers' intransigence. The result was the upsurge of disputes in the 1890s and a worsening climate of industrial relations which had led the TUC first to support the formation of a General Federation of Trade Unions to provide mutual support for unions engaged in strikes or lock-outs and then to join the socialist societies in setting up the Labour Representation Committee.

The events of the 1880s and 1890s had another important consequence too, in that the government became increasingly drawn into industrial affairs. Prior to this, state involvement had been confined mainly to the regulation of factory conditions for female and child workers. The governments of the 1870s had established a legal framework for industrial relations – through the passage of the Trade Union Acts and the employer and workmen legislation – but otherwise, apart from the specific area of employers' liability, had maintained only a watching brief. But as the signs multiplied that the voluntary system of collective bargaining was breaking down, and as the occurrence of national strikes in the coal industry and elsewhere threatened other sectors of the country's economy, gradually the state came to play a more active part. Compulsory arbitration of disputes was ruled out, but a Labour Department was established at the Board of Trade to monitor industrial disputes and to offer its services as conciliator, a system regularised by the Conciliation Act of 1896. Government ministers acted as go-betweens in the more serious cases, following a precedent set by the Liberal Foreign Secretary, Lord Rosebery, in the coal dispute of 1893. The industrialisation of politics was reflected in other ways as well. On a macroeconomic level, the early 1900s were marked by a lively debate over whether the Victorian policy of Free Trade should be abandoned in favour of Chamberlain's plans for protective tariffs to safeguard Britain's industries against foreign rivals.[35] There was much discussion, from the mid-1880s, of the extent to which the state should intervene to regulate the operation of the labour market and relieve unemployment. The legal decisions and industrial troubles of the 1890s also reopened the debate over the rights of the trade unions and how they could best be reconciled with the interests of the community at large. In all of these respects, the 'Labour question' had assumed a high priority on the political agenda by the time the Liberals came to power at the end of 1905.

With the Liberal victory in the general election of 1906, Free Trade was secured for the time being, although Tariff Reform continued to gather support in Unionist ranks. Unemployment remained a problem, since it was rising sharply in 1907–8. The Conservative government's 1905 Unemployed Workmen Act did something to alleviate distress, but it was the improvement in the economy after 1908 which reduced the political urgency of a solution. The Liberals nevertheless pushed ahead with the more interventionist measures which have already been described, namely the Labour Exchanges Act of 1909 and the National Insurance scheme of 1911. From the trade unions' point of view, however, the most important issue in 1906 was what the Liberals intended to do about the question of trade union law. The Taff Vale Judgement had left the unions in a vulnerable position, and attempts by backbench MPs to amend the law in the unions' favour had failed. The Balfour government had appointed a Royal Commission to consider the question but had not brought forward legislation at the time of its fall from office. Campbell-Bannerman's government was committed to some action on behalf of the unions, though not to the details of a particular plan. When the Liberal government duly published its Trades Disputes Bill early in 1906 the unions were disappointed to find that it proposed to give them only a carefully defined freedom from liability rather than the complete immunity from Taff Vale type prosecutions which they had sought. The debate on the Bill turned into an early trial of strength between the Liberal administration and the new Labour party, with the government eventually giving way in the face of Labour pressure. The Prime Minister abandoned the government's Bill, substituting instead a Labour measure which provided the unions with the total legal immunity that they wanted. There was some disquiet on the government benches about the sweeping nature of the new Bill, but it was passed by the House of Lords and became the basis of the legal framework which governed industrial relations for the remainder of the Edwardian period, and indeed for much of the twentieth century.

The critics of the Trades Disputes Act were concerned that the measure effectively placed trade unions 'outside the law' and provided inadequate protection for the community against abuses of trade union power.[36] This had not been a problem in the opening years of the century since the levels of industrial unrest between 1900 and 1906 were comparatively low, partly because the unions were cowed by the fear of punitive action by the courts. No sooner had the 1906 Act been passed, however, than a sea-change occurred in the industrial situation. Between 1906 and 1914, trade union membership increased from 2,210,000 to 4,145,000, the TUC's membership rising from 1,700,000 to 2,682,357. From a low point of 479 stoppages in 1906, the number of industrial disputes leading to strikes or lock-outs reached a peak of 1,459 in 1913. Only 2,150,000 working days were lost in strike action in 1907, whereas an unprecedented 40,890,000 were lost in 1912.[37] Of course, this was not simple cause and effect, and factors other than the change in the law were responsible for the more disturbed nature of the industrial scene. But the scale and variety of disputes generated a mood of crisis and tension that was not easily dispelled.

The strike wave began, somewhat abortively, with a threatened rail strike in 1907 which was averted by negotiation at the last moment. But this was followed in 1908 by a series of strikes in the cotton, engineering and shipbuilding industries, some of which continued into the following year. In 1910, a ten-month strike began in the South Wales coalfield, involving upwards of 30,000 men. Worse was to come in 1911 and 1912. In the summer of 1911 strikes broke out among dockers, seamen and other groups of workers in London, Liverpool and elsewhere. A national rail strike occurred in August, although it was settled after only two days. At the start of 1912 there was more trouble on the coalfields, leading to a national stoppage in March. Almost as soon as the coal strike ended, another strike began in the London docks, with the National Transport Workers' Federation calling, albeit unsuccessfully, for nationwide support. In 1913 there was a lengthy strike by transport workers in Dublin, with a large number of smaller-scale disputes in Britain, including the so-called 'prairie fire' strikes in the Midlands' metal trades. Another worrying sign to observers, apart from the extent of the unrest, was the re-marshalling of forces that was taking place on the union side. The formation of the Transport Workers' Federation in 1910 was one such step; in 1913 a National Union of

Railwaymen was created, leaving only the train drivers and railway clerks outside a single, all-grades union. In June 1914 the railwaymen, transport workers and the Miners' Federation made the agreement known as the 'Triple Alliance', as a possible prelude to offering sympathetic action in the event of future disputes.

The causes of this sudden explosion of unrest, and the motives of the workers involved, have been subjected to much scrutiny.[38] The Trades Disputes Act of 1906 was a contributory factor, in that it made it possible for the unions to take strike action without fear of prosecution, but it was not the sole, nor perhaps even the primary, cause. Economic conditions provide the best explanation for discontent. In 1908, for example, most of the strikes that occurred were caused by opposition to proposed wage reductions. From 1909, economic factors became more influential in two ways. First, the reduction in unemployment (from a peak of 7.8 per cent of trade unionists in 1908 to 2.1 per cent by 1913) increased the unions' bargaining power as the market for labour became more competitive. Secondly, workers found that their standard of living was under threat from rising prices and a falling level of real wages, so they may have been more willing to try to bolster their position by industrial action. In addition, there were causes of unrest in individual industries. In the engineering and metal trades there was resistance to the erosion of craft privileges and the spread of piece-work. The railwaymen were driven, in part, by a desire for the recognition of their union by the employers, and the national strike of 1911 was the direct result of the failure of the conciliation machinery established in 1907. On the coalfields, a variety of localised grievances (such as the rate for working 'abnormal places' which led to the Cambrian Collieries strike in South Wales in 1910) spilled over into the demand for a national minimum wage in 1912. Other causes may be adduced – such as the transferable momentum of strikes from one industry to another, or the release of pent-up frustrations (like those of the 15,000 Bermondsey women sweat-shop workers who went on strike in 1911) – but the underlying issues of wage rates, working practices and conditions are sufficient in themselves to account for most of the disputes that took place. Another important characteristic of many of the disputes was their apparent spontaneity. They were shop-floor strikes started by rank-and-file action, a sign of the extent to which discontent was swamping the existing negotiating and conciliation machinery and weakening the hold of union leaders over their members.

This is not to say that the labour unrest did not have a more specifically political dimension. It does not seem greatly, if at all, to have strengthened the Labour party.[39] It did, however, provide opportunities for those who wanted to outflank the Labour party and enlist the support of workers for a more militant political and industrial policy. The group best placed to achieve this, and the one to receive most attention from historians, were the Syndicalists.[40] Syndicalism as it developed in Britain was an amalgam of the ideas of the American union leader, Daniel de Leon, and those of French and Belgian Marxist and labour leaders such as Georges Sorel. It combined the concept of 'industrial' (as opposed to 'trades') unionism (that is, the notion that all the workers in a particular industry should be members of a single union) with the aim of achieving workers' control of industry, perhaps by using the weapon of a general strike to undermine the power of the employers and subvert the liberal-capitalist economic and political order. In Britain, the main exponent of Syndicalism was Tom Mann, one of the leaders of the 1889 London dock strike who had travelled widely in different parts of the world and who returned to England from Australia in 1910 to help found the Industrial Syndicalist Education League. A journal, the *Industrial Syndicalist*, was published (and later, from 1912, a newspaper, the *Syndicalist*), and through these organs Mann began his campaign for the formation of 'Amalgamation Committees' as embryonic industrial unions. Mann himself was active in many of the disputes of 1910–14, helping to form the Transport Workers' Federation and also the Workers' Union, which had over 150,000 members by 1914. He found support from other groups such as the Marxist-inspired Plebs League, which was strongest among the railwaymen and the miners, and the Syndicalist message won a ready audience in parts of the South Wales coalfield, where Noah Ablett and the members of the Unofficial Reform Committee of the South Wales Miners' Federation published their

Syndicalist manifesto, *The Miners' Next Step*, in 1912. It is hard to be certain exactly how much influence the Syndicalists had, or how far they were behind the disputes of the pre-war period, but their activities did lend colour to the view that the labour unrest with which the Liberal government was confronted was more threatening than a coincidental yet unconnected wave of strikes would have been.

The government's response to these mounting industrial problems was flexible but firm. In line with the policies pioneered by the Liberal ministries in the 1890s, and with the party's philosophical belief in the compatibility of the interests of capital and labour, every effort was made to encourage the settlement of disputes through a process of conciliation. Government ministers were prominent in the business of industrial diplomacy, Lloyd George, as President of the Board of Trade and later as Chancellor of the Exchequer, being especially to the fore.[41] It was his skills which averted the threat of a national rail strike in 1907 and which subsequently brought the strike of 1911 to an end after only two days. Under the Liberal administration, too, the Board of Trade made full use of the powers given it under the 1896 Conciliation Act to appoint mediators where the contending parties to a dispute were prepared to accept its services. G. R. Askwith, the Board's chief conciliator, and, from 1911, the Chief Industrial Commissioner, was heavily employed throughout the period, helping to negotiate settlements in a number of disputes, including those in the docks and the cotton industry. The Board of Trade also promoted the formation of permanent conciliation boards where conditions were right, and the number of these actually increased from 162 in 1905 to 325 in 1913.[42] Another innovation was the setting up in 1911 of the Industrial Council, a national body which brought together employers and trade union representatives in a kind of unofficial court of appeal for industrial disputes. In practice the Council was not particularly effective, largely because it had no formal authority and was usually by-passed by more direct or *ad hoc* forms of mediation. But these various initiatives showed that the government and its officials were seriously addressing the need for improved structures of industrial relations and that they were prepared to use their influence in the cause of preserving and promoting industrial peace.

Conciliation was accompanied by a policy of concessions to organised Labour, in an attempt to remove particular grievances or to deal with long-standing problems which could only be solved by summoning the power of the state to supplement the normal processes of collective bargaining. The Liberal government's general record in the field of social and industrial reform has already been surveyed, with reference to such measures as the National Insurance Act, labour exchanges and so on. In 1906–8, two measures were introduced in direct response to trade union pressure: the Trades Disputes Act of 1906 and the Mines Eight Hours Act of 1908.[43] The first of these gave considerable freedom to the unions, but it also reflected the Liberal belief that the existence of strong trade unions was a desirable component of a harmonious system of industrial relations. The Mines Eight Hours Act was passed at the behest of the Miners' Federation and was significant in that it marked the first substantial departure from the principle of non-interference with adult male hours of labour which had characterised government policy in the nineteenth century. It was not wholly successful, partly because not all miners had wanted it in the first place (those in Northumberland and Durham already had agreements which gave them a seven and a half hour day), partly because it left the way open for complex disputes about pay and productivity. Nevertheless, the government was endeavouring to use its interventionist powers for the benefit of the workers. The same was true of the Trade Boards Act of 1909, designed to improve the wages of low-paid sweat-shop labour, and the 1912 Miners' Minimum Wage Act. The last measure was extracted from a reluctant government by the miners' strike of March/April 1912. The miners were demanding 'five and two', a minimum wage of five shillings a shift for men and two for boys. Ministers were not prepared to write these figures into a Bill, and in any case were under pressure from the coalowners not to accede to the men's demands, but they did offer a legislative compromise based on the negotiation of agreed district minimum wages, adopting a position somewhere between what the unions wanted and what the employers had initially been willing to concede.

Concession and conciliation could be combined as a policy with at least the threat of coercion. Asquith's famous assertion to the railwaymen's leaders in 1911 that he would 'employ all the forces of the Crown'[44] to keep the railways open in the event of a strike has sometimes been taken as confirmation of the government's willingness to resort to force to overawe and defeat union unrest. In fact this is a misleading view. It is true that large numbers of police and troops were deployed during the disturbances of 1910–14. In 1911 gunboats and armoured cars were sent to Liverpool when there was the threat of rioting. It is also true that a number of clashes occurred between strikers, demonstrators and the forces of law and order. The Tonypandy riots of 1910 and the Liverpool and Llanelli riots of 1911 are perhaps the best known examples, and in the cases of Liverpool and Llanelli fatalities occurred when troops fired on demonstrators. Yet it would be wrong to deduce from this that the government was embarking on a deliberate policy of repression. Recent research has shown that Churchill, who was Home Secretary at the time of the Tonypandy riots, was a restraining rather than a warlike influence on events.[45] Similarly, the government as a whole was more concerned with the maintenance of order than with the systematic use of force to suppress industrial discontent. Problems arose from two associated factors. One was that, for instance at Llanelli, military force was used to protect blackleg workers being employed by the railway companies during the rail strike, giving the impression that the authorities were actively intervening against the strikers (perhaps in pursuance of Asquith's threat). The second problem was that, in many cases, local magistrates and employers (who were often the same people) were also prominent political figures in their localities, frequently linked to the Liberal party, thus adding credence to the feeling on the part of the workers that the government was on the side of capital rather than Labour, and not, as Asquith claimed, that it was simply trying to 'hold the ring' between the two contending parties.

Be that as it may, a case can none the less be made for saying that the Liberals had successfully contained the challenge of

Labour on both the industrial and political fronts. Politically the Labour party had been unable to break free of the progressive alliance, whatever pressures its leaders were under from their grass roots to do so. The more extreme socialist and quasi-revolutionary groups like the BSP had made only a limited impact on the margins of the political scene. Meanwhile, in the industrial arena, there were encouraging signs that the labour unrest had passed its peak after 1912. Although there were a larger number of disputes in 1913 than in the previous year (1,459 compared with 834), the number of working days lost fell by 75 per cent, from 40.8 to 9.8 million.[46] Throughout the pre-war period, government-union relations were being strengthened by the 'corporatism' of the Labour Department and by the recruitment of leading trade unionists like David Shackleton and Richard Bell to work as officials at the Home Office and the Board of Trade.[47] The unions had been integrated into the machinery of state welfarism by being allowed to register as 'approved societies' under the National Insurance Act, while more permanent schemes of industrial conciliation were being established at local and national level. The attitude of most trade union leaders, and of the TUC, still seemed to favour cooperation rather than confrontation, and even the formation of the Triple Alliance was seen more as a means of maintaining industrial discipline for purposes of negotiation than as a prelude to a politically-motivated general strike. It is true that violence had attended a number of disputes, especially in the docks and on the coalfields, but this was was far from being an indication of revolutionary pressures building up, as the restricted penetration of the union movement by the spirit of Syndicalism amply confirmed.

However, this is possibly to take too narrow or complacent a view. Just as the Labour party's potential for growth should not be underestimated, so too it would be wrong to play down the scale and seriousness of the industrial problems of Edwardian Britain. The strike wave of 1910–14 may have been 'economist' in its origins – concerned in the main with specific grievances rather than with more millenarian ideas of industrial or political transformation – but it did constitute the most widespread spell of labour protest since the Board of Trade had begun to keep records in the early 1890s. The simultaneous deterioration of relations in several key industries threatened to cause great harm to the country's economy, and there was sufficient evidence of continuing discontent to justify ministerial concerns about the likelihood of further trouble, whatever the appearances of short-term improvement. Indeed, reports were reaching the Cabinet Committee on Industrial Unrest predicting a resurgence of large-scale strikes in the autumn of 1914, organised by the big battalions of the miners and their allies in the Triple Alliance.[48]

What has to be appreciated, moreover, is that the disputes of the late Edwardian period were not unrelated occurrences: they were symptomatic of an underlying transition in the character of the Labour movement and its relationship with the rest of British society. Hitherto Labour had followed the path of accommodation in the industrial and political fields, in line with the essentially collaborative strategies of Lib–Labism. The trade unions of Victorian Britain had been representative mainly of the more aspiring groups of skilled workers who, concerned to protect their 'respectability' and craft privileges, had formed a natural affinity with other ruling groups in late nineteenth-century society. In the Edwardian years an important shift took place. The trade union movement itself was expanding to embrace a higher proportion of the semi-skilled and unskilled workforce. Simultaneously the introduction of new techniques of mass production was breaking down the distinctions between the 'labour aristocracy' and the bulk of the working class, at just the moment when the economic trends of the early twentieth century were threatening their incomes and their social aspirations. Industrial clashes such as those in the engineering industries and on the railways were indicative of a growing conflict of interest between capital and labour and of the gulf that was opening up between an increasingly militant rank-and-file and the more moderate, 'collaborationist' approach of the official union leaders. Even the encroachment of government-sponsored welfarism was undermining the status and social independence of skilled workers and contributed, along with the more conflict-oriented mood of the time, to a growing solidarity and community of outlook among all sections of the organised Labour movement.

The immediate consequences of this change were industrial rather than political, but they certainly had political implications and added to what one historian has called the sense of an 'impending clash' in the Labour history of the pre-war period.[49] By 1914 the Labour movement was immeasurably more powerful than it had been in Victorian times, and the unions had demonstrated their capacity to hold the government to ransom over issues like the miners' minimum wage and the reform of union law. Trade union militancy had not yet led to a direct access of support for the Labour party, which many trade unionists considered as ineffective or irrelevant to their needs. But it is reasonable to infer that as a political culture of 'Labourism' developed, the Labour party – as the only viable vehicle for national Labour politics – would reap the benefits, given the strength of the unions' basic commitment to parliamentary action. The ballots held to set up political funds under the 1913 Trade Union Act suggest that such a convergence of the political and industrial wings of the movement was occurring, helping to rebuild the unity of 1901–6. The repercussions of this development must remain, to some extent, conjectural. For the future, much would depend on how the established parties dealt with the unfolding problems of Britain's industrial decline. The skill of the government and the restraint of the unions had prevented an outright confrontation between Labour and the state prior to 1914, and steps had been taken to remake the relationship between unions and government to lessen the chances of the outright estrangement of organised Labour from the governing institutions of the country. Even so, there was a definite tension between the government's position as the mediator of divergent interests and Labour's necessarily more sectional concerns. Political and ideological considerations dictated that there were limits beyond which a Liberal government could not afford to go in satisfying Labour demands. Already, from Liberal and Conservative ranks alike, voices were being raised in favour of putting curbs on burgeoning union power. As the 'Labour question' increased in political importance, and the problems of British capitalism intensified, further conflicts were likely to arise, as indeed they did after 1918. In those circumstances, a more serious confrontation between organised Labour and the British state could not be ruled out. As a component in the Edwardian crisis, then, the challenge of Labour had been checked rather than surmounted. It remained to be seen whether the breakwaters erected by the Liberal governments before 1914 could cope with the electoral or industrial storms that might lie ahead.

5

IRELAND AND THE CRISIS OF NATIONALISM

The controversy over Irish Home Rule was undoubtedly the most serious of the domestic problems with which Asquith's Liberal government was faced between 1911 and 1914, dwarfing even those of women's suffrage and labour unrest. By the summer of 1914 Ireland appeared to be on the verge of a violent civil war between supporters and opponents of the government's Home Rule Bill, a conflict which threatened to destabilise the British political system itself. The 'Irish question' was at the same time part of a more complex 'crisis of nationalism' confronting Britain's imperial state at home and abroad. To understand the full significance of the divisions over the future of Ireland it is necessary not merely to study events in Ireland or the history of Anglo-Irish relations but to place these in the context of political developments on the British mainland and elsewhere, particularly the deepening rift between the Liberal and Unionist parties, the growth of a 'Radical Right' and the worsening international situation which led, in August 1914, to the outbreak of the First World War.

Nations and Nationalism

In European history, the late nineteenth century was the age of nationalism. Italy and Germany emerged as unified nation states. There were intensifying great power and imperial rivalries.

Multinational empires like Russia and Austria-Hungary struggled to maintain their integrity in the face of the destabilising forces of secessionist ethnic and national groups. Nationalism also became increasingly important as a cohering factor in political activity. Left-wing groups – whether liberals, radicals or revolutionary republicans – used 'nationalism from below' as a means of rallying disaffected opinion and challenging the position of ruling elites. Meanwhile the established regimes themselves, for example in Bismarck's Germany, used a state-sponsored 'nationalism from above' as an integrationist tool of social control.[1]

Britain, or, more correctly in this context, the United Kingdom, produced its own variant of these European trends and nationalism, in its different forms, was central to the late nineteenth and early twentieth-century British experience. Like the Russian and Austro-Hungarian empires, the United Kingdom was a multinational, multi-ethnic political community whose rulers were keen to establish a unifying identity. As an imperial power, Britain faced the problem of welding together a diverse and fragmented empire at a time of burgeoning colonial nationalism and growing external threat. Finally, after a century of 'splendid isolation' in which British governments had endeavoured to remain free of entangling foreign alliances, Britain by the early 1900s was being drawn more deeply into the tangled web of European great power diplomacy, a process which led eventually to her participation in the First World War. All of these long-term considerations had an impact on the domestic political crisis that developed in the years prior to 1914.

The main internal debate was over the future political organisation of the British Isles. The United Kingdom of Great Britain and Ireland had been a plant of slow growth. A formal union of England and Wales was effected in 1536, regularising a situation created by the elimination of the independent Welsh princedoms and assimilating Wales into the English shire system with representation in the English parliament. In 1707 England and Scotland had negotiated a Union, building upon the union of crowns of 1603 to create a single British state, Scotland's parliament being abolished, or rather united with the English parliament through the return of Scottish MPs and representative peers to

Westminster. Not until 1800 did Ireland follow the same path, paving the way for the emergence of a more centralised, unitary state in the nineteenth century. But the process of unification was neither smooth nor uniform. Ireland was never integrated into the structures of government as completely as Wales or Scotland, retaining a separate, albeit appointed, administration at Dublin Castle, ruled over by a Lord Lieutenant and a Chief Secretary who were, in effect, colonial governors in an alien land. The encouragement of a sense of 'British' loyalty proved problematic. Despite closer economic ties, improved communications and substantial internal migration, 'Britishness' remained an elusive concept. Irishness, Scottishness and Welshness – and for that matter Englishness too – were stubbornly ingrained, and the persistance of cultural, linguistic and religious distinctions ensured that they remained so, in some respects becoming even more pronounced as the nineteenth century progressed.[2] The task of reconciling conflicting perceptions of communal and national identity within the political and administrative framework of a unitary state became more and more difficult in consequence, especially when it seemed that London-based governments did not fully understand the needs and concerns of peripheral areas, and when the interests of England – the 'predominant partner' in the United Kingdom, demographically, economically and strategically – appeared to take precedence over those of the other regions.

It was in Ireland that the centrifugal tendencies of nationalism developed their earliest, fullest momentum.[3] The Union of 1800 came in the wake of the Irish rebellion of 1798 in which the mainly Catholic United Irishmen had, with French assistance, attempted unsuccessfully to secure simultaneously the overthrow of the minority Protestant Ascendancy in Ireland and Irish independence from Britain. Many Irishmen were never reconciled to the new arrangement, even after the granting of equal rights to Catholics in 1829. In the 1840s Daniel O'Connell led a mass campaign for the repeal of the Act of Union. His constitutional efforts were shadowed by a more romantic, conspiratorial and revolutionary tradition of Irish nationalism, drawing on the legacy of Wolfe Tone, Robert Emmet and the rebels of 1798 and

1803. Groups such as 'Young Ireland' in the 1840s and the Fenians in the 1850s and 1860s, encouraged by the nationalist ideas of continental Europe and by support from Irish exiles in the United States, and tapping a well of grievance deepened by the immense tragedy of the potato famine of 1845–9, staged a series of abortive insurrections and symbolic acts of violence in a bid to rouse the Irish people and coerce the British government into making concessions to nationalist demands. In the 1870s mass protest and constitutional action were revived in the activities of Michael Davitt's Land League (campaigning for help for tenant farmers hit hard by the effects of agricultural depression) and the organisation of an independent Nationalist party in parliament. The Irish Home Government Association was founded in 1870 by the Irish lawyer and MP Isaac Butt. At the general election of 1874 59 'Home Rule' MPs were returned. In 1879 the leadership of the Home Rulers passed from Butt to Charles Stewart Parnell, a charismatic figure who, despite being a landowner and a Protestant, was also President of Davitt's Land League.[4] The number of Home Rule MPs rose to 65 in 1880 (at least half of them staunch 'Parnellites') and the Irish National League, formed in September 1882 to provide the parliamentary party with an effective grass-roots machine, had 1,200 branches by 1885. The Nationalists benefited from the 1884 Reform Act, which in Ireland had the dramatic effect of almost quadrupling the electorate, and at the 1885 election the total of Nationalist MPs increased again to 86, an overwhelming demonstration of support which gave Parnell every right to claim a mandate to speak for Ireland at Westminster.

Ireland, though, was not the only part of the United Kingdom in which the stirrings of nationalism were being felt by the 1880s. In Scotland, a nationalist movement was coming into existence, partly in reaction to the centralising, anglicising tendencies of the British state. Discontented groups like the crofters and land reformers used nationalism as a vehicle for defending a traditional way of life against increasingly harsh and impersonal economic pressures. A Scottish Home Rule Association was founded in 1886, attracting support from a broad spectrum of radical and socialist opinion.[5] An even more emphatic nationalist revival was taking place in Wales, where its fortunes were tied to the rise of the Welsh Nonconformist middle class.[6] Here, as in Ireland, parliamentary reform played its part in enabling nationalism to assume a concrete political form. The election of 1868 was the first at which the Nonconformist majority were able to vote in large numbers and they used their new-found power to break the monopoly of the anglicised, Anglican squirearchy in the Welsh constituencies, a transition symbolised by the election of the Nonconformist Henry Richard as MP for Merthyr. Thereafter Welsh Nonconformists, in alliance with the Liberal party, set about creating a nationalist movement in their own image, skilfully identifying the issues they wished to prioritise – the disestablishment of the Welsh Church, temperance, education, land reform – with the interests of the Welsh 'nation'. The movement was cultural and linguistic as well as political. The Society for the Utilisation of the Welsh Language was founded in 1885; there was a remarkable upsurge of Welsh literature and journalism and a new interest was being taken in Welsh history and Welsh poetry. In the 1890s cultural and political nationalism overlapped in the organisation known as *Cymru Fydd* ('Wales of the Future') which attracted the support of a younger generation of nationalist Liberal politicians, among them Tom Ellis (MP for Merioneth, 1886–99) and David Lloyd George (elected MP for Caernarfon Boroughs in 1890). Lloyd George, indeed, attempted in the mid-1890s to use *Cymru Fydd* as a launching pad for a separate 'Welsh party' on the Irish Nationalist model, campaigning for disestablishment of the Church and Welsh Home Rule. The attempt failed, but that such a departure could even be contemplated was a testimony to the strength of nationalism in Wales as the nineteenth century drew to its close.

In response to the growth of nationalism, British governments adopted a familiar policy of containment and concession.[7] Attempts were made to redress outstanding grievances in areas such as religion, education and land reform in an effort to prevent nationalism from developing into outright separatism. In Ireland Catholics were appeased by the disestablishment of the Anglican Church in 1869 and by government assistance for the expansion of higher education. Gladstone introduced two Irish Land Acts, in 1870 and 1881, to extend the rights of tenant farmers, control rents and reduce the number of evictions. A similar strategy was pursued in Wales. Nonconformist demands for disestablishment were not met, although the Liberals made Welsh Disestablishment party policy in 1887 and introduced an unsuccessful Bill in 1894–5. But measures such as Osborne Morgan's Burials Act of 1880 and the Welsh Sunday Closing Act of 1881 were important victories for Nonconformist opinion. Successive governments sponsored significant education reforms in the Principality, notably the Welsh Intermediate Education Act of 1889 and the granting of a royal charter to the University of Wales in 1893. In Wales and Scotland, as in Ireland, land reform was also a major issue. The discontent of Scottish crofters was sufficient to provoke the 'Battle of the Braes' on the Isle of Skye in 1882 and the election of a number of independent crofter MPs in 1885. A Scottish Land Act was duly passed in 1886, while the Welsh 'tithe war' of 1887 led eventually to the appointment of a Welsh Land Commission in 1893.

These and other reforms helped to forestall the growth of genuinely separatist movements in Scotland and Wales, though other factors also came into play. Scotland had become in many ways reconciled to the Union and the advantages which it could bring. This is not to underestimate the vitality of the Scottish sense of national identity, but that identity was already effectively preserved in those distinctively Scottish institutions which had survived the Union of 1707 – the Scottish Church, the legal system and the separate educational structure. The appointment of a Secretary of State for Scotland in 1885 added a measure of administrative devolution to offset the centralising tendencies of government from London. Otherwise most Scots were content to participate in the British state on equal terms with their English partners, playing their full part in party politics, economic and intellectual life, and the opportunities of Empire. The Welsh case was rather different, since Wales lacked the institutional separateness of Scotland, save for its churches, its University and, later, a National Museum and Library. However, the establishment of elected county and district councils in the 1880s and 1890s provided Nonconformists and nationalists with a substantial power base in the localities which did much to undermine demands for a further devolutionary instalment of Home Rule. Wales was, in any case, economically so interdependent with England that only a few visionaries contemplated a more far-reaching political change, let alone a complete severing of ties between the two nations.

Ireland, on the other hand, while sharing some of the charac-teristics of Scotland and Wales, was a land apart, both literally and figuratively. Perhaps because of Ireland's more obviously colonial status, although individual reforms were welcomed they did not suffice to remove the sometimes violent edge of Irish discontent. Throughout the 1880s Coercion Acts were employed to try to quell disorder, but they could not prevent terrorist outrages such as the murder of the Chief Secretary, Lord Frederick Cavendish, in Dublin's Phoenix Park in May 1882. Nor did ameliorative legislation solve the underlying problem of Ireland's constitutional position in relation to the rest of the United Kingdom which the success of Parnell's Nationalist party at the general election of 1885 brought squarely to the fore.

The Home Rule crisis of 1885–6 made the future of the Anglo-Irish Union a more urgent question than it had been at any point since the time of Pitt, Grattan and George III. It also decisively reshaped the pattern of British politics in a way that was subsequently to have an intimate effect on the conflicts of the Edwardian era.[8] Gladstone's open espousal of Home Rule after the victories of the Parnellites in the 1885 election cemented a Liberal–Nationalist alliance, splitting the Liberal party in the process and dividing party politics in Britain along a Home Rule–Unionist axis similar to that which had existed in Ireland since the 1870s. The defeat of Gladstone's first Irish Home Rule Bill in June 1886 precipitated a further general election which opened the way to twenty years of Unionist hegemony in Britain, finally brought to an end only by the Liberal landslide of 1906. The irony in all of this was that neither of the British parties actually wanted to see the United Kingdom dismantled. Their disagreement was not over whether the Union should continue, but over how best it could be preserved. Gladstone argued that only a generous concession in recognition of Ireland's separate political identity could reconcile the Nationalist majority to the continued existence of the United Kingdom. The Unionists believed that the establishment of a parliament in Dublin, even if at first its powers were limited, would lead inevitably to demands for eventual independence and must therefore be resisted at all costs. In accordance with this latter view, while Gladstone introduced a second Home Rule Bill in 1893, the Salisbury–Balfour governments of 1886–92 and 1895–1905 reverted to the combination of coercion and social reform which had characterised the earlier phase of Gladstone's Irish policy. The centrepiece of their so-called 'constructive Unionism' was provided by a series of Land Purchase Acts (in 1885, 1891 and 1903) and by infrastructural investment in rural Ireland to stimulate hardpressed local economies.[9] Yet while these measures were of practical benefit and did something to reduce discontent among tenant farmers, they did not address the Nationalists' political demands. Elected county councils were established in Ireland in 1898, but the desire for a separate national parliament still remained strong. In the meantime, the failure of constitutional methods to achieve this goal encouraged more extreme nationalist groups and strengthened precisely those separatist tendencies which ameliorative policies were intended to contain. The 1890s were not only the period of the 'Gaelic revival' in nationalist Ireland, but they also saw growing disillusionment with the Irish Parliamentary Party as a vehicle for change, leading, among other things, to the founding of the pro-independence Sinn Fein by Arthur Griffith in 1905.[10]

The future of Ireland aroused fierce passions in Britain partly because of its intrinsic importance, partly because of the way in which Irish questions interacted with other causes of unease. English landlords with Irish estates feared that the rights of property would be flouted by a Nationalist parliament in Dublin. Anti-Catholic feeling was a factor influencing British Protestants in their opposition to their co-religionists in Ireland being placed under 'Rome rule'. There was genuine concern that if a Home Rule Ireland moved towards independence the economic integrity of the United Kingdom would be threatened (a particular worry for those with business links with Ireland's industrial

North) and that Britain's strategic security could also be put at risk. In addition, there were two further areas of policy in which divisions over Ireland helped to widen the differences between the British political parties and consequently to exacerbate the rivalries of the Edwardian period.

The first was that of the Empire. As has been suggested, there were fears among Unionists that the granting of Irish Home Rule would lead to the break-up of the United Kingdom. In the 1880s there were signs that the success of Irish nationalism was encouraging the growth of nationalist movements in Scotland and Wales. This, in turn, was only part of a wider problem of nationalism developing within the British Empire as a whole. The 'dominions' of Canada, Australia and New Zealand had already attained self-government. Local nationalisms were becoming a significant force elsewhere: in Egypt, occupied as recently as 1882; in India, where the Indian National Congress was founded in 1885; and in South Africa, where the Transvaal had fought a successful secessionist war in 1880–81 and been granted effective independence in 1884. The enactment of Home Rule for Ireland would not only stimulate future breakaway movements; it would also, by weakening the United Kingdom, undermine Britain's capacity to maintain the unity of the Empire itself. This, at any rate, was the message which Unionist politicians were eager to convey, building upon Disraeli's legacy of popular imperialism sketched out in his Manchester and Crystal Palace speeches of 1872 and the policies of his government of 1874–80.[11] In the late 1880s and 1890s, imperialism, invested with the full pageantry of Victoria's golden and diamond jubilees, became the Unionists' most successful electoral weapon.[12] They portrayed the Liberals, largely on the strength of their Irish plans, as unsafe custodians of the imperial heritage; dangerous radicals who would squander the hard-won victories of British arms and British enterprise. This picture was not, of course, entirely fair. The Liberal party had its Roseberyite 'Liberal Imperialist' wing. There were few outright anti-imperialists in the Liberal ranks, even among the Welsh and Scottish nationalists. But the Liberals' alliance with the Irish party, together with the opposition of Liberals like Morley and Lloyd George to the South African War of 1899, lent colour to the Unionist charge. Liberal support for Home Rule, and their opposition to Chamberlain's plans for imperial federation through Tariff Reform, in any case made it clear that there were underlying differences over imperial policy, although without the emotions aroused by the Irish question it is doubtful if these would have seemed anything like as pronounced.

A second complicating factor was that, from the turn of the century, the idea of a strong, united Empire became linked to concern over Britain's national defence, particularly in view of the perception of the growing threat from Germany, embodied in the latter's naval building programme, the expansion of German interests in Africa, the Pacific and the Near East, and the instability of German policy represented by the Moroccan and Agadir crises of 1905 and 1911. Balfour's government instituted a Committee of Imperial Defence in 1902 to build on lessons of imperial cooperation learned during the Boer war. Programmes of army and navy reform were set in train, and these were carried forward by the Liberals after the election of 1906. Despite an apparent continuity of foreign and defence policies, however, there were those on the Unionist right who wanted a more thorough going militarisation of national life than the Liberals were willing to endorse. From the publication of Erskine Childers' *The Riddle of the Sands* (a novel warning of the threat to England from the Kaiser's expanding battle fleet) in 1903,[13] popular fears of German invasion were exploited by the Unionist right, and by organisations like the Navy League, to press for more rapid naval expansion, including the demand for the building of larger numbers of 'dreadnought' battleships which culminated in the war-cry 'We Want Eight and We Won't Wait' in 1909. Behind the 'scaremongers', as they have been called, were right-wing journals such as Leo Maxse's *National Review*, and a body of intensely patriotic public opinion.[14] Lord Roberts, former Commander-in-Chief of the army, was one of the founders of the National Service League which campaigned throughout the Edwardian period for the introduction of compulsory military training. Another initiative to strengthen the sinews of the nation's manhood, or at least its boyhood, was undertaken by the hero of the siege of Mafeking, Sir Robert Baden-Powell, whose Scout movement became the 'character factory' of a large segment of Edwardian youth.[15]

The point about these developments in the present context is that, almost to a man, the supporters of these military, patriotic causes were staunch opponents not just of the Liberal governments of 1906–14 but of the proposal to grant Ireland Home Rule in particular.[16] For many of them, Ireland became the keystone in the arch of Empire and national security, without which collapse and ruin would inevitably follow. The reasoning behind this line of argument may have been fallacious, as the Liberals claimed, but it highlighted the degree to which by the early twentieth century Britain was becoming a battleground between two opposing concepts of nationalism. The Liberals and their allies believed in unity through diversity, a peaceful devolution of power which would satisfy the aspirations of nationalists for greater autonomy without encouraging separatism. As a counterweight to this, the Unionists were articulating an imperial nationalism which advocated a much more central role for the British state. Even without the re-emergence of the Irish question in British politics after 1900 this was a potentially combustible mix. With Ireland once again back on the agenda, and an international situation deteriorating towards war, its implications were explosive indeed.

The Liberals and Ireland, 1906–14

The issue of Home Rule had been pushed into the background following the defeat of the second Home Rule Bill in the House of Lords in 1893 and the return of a Unionist government at the election of 1895. The re-election of the Unionists in 1900, coupled with the internal problems of the Irish Nationalist party and the success of the ameliorative policies of the Salisbury and Balfour ministries, ensured that this remained the position at least until the Liberals' landslide victory in 1906. Even the Liberal commitment to Home Rule showed signs of weakening. Lord Rosebery, on becoming Prime Minister in 1894, had suggested that Home Rule should not be introduced against the wishes of the 'predominant partner' in the United Kingdom, namely England. In his Chesterfield speech of December 1901 he had gone further, urging the party to adopt a 'clean slate' and abandon its unpopular and outdated policies, Home Rule among them. Other Liberals were sympathetic to the idea of concentrating on matters more directly relevant to the British electorate and in any case realised the impossibility of proceeding with Home Rule while the Lords retained a veto on constitutional reform. Consequently, although Home Rule remained official Liberal policy, Campbell-Bannerman's incoming administration, with its large, independent Commons majority, pursued no more than a cautious, 'step-by-step' approach to Irish affairs. This intention was emphasised by the appointment first of James Bryce and then, in January 1907, of Augustine Birrell as Chief Secretary, rather than the staunch Home Ruler John Morley, who had held the post in Gladstone's last cabinet.[17] Indeed, the Liberals' immediate policy showed little change from that of their Unionist predecessors, the latter having introduced elected county councils to Ireland in 1898. In 1907 the Liberal government published its own Irish Council Bill, which would have set up a partially elected Executive Council in Dublin, but since the Bill met considerable hostility from the Nationalists and aroused no compensating enthusiasm elsewhere it was withdrawn.

As historians like Alan O'Day and George Boyce have pointed out, the failure of the Irish Council Bill, and of the gradualist devolutionary strategy which it embodied, left the government with only two realistic options: the maintenance of the status quo or the return to a policy of fully-fledged Home Rule.[18] Pressure to adopt the second course came from the Irish Nationalist party, reunited and reinvigorated under the leadership of John Redmond, and themselves trying to fend off an electoral threat in Ireland from Arthur Griffith's Sinn Fein. But it was not until the constitutional crisis of 1909–11 that the general political situation developed favourably from the Home Rulers' point of view. In January 1910 the Liberals lost their overall Commons majority, giving added leverage to the Nationalists who effectively held the balance between the two major parties. Redmond and his colleagues were able to use this altered state of affairs to their advantage. Despite their initial opposition to some aspects of Lloyd George's 1909 budget, in 1910 they supported the budget in return for an undertaking that the Liberal government would act decisively to remove the Lords' right of veto. As all the participants in the constitutional debates of 1910–11 were aware, the abolition of the veto would open the way to the introduction of Home Rule, leaving only the King's opposition or the exigencies of parliamentary and electoral politics as possible obstacles to the passage of legislation. This was one reason why Unionist resistance to the Parliament Bill was so prolonged, and it was a major factor behind the enthusiasm shown on the Unionist side for the use of the referendum in cases of 'organic' or constitutional reform. The passing of the Parliament Act in 1911, by ending the veto, placed the question of Home Rule once more firmly in centre stage.

It came as no surprise, therefore, when, in the King's Speech in February 1912, the government announced its intention of introducing a Home Rule Bill. When the Bill was published in April it was similar, in its essentials, to the measure which Gladstone had proposed, and which had been defeated by the Lords, in 1893. It provided for the establishment of a two-chamber Irish parliament, comprising an elected House of Commons of 164 MPs (59 from Ulster, 41 from Leinster, 37 from Munster, 25 from Connacht and two from Dublin University) and a 40-member Senate, nominated by the government. A quarter of senators were to retire every two years; the Commons would have to present itself for re-election at least once every five years; disputes between the two Houses would be resolved by a joint sitting and a majority vote. The parliament would have competence to deal with most of Ireland's internal affairs, though not with social welfare policies such as pensions and national insurance, nor, for six years, the direction of policing. Foreign affairs, overseas trade and taxation would remain the preserve of the United Kingdom parliament at Westminster (where a reduced contingent of 42 Irish MPs would sit), although the Irish parliament would have the discretionary power to add up to ten per cent to the level of income tax, death duties and customs, and was to be given additional revenue raising powers of its own. In a further delicate balancing of the imperial and local interest, the Irish parliament would have no role in determining the succession to the throne. There was to be an Irish executive responsible to the Dublin parliament, but the chief executive authority remained the Lord Lieutenant, appointed on the recommendation of the London government as the representative of the Crown.[19]

Whatever the intrinsic merits of these proposals, the government knew that any attempt to legislate for Home Rule was bound to be controversial and to arouse fierce opposition. The difficulties of securing the passage of the Bill were enhanced by the terms of the Parliament Act which, while it removed the Lords' right of veto, gave the Upper House delaying powers which effectively condemned the Liberals to piloting the Bill unchanged through three successive sessions of parliament before it could become law. Ministers, moreover, made their task even more onerous by refusing to offer any concessions to Unionist opinion in the form of special provision for Ulster. This won them the backing of the Nationalist party, was consistent with the Gladstonian policy of treating Ireland as a single entity, and may have been done with a view to keeping a bargaining counter in reserve for a subsequent compromise, but in the short term it was certain to increase resistance to the Bill. Ulster, with its large Protestant community and historic Unionist tradition, was the stronghold of opposition to Home Rule, which the Northern Protestants feared would place them under the jurisdiction of a Catholic-dominated Dublin parliament. Admittedly the situation in regard to Ulster was not quite as clear-cut as the conventional picture implies. Unionism was a force, albeit a minority one, in southern Irish politics as well, and was not confined to Ulster. In Ulster itself the population was fairly evenly divided between Catholics and Protestants, and in 1911 Ulster was represented by 17 Unionist MPs and 16 Nationalists. But since 1886, when Lord Randolph Churchill had spoken of playing the 'Orange card' and declared that if a Liberal government tried to impose Home Rule on an unwilling Ulster, 'Ulster will fight and Ulster will be right', it had been obvious that the Ulster hurdle would have to be cleared if a workable solution to the problem of devolution were to be found, regardless of any measures taken to safeguard the interests of Protestants in Ireland as a whole.[20]

The spectre of Home Rule had caused the Ulster Protestants to mobilise in opposition even before the Asquith government was publicly committed to proceeding with a Bill. In 1905 the Ulster Unionist Council had been formed to bring together 'loyalist' Protestant organisations and to provide grass-roots support for a parliamentary campaign. In 1910 the Irish Unionist MPs elected Sir Edward Carson as their new leader, a decision which was to have a powerful influence on the course of the Home Rule struggle.[21] Carson was one of the ablest figures on the Irish political scene. By birth a southern Irish Protestant and by training a barrister, he had earned himself respect and hatred in equal measure by acting as crown prosecutor for Dublin Castle during Balfour's term as Chief Secretary. In 1892, 'coercion Carson' was returned as one of the two MPs for Trinity College, Dublin, and rapidly established a reputation as a brilliant parliamentary speaker and a resolute critic of the Liberals' Irish policy. He sacrificed a lucrative practice at the English bar to become Solicitor-General in Lord Salisbury's government and seemed destined for high office in any future Unionist administration. Yet it was the Ulster crisis of 1912–14 that stamped his destiny. Carson and his fellow Irish Unionists knew that the results of the 1910 elections and the placing of the Parliament Act on the statute book meant that the introduction of a Home Rule Bill could not be long delayed. They saw, too, that Ulster was going to be the chief battleground in the conflict which would ensue. Accordingly, on 23 September 1911, they arranged a massive demonstration at Craigavon, the home of Sir James Craig, himself an Ulster MP and Carson's deputy, to show the depth of Unionist hostility to the idea of Ulster being incorporated in a Home Rule Ireland. Carson denounced the government's plan to introduce Home Rule as 'the most nefarious conspiracy that has ever been hatched against a free people' and gave notice of Protestant intentions by initiating preparations for setting up a separate provisional government for Ulster outside the working of a Home Rule scheme. The strength of Protestant feeling was shown again in February 1912, when

Winston Churchill was forced to cancel a meeting at Belfast's Ulster Hall (where his father had spoken in 1886 and where Churchill planned to defend the government's policy), having to address his audience instead at the Celtic Park football ground in the Catholic part of the city before being spirited away under police guard to avoid serious injury at the hands of outraged Protestants.[22]

It was partly in order to channel this Protestant hostility into a more disciplined, peaceful campaign, and to contain the upsurge in sectarian violence, that the Unionists organised their famous 'Ulster Day' in September 1912. A series of mass meetings throughout the province culminated, on 28 September, in the ceremonial signing of the 'Ulster Covenant', the signatories pledging themselves to use 'all means which may be found necessary' to defeat Home Rule and to refuse to recognise the authority of a Home Rule parliament.[23] The whole occasion was stage-managed with an impressive degree of solemnity and demonstrated Protestant solidarity in the face of the Home Rule threat, with over 200,000 Ulstermen coming forward to put their names to the Covenant roll. Equally impressive in its way, and of some concern to the Liberal government, was the support which the Ulster cause received from Unionists in Britain. Signatures for the Covenant were collected in Glasgow, Edinburgh, London, Manchester, Liverpool, Bristol and York. Rudyard Kipling offered £30,000 to the Ulster Unionists' 'fighting fund'.[24] A British League for the Support of Ulster and the Union, founded in March 1913, received the backing of 100 peers and 120 MPs and had over 10,000 members by 1914. Most importantly of all, Ulster's defiance of the government received the imprimatur of the official leadership of the British Unionist party.[25] Bonar Law addressed a meeting of more than 100,000 Ulster Unionists at Balmoral outside Belfast on Easter Tuesday 1912, expressing his support for their stand and assuring them that they could 'save the Empire' by their example. At a rally at Blenheim Palace in July he went even further and pledged his party to unspecified but nevertheless unstinting extremes of opposition to Home Rule. He characterised the Liberal government as 'a revolutionary committee which has seized by fraud upon despotic power' (a reference to the fact, in his view, that Home Rule had not been placed properly before the electorate in 1910 and that the Liberals were only introducing it because of their reliance on the Nationalist party in the House of Commons). Vaguely yet ominously he warned the Liberals that there were 'things stronger than Parliamentary majorities' and that, in this particular conflict, the Unionist party would 'not be guided by the considerations . . . which would influence us in any ordinary political struggle'. 'I can imagine no length of resistance to which Ulster can go,' he asserted, 'in which I should not be prepared to support them, and in which, in my belief, they would not be supported by the overwhelming majority of the British people.'[26]

How seriously Bonar Law's rhetoric should be taken, and precisely what construction should be put on it, is a moot point to which it will be necessary to return. Stripped of its hyperbole, the Unionist leader's speech nevertheless exposed a weakness in the government's position. Home Rule had been a subsidiary issue in the 1910 elections (only 84 of the 272 Liberal candidates successful in December 1910 had mentioned it in their election addresses). The Liberals were not acting 'unconstitutionally' by the conventions of parliamentary government, yet equally they knew that Home Rule was not popular with the British electorate (which was one reason for their rejection of the idea of a referendum). Even within the Liberal party complaints were heard that too much time was being spent on Home Rule, to the exclusion of British issues. Under the terms of the Parliament Act this was inescapable. The Liberals introduced the Home Rule Bill in April 1912. When it was rejected by the House of Lords (by 326 votes to 69) in January 1913, the whole process had to be started again, only for the Bill to be defeated in the Lords a second time in July. Meanwhile in Ireland, and especially in Ulster, organised opposition gathered momentum. The Unionists suffered one embarrassment when a Home Rule candidate won a by-election in Londonderry in January 1913 (albeit by only 57 votes), thus giving the Home Rulers a majority of Ulster seats. But this was brushed aside as no more than a temporary setback and if anything strengthened Unionist resolve. The Ulster Unionist Council formally established the Ulster Volunteer Force in

January 1913. Drilling, manoeuvres and paramilitary training based on the UVF, the Ulster rifle clubs and the lodges of the Orange Order were stepped up; plans were laid to arm the Volunteers and to place them under military command. They continued to receive high level support from sympathisers in Britain. The Union Defence League, founded in 1907 by Walter Long, and including Lord Milner among its members, organised a 'British Covenant' in March 1914 which was signed by an estimated two million people, many of them prominent in politics, the armed services or the arts, such as Lord Roberts (former Commander-in-Chief), Lord Balfour of Burleigh, Kipling, Elgar and A. V. Dicey, the constitutional historian. Support was enlisted in the Dominions and funds were raised to provide weapons for Ulster if armed resistance became necessary.

These preparations provoked a corresponding reaction on the Nationalist side. The 'Irish Volunteers' were constituted as a paramilitary force in opposition to the UVF. The secret Irish Republican Brotherhood and the pro-independence groups like Sinn Fein readied themselves for the coming struggle. Attempts were made to exploit other forms of popular unrest for nationalist purposes, most notably in the transport workers' strike of 1913. John Redmond, the leader of the Irish Parliamentary party, was personally opposed to the use of violence and strove to restrain his followers, but the possibility of serious conflict existed if a political solution to the crisis could not be found. Any compromise had to provide special treatment for Ulster. Significantly, when, in June 1912, the Liberal MP, Agar-Robartes, had proposed an amendment excluding four Ulster counties from the original Home Rule Bill he had received substantial Unionist support. The Unionists may on this occasion simply have been trying to embarrass the government, who were not yet ready publicly to consider exclusion, but the idea offered at least a possible way forward. Politicians returned more seriously to the issue in the summer of 1913, after the second rejection of the Home Rule Bill by the Lords and the publication of a pro-exclusion letter in *The Times* from the former Liberal Lord Chancellor, Lord Loreburn. The King suggested to the Prime Minister that an election should be held before Home Rule was introduced. Asquith was unwilling to agree, both on constitutional grounds and because any election held over Home Rule would favour the Unionists. He nevertheless had private discussions with the Unionist leaders to see whether exclusion could provide a basis for a settlement. The signs were hopeful. Carson and Bonar Law knew that this was the best they could realistically expect to gain from the government, even if it meant abandoning the southern Unionists to a Home Rule parliament. However, when Asquith made a formal proposal to the Commons on 9 March 1914, suggesting that the counties of Ulster should be allowed to 'opt out' of Home Rule for six years, at the end of which (unless parliament in the meantime decided otherwise) they would be included in a united, 'Home Rule', Ireland, his offer was less generous than the Unionists had anticipated and it drew a hostile response. Carson demanded the right of permanent exclusion, saying bluntly, 'We do not want a sentence of death with a stay of execution for six years.'[27]

There has been speculation that the Liberals anticipated, or even deliberately courted, this rejection, which, by revealing the intransigence of their opponents, could be seen as giving the government an excuse for imposing its own solution on the Ulster problem. It is true that Asquith's immediate reaction to the snub was less than decisive: he appointed a cabinet committee under Lord Crewe to consider the government's next move. On 14 March, however, after Crewe had been taken ill, Winston Churchill made a speech at Bradford (described by the Prime Minister as 'quite opportune'[28]) in which he attacked the Unionist party for fomenting 'civil war' by the support they were giving to the Ulster rebels. Setting himself firmly against this attempt, as he claimed, 'to subvert Parliamentary government and to challenge the civil and constitutional foundations of society', he cautioned the opposition that 'Against this mood . . . there is no lawful measure from which the Government should shrink', even, he implied, if it meant 'bloodshed . . . on an extensive scale.' There were echoes here of the heated exchanges during the budget crisis of 1909, and Churchill went out of his way to link the Irish question to other issues which aroused the hostility of 'the propertied classes', portraying the government as reasonable men pushed to the limits of endurance by factional and unconstitutional obstruction.[29]

Perhaps this was intended merely as a warning shot across Unionist bows. Alternatively, it may have been designed to justify a pre-emptive strike against Ulster, to nip any incipient rebellion firmly in the bud. Certainly in the few days following Churchill's speech military steps were taken. The army was ordered to move additional troops to Belfast to increase guards at strategic points such as arms depots. Naval reinforcements (including the Third Battle Squadron) were sent to Irish or adjacent Home waters. Ulster leaders feared their own imminent arrest and a government coup against the UVF (similar to the blow which Pitt's government had struck against the United Irishmen in 1795–6). However, the main outcome of the crisis – or 'The Plot That Failed', as it was dubbed by *The Times* – was not to break Unionist resistance but to put extra strain on relations between the government and the army. The Commander-in-Chief in Ireland, Lieutenant-General Sir Arthur Paget, had initially opposed the troop movements and had acceded to them only after a two-day conference at the War Office in London on 18–19 March. He had, at that time, secured the verbal concession that, while officers must obey their orders or be dismissed the service, those with Ulster connections would be allowed to 'disappear' for the duration of the operations. This introduced a complicating element into proceedings which already, in some eyes, had sinister connotations. If the troop movements were only 'precautionary', as the War Office claimed, why should Ulster-born officers object to being involved? Did the government therefore intend to coerce Ulster after all? That was how it appeared to Paget and to many of his officers, among whom there was already strong opposition to Home Rule and a reluctance to be used as a weapon in a domestic political conflict. The upshot was that a number of officers in Paget's command at the Curragh, mostly from the Third Cavalry Brigade, indicated that they preferred dismissal to the possibility of being asked to lead their men in what they believed might easily develop into a civil war.[30]

Although only a small-scale affair, caused in part by Paget's mishandling of the situation, the 'Curragh mutiny' reflected widespread discontent among the officer corps. Matters were made worse by the subsequent actions of the Secretary for War, Seely, who attempted to overcome the scruples of one of the 'mutinous' officers, Brigadier-General Hubert Gough, by giving a written assurance that the army would not be used to impose Home Rule on Ulster.[31] Asquith, who had taken a back seat in the crisis, was forced to intervene to disavow Seely's assurances, just as he had previously intervened to countermand the naval and troop movements. Seely resigned, as did the Chief of the Imperial General Staff, Sir John French, and Asquith himself took over the running of the War Office, but considerable damage had been done, both to the Liberal government's relationship with the army and to the position of moral superiority which ministers had tried so carefully to build up with their offer of exclusion in early March.

In the wake of these events a solution to the Ulster crisis was more imperative than ever, yet with the Unionists cock-a-hoop over what they saw as the government's bungled attempt at coercion a settlement had at the same time become more difficult to achieve. In Ireland, preparations for armed resistance continued unabated, the UVF successfully landing 20,000 illegally imported rifles at Larne, Bangor and Donaghadee on the night of 24 April.[32] Unionist leaders were reviewing any expedients by which they might still block the Home Rule legislation, including obstructing the annual Army Act and calling on the King to use his power of veto. The Liberals, for their part, attempted to effect an eleventh-hour compromise by introducing an Amending Bill in the House of Lords, offering the Ulster counties the six-year, county-by-county opt out which had first been proposed in March. When the Lords inserted a provision for permanent exclusion into the Bill, however, they went further than either the government or the Nationalists were willing to accept and the initiative came to nothing. A further effort to break the deadlock, through the 'Buckingham Palace Conference' of July 1914, also failed. Asquith and Lloyd George met with the Unionists Bonar Law, Lansdowne, Carson and Craig, and with the Nationalist leaders

Redmond and Dillon, in talks sponsored by the King and chaired by Speaker Lowther, but yet again the discussions foundered, the participants being unable to reach agreement on the extent and terms of any exclusion provisions.[33] Two days after the breakdown of the talks, the tension of the situation in Ireland was increased when, having thwarted a plan by the Irish Volunteers to mount a daylight gun-running mission, British troops fired on a crowd of nationalist sympathisers at Bachelor's Walk in Dublin, killing three people and wounding 38 more. As the Home Rule Bill made its way inexorably towards becoming law, Ireland teetered unsteadily on the verge of serious civil strife.

It was at this point that the immediate prospect was transformed by the outbreak of the First World War. The same cabinet meeting which on 24 July received Asquith's report on the failure of the Buckingham Palace Conference also received news from the Foreign Secretary, Sir Edward Grey, of the Austrian ultimatum to Serbia arising from the assassination of the Archduke Franz Ferdinand, the heir to the Austrian throne, in Sarajevo at the end of June. As Winston Churchill memorably described it in his book, *The World Crisis*, 'The parishes of Fermanagh and Tyrone faded back into the mists and squalls of Ireland, and a strange light began . . . to fall and grow upon the map of Europe'.[34] Within days, the Great Powers of Europe were at war and domestic conflicts were pushed temporarily into the shade. On 30 July, Asquith agreed to postpone further discussion of the Amending Bill because of the severity of the international crisis. The government still insisted on the Home Rule Bill receiving the royal assent, much to the anger of the Unionists, but agreed, with Redmond's concurrence, that it would not become operative until after the war, so giving time for another attempt at settling the exclusion question. These assurances, together with the seriousness of the external threat to the United Kingdom and its Empire, were enough to persuade the Ulster loyalists to throw their support behind the war effort. Ulstermen rallied in large numbers to the Union flag, and for many of them the battles for which they had trained in the fields and by-ways of northern Ireland became reality, two years later, on the Somme.[35]

Home Rule and the Revolt of the Right

The big imponderable about the Home Rule crisis of 1912–14 is what would have happened if a European war had not broken out in August 1914, or if Britain had not joined her French and Russian allies in the struggle against Germany. The Liberal government was still honestly seeking alternatives to confrontation with the Ulster rebels. After the collapse of the Buckingham Palace talks the cabinet decided to press ahead with the Amending Bill, a Bill which now provided for indefinite exclusion of the four Protestant-dominated counties of northern Ireland (and possibly parts of Fermanagh and Tyrone) rather than the temporary opt-out previously considered. This was sufficiently close to what Carson had been prepared to settle for in earlier negotiations to remove much of the justification for a full-scale rebellion against the Home Rule Bill. Bonar Law was already looking for a compromise and might well have thrown his weight behind an agreed solution to the Ulster problem, so long as it could be packaged to appear as a victory for Unionist firmness. A peaceful resolution of the Irish impasse was thus in sight, if only the Nationalists did not baulk at the effective partition of their island between the pro- and anti-Home Rule factions, and the Unionists and their allies were willing to concede the principle of Home Rule in return for limiting the territorial jurisdiction of a Dublin parliament.

Yet this may be too optimistic a scenario. The battle lines were tightly drawn in Ireland in the summer of 1914 and Carson's followers were ready to fight for their independence if final talks with the government broke down. Even if a compromise had been reached, it would not necessarily have been the end of Ireland's political problems. There would still have been a feeling of betrayal among Ulster loyalists, particularly among those Protestants who lived outside the areas proposed for exclusion. The treatment of Southern Unionists in the civil war after the conclusion of the Anglo-Irish Treaty in 1921, and indeed the high levels of sectarian violence which existed in places before 1914, showed that high-political agreements were not easily translated into peaceful solutions on the ground. On the Nationalist side, it would have been difficult for Redmond and his party to have accepted the permanent exclusion of the Northern Counties, with their large Catholic populations, from a Home Rule Ireland. Had they done so, there were hotter heads, especially in Sinn Fein and the Irish Republican Brotherhood, who would have been loath to acquiesce in what they considered a 'sell-out' of the nationalist cause. On this more pessimistic reading, further conflict in Ireland was inevitable, either between Nationalists and Unionists or among the various factions of the nationalist movement, with every prospect of a recrudescence of the Irish question in British politics as the modified Union came under attack – whether constitutionally or militarily – from its dissatisfied critics.

The unpredictability of its outcome is only part of the difficulty of gauging the seriousness of the situation in Ireland in 1914. In the broader context of imperial politics, an equally important factor is the extent to which the affairs of Ireland were entangled with the other problems of pre-war Britain. Dangerfield's account of the Edwardian period emphasised the similar characteristics, if not the actual interconnectedness, of the three 'rebellions' of the Ulster Unionists, the suffragettes and the working class, drawing attention to what he saw as their common challenge to the authority of parliament and the rule of law. His portrait is not without a modicum of truth. Neither the suffragettes nor the trade unions contemplated the use of armed force against the elected government, but they did employ various types of direct action, and made skilful use of the threat of disruption, in an attempt to bend parliament to their will. The suffragettes, certainly, were prepared to use at least a limited amount of violence and to defy the law in order to promote their cause. There were also some instances of cooperation between the different groups of campaigners. The existence of an alliance between the women's suffrage organisations and the Labour party has already been described.[36] Interaction between the Labour and suffrage movements and the Irish conflict is more complicated to unravel, because of the political cross-currents involved. For one thing, the symathies of the British Labour movement tended to be with the Nationalist Home Rulers rather than the Ulster rebels. In Ulster, however, Carson received the backing of the Protestant-controlled trade unions, which formed the Ulster Unionist Labour Association to demonstrate their support for the anti-Home Rule campaign. The women's movement was similarly divided over the Home Rule issue, socialist and Liberal women being inclined to back the Nationalists while Conservative women were more likely to be drawn to the Unionist camp. For most of the leading suffrage campaigners, Home Rule was a distraction from the main task in hand, that of securing votes for women. Alliances were made and broken insofar as they advanced or hindered the central objective. For example, the Irish nationalists forfeited some suffragist support when they withdrew their endorsement from the Conciliation Bill in 1912 (one reason for the WSPU's extension of its arson attacks to Dublin). In Ireland, though, especially in Ulster, the Home Rule crisis played a significant part in the politicisation of the female population, attracting some of them to the suffrage movement. The Ulster Women's Unionist Council had 40,000 members by 1912. When the Ulster Covenant was signed in September 1912, 228,991 women signed a corresponding Declaration of opposition to Home Rule. They also gave practical help to Carson's movement, including the formation of ambulance and nursing auxiliaries to assist the Ulster Volunteers. Carson reciprocated by declaring his commitment to female suffrage in the election of an Ulster parliament, although he subsequently went back on this pledge, prompting the establishment of an Ulster Women's Suffrage Society.[37]

But while these individual points of contact existed, there was insufficient unity of purpose among the disparate movements to enable them to make common cause. In Ireland, labour and gender issues were very much subordinate to the nationality question, and political and sectarian differences hampered attempts to create united trade union or suffrage organisations. Nor, in the case of Labour, was class solidarity easy to preserve across St George's Channel. Although there had been personal and institutional links between British and Irish Labour since the 1830s, with many British unions having an Irish membership, the British TUC was alarmed at the growth of more extreme, socialist-syndicalist tendencies in Ireland, particularly among the Dublin dockers and transport workers mobilised by Larkin and

Connolly in the disputes of 1912 and 1913. By 1914, consequently, clear divisions had opened up between the British and Irish trade union movements and the leadership of the organised Labour movement in Britain was doing its best to distance itself from the Home Rule controversy.[38] Suffrage campaigners in Britain likewise, though welcoming any support they received from Ireland, refused to become embroiled in the Home Rule struggle, simply wanting the issue cleared from the path so that the suffrage question could take its place at the top of the political agenda. It is possible that Labour and suffragist leaders were encouraged to redouble their own efforts to pressurise the government by the example of Irish success, but they were essentially competitors for attention with the Nationalists and Ulster Unionists rather than their allies. For that reason it is unlikely that, even if a civil war had broken out in Ireland in 1914, there would have been any sympathetic action to assist the Irish factions from any of the principal women's or labour organisations in Britain, except perhaps in cities like Glasgow and Liverpool which had large Irish working-class populations traditionally divided along sectarian lines.[39]

A civil war in Ireland was actually more likely to find a sympathetic echo on the right than on the left of the British political spectrum. This was at least partly because of the way in which the Irish question continued to be enmeshed in the more general debate about Britain's constitutional and imperial future. The revival of Home Rule as an issue had sparked a corresponding revival of nationalism in Scotland and Wales, and there were a number of unsuccessful attempts by backbench MPs to introduce Scottish and Welsh Home Rule Bills between 1908 and 1914.[40] These campaigns prompted proposals for a move towards a federal constitution, in which the demands of Ireland, Scotland and Wales could be met by the granting of 'Home Rule All Round'. The idea received some backing from the Unionist camp. F. S. Oliver ('Pacificus') wrote a series of pro-federal articles in *The Times* in October and November 1910. But it was the Liberals, with their electoral roots in the 'Celtic fringe', who responded most warmly. Asquith, when introducing the Third Home Rule Bill in April 1912, described Irish devolution as 'the first step in a larger and more comprehensive policy'.[41] Although his government made no practical moves towards the implementation of this 'larger policy', its very adumbration was enough to arouse considerable Unionist hostility. Even more contentious in this respect was the question of Welsh Disestablishment. As with Irish Home Rule, the removal of the Lords' veto in 1911 had lifted the barrier to the fulfilment of this long-standing Liberal pledge. When the Disestablishment Bill was introduced in 1912, however, the Unionist party, supported by the full weight of the Church, decided not only to use the machinery of the Parliament Act to delay the measure for as long as possible, but waged a fierce public onslaught on its provisions, especially regarding the disposal of Church endowments. The Bill had still not reached the statute book in the summer of 1914 and was another factor embittering the political mood in the latter stages of the Irish crisis.[42]

Arguments over the constitutional future of the United Kingdom were closely linked to the debate about the future of Britain's Empire overseas. The Liberals had already extended their devolutionary policies beyond the British Isles before they turned their attention to Ireland. Australia and New Zealand were granted dominion status in 1907. The Indian Councils Act of 1909 enabled Indians to participate in provincial councils, holding out the prospect of a greater role for them in the administration of their own country. In South Africa, the Chamberlain–Milner plan to incorporate the Orange Free State and the Transvaal into a British-dominated territory ruled from the Cape was reversed by Campbell-Bannerman's concession of self-government to the two Boer states in 1906 and 1907, a Gladstonian-style policy continued by Asquith, who, in 1910, presided over the creation of a Union of South Africa as a new dominion in which Afrikaners outnumbered Whites of British descent.[43] These measures were not motivated by anti-imperial sentiment or 'Little Englandism'.[44] As with the devolution of powers to Dublin, the Liberal contention was that decentralisation would strengthen the Empire rather than weaken it. But the path of imperial development which the Liberals had in mind was very different from the closer political and economic integration to which Chamberlain had committed the Unionist party with his plans for imperial federation and preferential tariffs. The confrontation with the Liberal government over Ireland was the latest engagement in a running battle to determine imperial policy, in the light of which Bonar Law's exhortation to Carson's Ulstermen to 'save the Empire' by their example was more than merely a rhetorical flourish.

Indeed, resistance to Home Rule became the linchpin of an increasingly desperate rearguard action being fought by the Unionists against the Asquith government on both the imperial and domestic fronts. Since 1905 the Unionists had suffered a succession of defeats at Liberal hands, the cumulative effect of which was to sap Unionist morale and weaken the unity of the party. After their victory over the Parliament Act in 1911 the Liberals pressed ahead with the next phase of their assault on entrenched interests through measures such as Welsh Disestablishment and Land Reform. The Unionists, meanwhile, were divided and on the defensive. The constitutional crisis of 1909–11 and the events leading to Balfour's departure from the leadership had opened wounds in the party which Bonar Law could heal only by rallying his followers behind a policy to which they were all committed and which gave them a chance of levering their way back to power. Tariff Reform was inadequate for this purpose because there was no unanimity of view as to how and in what form it should be introduced, and in any case it was not electorally popular. Opposition to Home Rule, on the other hand, enabled the Unionists to appeal to the atavistic forces of English nationalism against Celtic particularism, thereby reviving a vital component in the popular imperialism which had contributed to their electoral success in the 1890s. More importantly, perhaps, it was a policy which had the unequivocal backing of Unionist MPs and peers. Although 'Unionism' had taken up a variety of causes – 'National Efficiency', Tariff Reform, Imperial Federation – the preservation of the Anglo-Irish Union of 1800 was still very much the Unionist party's *raison d'être*. The Irish question drew upon deep-rooted emotional, religious and family loyalties which went beyond the calculations of purely rational political debate and gave the defence of the Union a symbolic, almost talismanic, status in Unionist politics which no other issue even remotely possessed.

Nevertheless, a strategy of staking everything on defeating Home Rule, or precipitating an election which would allow the English electorate to defeat it, was not without risk. If it failed, the spirit and cohesion of the party might be fatally weakened. There was the possibility, too, of renewed dissent in Unionist ranks if the party's leaders eventually accepted a compromise which did not commend itself to their more militant supporters. The position was made more difficult by the emergence of what historians of the Edwardian period have termed the 'Radical Right' within the Unionist party and on its fringes.[45] This tendency culled its membership mainly from the party's 'diehard' wing, still smarting from its defeat over the Parliament Act and the People's Budget. The diehard members of the 'Reveille' movement had played a key role in ousting Balfour from the Unionist leadership in 1911, and although Reveille was disbanded in the wake of this victory successor groups like the 'Halsbury Club', formed in November 1911, acted as an organisational focus for diehard opinion. The diehards were not an entirely negative political force. Many of them believed in 'constructive' policies such as Tariff Reform and their ideas had some affinity with those of the Milnerite 'national efficiency' movement. But they were staunch in their resistance to what they saw as the revolutionary radicalism of the Asquith government, and they wanted to preserve as much as possible of the traditional social and political order from the depradations of socialism, Liberalism and nationalism which they believed were undermining the stability and cohesion of British society and thus threatening Britain's place in the world.

Bonar Law shared some of the diehards' fears but he did not necessarily approve their political methods, despite the impression created by some of his hard-line rhetoric. He knew, though, that the diehards were a significant strand in Unionist politics, and he could not afford to override or ignore their views lest they carry through another palace revolution against the party leadership or seceded from the Unionist ranks altogether to form their own 'National' party.[46] The aristocratic diehards, moreover, were reinforced on the political right by a variety of patriotic or quasi-military pressure groups and by an increasingly vociferous right-wing press. As has been seen, journals like Maxse's *National Review* (which in 1912 accused the Liberal government of promoting 'national anarchy') and organisations like the Navy League and the National Service League were drawing together imperialist, anti-Liberal opinion, and they formed a natural alliance with the diehards against what they regarded as the symptoms of a potentially catastrophic national decline.

The importance of the Radical Right, and of the creeping 'militarisation' of right-wing politics, in the context of the party battle over Irish Home Rule was considerable. First, the Radical Right provided many of the most committed supporters of the Ulster cause. Diehards like Willoughby de Broke and Milner took a leading part in pro-Ulster organisations such as the British League, while those on the 'military right', including the influential Roberts, assisted Carson and Craig in setting up the Ulster Volunteers. Such support stiffened the fibres of Ulster resistance and helped to make armed rebellion a practical possibility. It may also have encouraged the Ulster leaders to believe that, in the event of a civil war, the army would either remain neutral or actively take a more sympathetic role. Politically, the antics of the right forced Bonar Law to adopt an outwardly tougher stance and made the search for a compromise an even more delicate operation. A further dangerous sign in these increasingly tense circumstances was the spread of overtly anti-parliamentary ideas among some of the more extreme right-wingers, with apparently serious consideration being given to the use of violent, insurrectionary methods for the attainment of political ends and the replacement of a worn-out, effete and corrupt party system by a more authoritarian, dictatorial form of government by patriotically-minded 'strong men'.[47]

These factors all have to be borne in mind when assessing the seriousness of the Irish crisis and the threat which it presented to the constitutional authority of the Liberal government. Opposition to Home Rule was not in itself unconstitutional of course, even where it involved campaigns of mass protest and the full exploitation of the powers of tactical delay contained in the

Parliament Act. Where the opponents of Home Rule in Ulster went beyond the bounds of constitutionality was in their plan to establish a provisional government without parliamentary approval and their determination to defend that government by military action against the forces of the Crown.[48] There can be little doubt that if the Liberals had gone ahead with their Home Rule Bill without securing agreement on exclusion a violent rebellion in Ulster would have resulted, with every likelihood of nationalist paramilitaries becoming involved in a virtual civil war. In that event, the key question then becomes what response this would have occasioned among Unionists in Britain. The British Unionist party had supported, condoned and encouraged the Ulster rebels – partly because of a common opposition to Home Rule, partly because of the exigencies of domestic British politics. This may, as some historians have argued, all have been part of a strategy of 'bluff and brinkmanship' designed to maintain party unity and squeeze concessions from Asquith's beleagured administration, though that is far from certain.[49] Yet even if that were the case, there might still have been those who were prepared to go over the brink if the situation arose, either carrying Bonar Law with them or defying him if he tried to exercise restraint. Another area of uncertainty concerns the role of the army. Confidential discussions took place throughout the spring and early summer of 1914 between Unionist politicians and army leaders, including the Ulster-born Sir Henry Wilson, Director of Military Operations at the War Office. The Curragh 'mutineers' had been fêted in Unionist circles and many Unionists believed that the army would be justified in standing aside from any conflict in Ireland brought about by government policy. Some officers were reportedly prepared to throw in their commissions and join the Ulster Volunteers rather than help to impose Home Rule on an unwilling North.[50] This is not to say that the army as an organisation would necessarily have refused to obey the orders of the Liberal government in Ireland, or to claim that army officers were actually involved in any ill-conceived plans for a military *coup d'état*. But the very fact that such contingencies can legitimately be speculated upon indicates the fine line that was being trodden between constitutional and unconstitutional action.

In the final analysis, the truth is probably that some form of last-minute deal would have been struck in August or September 1914 and that the parliamentary system would have survived intact. This should not, however, be allowed to conceal the depth of what *The Times* referred to as 'one of the greatest crises in the history of the British race'.[51] Between 1911 and 1914 the stability of British institutions and the integrity of the British state had been tested to their utmost and the British Isles had been brought measurably closer to civil war than at any time since the conflicts of the seventeenth century or the Jacobite rebellions of the eighteenth. There can be no absolute certainty about how events in the United Kingdom would have developed if Britain and her Empire had not been drawn into the even deeper crisis of nationalism which was about to engulf the whole of the European world.

CONCLUSION

As was indicated at the outset, it is possible to paint two very different pictures of Edwardian Britain. One is of a society riven by conflicts of class, gender and nationality, in which the liberal parliamentary system was being simultaneously undermined and overwhelmed and the country was sinking into ungovernability; the other emphasises rather the elements of stability and continuity which underlay the superficial appearance of disorder. Both pictures represent an aspect of the truth. Undoubtedly serious problems did exist, and some, like that of Irish Home Rule, were reaching a noisy and potentially violent climax. Yet this does not mean that the United Kingdom as a whole was on the eve of revolution or social collapse. It has been shown that the extent to which the various movements of the pre-war period were connected can easily be overstated, as can their spirit of revolt. Only a small number of syndicalists and extreme socialists – and perhaps a few on the radical right – contemplated the overthrow of parliamentary government. There were plans for rebellion in Ireland, but the Ulster Unionists protested their loyalty to the Crown; only the Sinn Feiners and the nationalist Irish Republican Brotherhood thought in more revolutionary, republican terms. Significantly Ireland was the one part of the UK which did experience a revolution during and after the war. In Britain, apart from one or two hotbeds of discontent on the coalfields, Clydeside and elsewhere, an outright rejection of the existing system was never likely and the use of violence for political ends was strictly limited. By the same token, it would be unconvincing to talk of a general social or economic crisis or a complete breakdown in class or gender relations. There were some signs that the material gulf between classes was widening, and the industrial troubles of the pre-war decade suggested that class antagonisms were reaching a higher pitch – perhaps more so as the downturn in living standards frustrated long-held expectations of continuing improvement. But unemployment rates remained low, the government's welfare measures alleviated some of the worst effects of poverty and the foundations of a basically cohesive society remained firm. A few cracks in the edifice were beginning to appear, but they were not yet wide enough to threaten the integrity of the social fabric.

Nevertheless, the concept of an 'Edwardian crisis' should not be dismissed as altogether a myth. At the very least, in the summer of 1914 there was a serious short-term political crisis over the Liberal government's Home Rule Bill and the future of the Anglo-Irish Union. This in turn was part of a more extended crisis in parliamentary politics which had lasted since the introduction of Lloyd George's 'People's Budget' in 1909 and arguably since Balfour's decision to use the Conservative majority in the Lords to block Liberal legislation after the election of 1906. At the same time other issues were coming to a head in ways which intersected, directly or indirectly, with the main thrust of the Liberal versus Unionist battle. The confrontation between the Liberals and the House of Lords provided a denouement to the nineteenth-century contest between the principles of aristocratic and those of representative government, while the campaigns for female and adult suffrage were the culmination of a long struggle to democratise the political system, a struggle of which the desires of nationalists for self-determination could also be seen as being a part. The emergence of the Labour party was another facet of the democratisation process, and Labour's electoral success, coupled with the growing strength of the trade unions, posed fundamental questions for politicians and industrialists alike. Allied to these domestic concerns were the problems of foreign policy, as Britain's century of imperial and naval supremacy came to an end and she was drawn inexorably into the affairs of continental Europe, sacrificing global independence for a measure of national security. Even then, peace, which, along with 'retrenchment' and 'reform' had been one of the axioms of nineteenth-century liberal statesmanship, could not be guaranteed. The ententes with France and Russia settled outstanding colonial differences and reduced the chances of war with traditional rivals, but they increased the risk of a European confrontation with Germany. From 1911 Britain and France were preparing in detail for the possibility of a German war, and in so doing contributed to precisely that fear of encirclement on the part of Germany which made war more likely.[1]

These developments placed a considerable strain not only on the Asquith government but on the political parties, on the workings of the parliamentary system and on the relationship between society and the state. Contrary to Dangerfield's view, there was no widespread rejection of the parliamentary process in these years and the high turnouts in the elections of 1906 and 1910 reflected an impressive level of voter commitment. All the same, the events of the pre-war period did raise doubts about the legitimacy of parliamentary institutions and their ability both to command continuing confidence and to cope with the manifold social and political problems of the day. The unrepresentative nature of the electoral system was attacked by female suffragists because it discriminated against women, and by Labour (and some Liberals) because it discriminated in favour of the propertied middle and upper classes. The use of syndicalist-type direct action, although a minority trend, was a reaction against what was perceived as a 'bosses' parliament' and an index of the frustration felt in some quarters at the limited progress made by a staunchly parliamentarist Labour party. Within parliament, the Liberal government found its legislative programme obstructed by an unelected hereditary chamber which the Parliament Act of 1911 reduced in power but left otherwise intact. Between 1906 and 1914 accusations and counter-accusations of 'unconstitutional' behaviour embittered relations between government and opposition, culminating in Bonar Law's declaration that there were things stronger than parliamentary majorities and in Ulster's rebellion against the Home Rule Bill. The cumbersome machinery of the Parliament Act itself brought further discredit on parliament because of the way in which it delayed the passage of laws and hamstrung the transaction of government business. Ministers were consequently encouraged to by-pass the parliamentary logjam wherever possible, acting by administrative fiat, setting up non-parliamentary bodies and treating separately with extra-parliamentary interest groups. In the context of the time, a particularly worrying aspect of the decreasing centrality of parliament to the decision making process was the lack of any properly sustained consideration of foreign affairs, with MPs (and even some ministers) being kept in ignorance about key areas of policy.

The crisis in the country's governing institutions was made more serious by the fact that the 'decline' of parliament was accompanied by the rise of the state. Already in the late nineteenth century the mid-Victorian ideal of the minimal state had been gradually eroded. In the Edwardian period it was finally abandoned. True, in economic policy Free Trade withstood the assault of Tariff Reform. But in other respects the state moved further away from its nineteenth-century liberal roots. The expansion of welfare provision, the introduction of new forms of redistributive taxation and the passage of more interventionist industrial and labour legislation was only part of the process, and the one that could most easily be reconciled with liberal (or at least Liberal) principles. However, the Edwardian period also saw the enhancement of the state's regulatory or coercive role, in response to rising levels of popular protest and civil disorder. The government was increasingly involved in the settlement of industrial disputes; it used the full rigours of the law against suffragette militancy and deployed the police and the army to combat labour unrest. It changed its character even more markedly in two other ways. One was the massive increase of public spending on armaments and preparations for war, which contributed to the 'militarisation' of the state and government machine. The other was the emergence, in embryo, of what historians have called the 'secret state' – the employment of the Scotland Yard Special Branch and the newly-formed MI5 to counter domestic subversion and the suspected activities of foreign spies, a system of intelligence backed by the passage of the 1911 Official Secrets Act which imposed blanket restrictions on access to government information and shielded the inner workings of the state from too close a public scrutiny.[2]

It would be a mistake to exaggerate the significance of these changes and the dangers they posed. Britain was still a more open, less regimented society than many of the states of continental Europe. There was no military conscription; the organs of censorship and the police state were less fully developed than elsewhere – less so, indeed, than they had been in earlier periods of British history such as the 1790s. Similarly, some of the instances of state intervention – for example the provision of old age pensions – were widely welcomed, making it melodramatic to talk in terms of an outright antagonism in relations between society and the state or the state and the individual. Yet as the state extended the range of its functions, the potential for confrontation inevitably increased, whether with organised interest groups like the Labour movement or individuals resisting the demands of the state in other ways. A crisis of sorts had been reached, in the sense that the statist trend was building up a momentum of its own and it was doubtful how far the actions of the state could be kept under any meaningful kind of popular control. Already a clear division was opening up in Edwardian politics between the advocates of a technocratic regime of national efficiency, staffed by 'experts', and progressive thinkers who wanted a more 'social democratic' state which could act as the executive expression of the communal will. The precedents of the early 1900s, which delegated considerable powers to civil servants and quasi-governmental bodies, suggested the former view was prevailing over the latter, with the state taking on a less liberal, more counter-democratic role.[3]

The problem of what, in more recent terminology, might be described as a 'democratic deficit' was complicated by the unsettled condition of the party system, hitherto the cornerstone of the British system of representative government, the channel through which popular discontents were mediated and the means by which an over-zealous executive could be brought under parliamentary control. But in the Edwardian period the upsurge in extra-parliamentary protest and the expansion in the role of the state coincided with a phase of extreme volatility in party politics, with both of the major parties facing serious difficulties in their internal affairs as well as in their relations with each other and with the wider electoral community. On both sides of the political divide there seemed to be a tendency towards fragmentation which the party leaders were unable to check and which called into question their ability to provide a stable platform for the government of the country.

Perhaps understandably, the greater weight of historiographical attention has fallen on the problems of the Liberal party. The Liberals, after all, were in government for most of the Edwardian period and might have been expected to feel the sharpest blasts from the wind of change. The crisis of the 'liberal' state could be seen as one aspect of a more generalised crisis of liberalism and liberal values, the effects of which were likely to be greatest on the party which by its name and traditions was most closely associated with them. Furthermore, the rapid decline of the Liberal party after the First World War, and its replacement by Labour as the principal opposition to the Conservatives, led some writers to assume that there was already something anachronistic about Liberalism before 1914, as its fundamental individualism was assailed by the collectivities of class and its moderate, rational approach to the tasks of government was rendered untenable by the growing extremism and violence of an increasingly unstable society.

Of late this rather simplistic view has undergone considerable revision and there has been more emphasis on the resilience of the Liberal party than on the inevitability of its decline.[4] The revisionist case finds support from contemporary testimony. Liberals in Edwardian Britain were certainly aware of the problems facing their party (J. A. Hobson published his seminal *The Crisis of Liberalism* in 1909), but they firmly believed that these problems could be overcome. Liberal politicians approached the difficulties of the pre-war era as manageable tasks of statecraft, not as symptoms of an untreatable social or psychological malaise. The advent of the New Liberalism, and its practical expression in a range of industrial and welfare reforms, demonstrated the adaptability of Liberal ideas and the ability of Liberals to redefine their creed in accordance with a developing interventionist consensus. In Lloyd George the party found a leader who could successfully blend the 'Old' Liberalism and the New, and so maximise the party's electoral appeal. The results of the general elections of 1910, and of the by-elections of 1911–14, suggested that the challenge of Labour had been held at least temporarily in check – a testimony either to the fact, as Peter Clarke has argued, that the Liberals had managed to reorientate themselves in relation to a political system divided more completely along lines of class, or else that before 1914 the electoral importance of class (as opposed to other factors such as religion, or local and regional loyalties) was more limited than was previously supposed.[5] Whatever the reasons, in 1914 the Liberal party was still a vibrant and viable political force, with its appetite for power undiminished and the reins of government held firmly in its hands. Indeed, there is a strong case for saying, as one recent study has done, that of the two major parties, it was the Conservatives, not the Liberals, who were facing the deeper crisis in the Edwardian period.[6]

Yet the revisionist arguments are not entirely convincing. It is valid to point out that the erosion of 'liberalism' in its broader Victorian sense was something which affected parties across the whole political spectrum and not just the Liberal party alone. But a growing disjunction between 'liberalism' and 'Liberalism' nevertheless posed particular problems for politicians who espoused the Liberal cause. Much of the electoral strength of the Edwardian Liberal party in the constituencies depended on the continuing appeal of the individualist, Nonconformist Liberalism of Gladstone's day. The 1906 election victory was demonstrably a triumph for the old Liberalism rather than the New. After 1906, however, at least at national level, Gladstonianism was in retreat. Asquith and Lloyd George developed a strategy for keeping the different wings of their party together, but their temporary success could not disguise an underlying difficulty. As they gradually liquidated their commitments to the old radicalism, and the New Liberalism moved into the ascendant, it became harder to maintain the enthusiasm of traditional supporters at the grass roots. Middle-class Liberals were resistant to the demands for higher taxation and concessions to the trade unions, while there were few indications that the working classes were being won over by a policy of improved welfare provision. This was a worrying trend which Lloyd George's Land Campaign, for all its potential as a rallying point for all shades of radical opinion, failed wholly to reverse.[7] Added to this were the problems arising from the Liberal government's alienation of its former supporters on the feminist and Labour left. By 1912–14 there was a growing frustration among suffragists because of the government's prevarication over the introduction of votes for women. On the industrial and political front there were signs of a rift between the Liberals and Labour which threatened the future of the progressive alliance. The Liberals were already a minority in parliament after the elections of 1910 and any further defections from their ranks plainly endangered their status as a party of government, especially once the Irish Nationalist representation at Westminster had been reduced by the introduction of Home Rule. This is not to say that the Liberal party was doomed in 1914, or that its eclipse was inevitable. But it had reached a turning point in its fortunes. If it was not to become the victim as well as the agent of the process of democratisation which it had initiated in the nineteenth century, a good performance in the approaching general election was essential, since defeat was likely to plunge the party once more into the morass of internecine conflict which had almost led to its extinction in the 1890s.

On the other hand, the revisionists are right to stress that it was not only the Liberals who had problems or for whom the general election of 1915 would have been a potentially decisive test. The Labour party was still far from securely established on a national basis and, whether or not it chose a fully independent course, its leaders must have been anxious to recapture their earlier momentum after a run of by-election defeats. The Conservatives were in an even more perilous position. Having lost three successive elections the party was beset by factionalism and committed to supporting an anti-government rebellion in Ulster which might at any moment explode into violence. Bonar Law had

either to accept a compromise over Ulster, which might alien-
ate his right wing, or to take the responsibility of endorsing a
civil war against the wishes of more moderate opinion. In either
case his party was likely to be torn by further conflict which
nothing less than a Unionist victory at the polls would be likely
to contain.

The crisis of the pre-war years can thus be interpreted not
merely as a 'crisis of Liberalism' but as a crisis for all the political
parties, and perhaps for the party system as a whole. Politics had
been becoming increasingly polarised since the 1860s. By the
early 1900s the two major parties were in danger of fragmenting
under the weight of a variety of internal and external pressures.
The viability, or desirability, of party government was being
called into question by those who favoured either a government
of national unity or some kind of 'Caesarist' dictatorship. The
significance of these trends is difficult to assess. Some writers
would play down the extremities of partisanship which characterised the party battles of these years, highlighting instead the
continuing existence of an underlying high-political consensus
about the limits beyond which party conflict should not be taken,
the compromise solution of the constitutional crisis being a case
in point. Again, there are those who would argue that the leaders
of the Liberal and Conservative parties were so alarmed by the
growing extremism coursing through the body politic – on the
right as well as the left – that they would have been driven to
compose their differences in order to present a united front
against a common enemy. Yet before the summer of 1914 the
causes making for conflict were stronger than those for coalition.
The traditional – even ritual – battles were fought out with
increasing ferocity: over education and Tariff Reform; over the
People's Budget and the House of Lords; over Welsh Disestablishment, the Land Campaign and Irish Home Rule. In this
atmosphere the unifying rhetoric of 'national efficiency' remained
just that. Lloyd George's coalition proposal, while not forgotten,
was cast aside and pushed into the background by the febrile
excitement surrounding such *causes célèbre* as the Marconi scandal[8]
and the Ulster rebellion. As the politicians berated one another,
however, and tried to marshal their supporters behind the old

banners, they laid themselves open to dangers which their more integrationist strategies had been designed to avoid. The violence of their language encouraged a corresponding violence of outlook elsewhere. At the same time the established parties risked being outflanked by the newer forces which were arising to challenge the previously all-inclusive duopoly. The Liberals faced competition from Labour, and from the more extreme socialist groups. The Unionists had to cope with the rise of the patriotic and radical right. At best the mood of crisis and controversy was likely to intensify as the general election approached, with the dividing lines between parties becoming more and more firmly drawn. At worst there was the possibility that the Edwardian party system might collapse altogether, creating a vortex of instability in which majority party government ceased to be viable and fundamental realignments had to take place.

It is often said that the outbreak of war transformed the domestic scene. Within a matter of weeks, the trade unions had agreed to curtail their campaign of industrial action and the prospect (admittedly remote) of a general strike had been lifted. The suffragettes had suspended their militant activity and declared their backing for the war effort. The Irish Nationalists accepted that while the Home Rule Bill would be placed on the statute book its implementation should be delayed until after the conclusion of hostilities in Europe. It would be misleading, though, to imply that the war suddenly solved all of the country's pre-war problems, just as it would be incorrect to claim that the Liberal government deliberately courted a European war as a way of escaping from troubles at home.[9] Even had they done so, the benefits were short-lived. Suffragette militancy did not revive, and the suffrage question was duly settled on a non-partisan basis in 1918.[10] But both labour unrest and Ireland caused considerable trouble during the war and immediately afterwards. Despite the 'Treasury Agreement' which Lloyd George negotiated with trade union leaders in March 1915, strikes and industrial disputes continued throughout the war, the level of discontent rising in 1917–18 as pent-up frustrations boiled over and an expanding Labour movement became more conscious of its growing industrial and political power.[11] In Ireland, the main consequence of

Redmond's self-denial over Home Rule in 1914 was that his Nationalist party lost ground to Sinn Fein. The Dublin Rising of Easter 1916 showed that the revolutionary, insurrectionary strand of Irish nationalism was coming to the fore, and at the election of 1918 Sinn Fein emerged as by far the largest political party in Ireland, winning 73 seats to the Nationalists' seven. They immediately established their own independent parliament, the Dail, and embarked on a three-year war of separation which was finally brought to an end only by the Anglo-Irish Treaty of 1921, which led to the setting up of the two separate entities of Northern Ireland and the Irish Free State. Thus the partition which had been discussed before the war had come about, but by an even more tortuous and bloody path than that which had beckoned in 1914.[12]

In this way it could be said that the First World War intensified the Edwardian crisis rather than bringing it to an end. What the war did do, however, was alter the political context in which problems like Ireland, labour unrest and women's suffrage were dealt with, in two important respects. First, it created a climate in which an extension of state intervention in the life of the community was more generally acceptable, in the process tipping the balance in favour of the more 'authoritarian' state which libertarians and social democrats had resisted before 1914.[13] Secondly, it helped to defuse the partisanship which had built up between 1906 and 1914, creating a sense of national unity which cut across party boundaries and facilitating a party truce under which electoral competition was suspended and the life of the 1910 parliament was prolonged until after the end of the war.[14] In May 1915 Asquith invited Conservative and Labour leaders to join a coalition government, which they did. This in turn was only the prelude to an even more momentous change, the formation of a second coalition in December 1916 with Lloyd George as Prime Minister and Asquith returning to the opposition benches at the head of those Liberals who would not accept Lloyd George's leadership. The creation of this broadly-based 'national' government broke the mould of Edwardian politics, providing the Conservatives with a means of rehabilitating themselves as a party of government and fatally weakening the

Liberals, who never recovered from the effects of the Asquith – Lloyd George split. The Lloyd George coalitions of 1916–18 and 1918–22 (the latter without the support of Labour, which fought the 1918 election as an independent party) provided stable, centre-right government and a secure parliamentary base from which the various problems inherited from the pre-war era could be addressed. The Representation of the People Act of 1918 enfranchised women over 30 and introduced virtual adult suffrage. The government negotiated a settlement of the Irish question which had eluded the Asquith cabinet in the partisan atmosphere of 1914. Lastly, when the confrontation between organised Labour and the state which had been brewing before 1914 occurred in the near-revolutionary conditions of 1919–20 the government held firm, partly because, unlike its Liberal predecessor, it could afford to ignore the electoral implications of standing up to trade union unrest.[15]

With this aftermath in mind, how, then, should the Edwardian crisis be viewed and its character evaluated? More than anything else, it was a crisis in the development of the political institutions of the country and in the relationship between those institutions and the community as a whole. The short-term problems of pre-war Britain were undoubtedly serious, but their full significance becomes apparent only when looked at in the context of a more extended period of adjustment for British society stretching from the 1880s to the 1920s: a period in which the transition from aristocratic to democratic politics was completed; the role of the state was expanded; and movements such as nationalism, feminism and organised Labour were either incorporated or appeased by the creation of a new governing dispensation. In this process, the historic Union with Ireland was broken; the framework of a socially-integrationist welfare system was put in place; and the Liberal–Conservative two-party configuration of nineteenth-century politics was replaced by a different alignment of parties organised more explicitly on lines of occupation or class. Britain, meanwhile, was simultaneously grappling – not altogether successfully – with the external challenge of remaining a major economic and imperial power in an altered and increasingly competitive world environment.

In all of these changes the First World War played an important part, and without the war the twentieth century would have been different in detail, and probably in more fundamental ways as well. Within the longer period of adjustment the years between 1901 and 1914, and more especially those from 1909 to 1914, nevertheless occupy a crucial place, since the events and decisions of those years made possible the profounder changes which followed. In one sense, they can be seen as constituting a bottleneck or pressure point in the process of historical development analogous to that represented by the Reform crisis of 1830–32 in the previous 'crisis of adaptation' which Britain had undergone in the early nineteenth century. Then too the nation's political and constitutional structure had been under extreme strain and a crisis of the party system had coincided with, and to some extent been brought about by, popular protest arising from a variety of interlinking economic and democratic pressures.[16] In the 1830s the crisis had found a natural resolution, and an essentially evolutionary (though not entirely non-violent) pattern of progress had been confirmed which was to colour the thinking not only of the Victorians but also of later historians about Britain's characteristically constitutional methods of managing change. An equally natural resolution of conflicts might well have taken place in 1914–15, yet in neither case does the comparatively peaceful settlement of problems diminish the depth of the crisis which had been overcome.

A similar point can be made about the validity of comparisons between Britain's problems and those of other European countries in the early twentieth century. Across the continent, hereditary ruling elites were striving to contain movements of social protest and to control the democratic tendencies inherent in the growth of complex urban, industrial societies.[17] Throughout Europe there was widespread labour unrest, revolutionary socialist and nationalists movements were at work and moderate, middleclass liberalism was on the defensive. In a number of countries the movement towards parliamentary government had been either suspended or aborted. Traditionally Britain has been seen as following a qualitatively different path, because of the strength of its representative institutions and its avoidance of revolutionary situations. Yet it could be that any difference which existed was one of degree rather than kind. Britain's problems may indeed have been less severe than those experienced elsewhere, with the gulf between rulers and ruled less marked and the parliamentary system acting as a safety valve for discontent. In Britain too the situation was distinguished by the fact that the ruling elite exercised its power through the competitive mechanism of party politics, which helped to mask the nakedness of class struggles. But, when allowances have been made for all of the necessary variations inherent in national diversity, common features between the British and continental cases remain. It is at least worth pointing out that the political systems in Russia, Germany and Austria ultimately collapsed only after those countries had been defeated in war, so that the margin by which Britain avoided a similar fate may have been narrower than hindsight would suggest.

All of this is inevitably, if frustratingly, inconclusive. How the British variant of the European crisis would have been resolved had it not been for the First World War must remain a matter of speculation, because in August 1914 the future which the Edwardians had planned for themselves came suddenly to an end. The result was not only to create a retrospective picture of an 'Edwardian' age which the citizens of George V's Britain and Ireland might have failed wholly to endorse, but, more importantly, to deprive them of the opportunity to solve the problems of their society in the way and at the pace they would have chosen to do. Instead, the essentially sectional conflicts of the pre-war period were subsumed in the larger upheavals of the war itself. For better or worse, the inhabitants of twentieth century Britain had to live with the consequences of that unexpected reverse.

APPENDIX 1

Chronology

1901 Death of Queen Victoria; accession of Edward VII
Publication of Rowntree's *Poverty, A Study of Town Life*
Taff Vale Judgement

1902 Anglo-Japanese alliance
End of South African War
Education Act
Balfour succeeds Salisbury as PM

1903 Formation of Women's Social and Political Union
Electoral agreement between Liberals and LRC
Chamberlain launches campaign for tariff reform and resigns
from government

1904 *Entente cordiale* with France
Report of Inter-Departmental Committee on Physical
Deterioration

1905 Foundation of Sinn Fein and Ulster Unionist Council
WSPU begins disruption of political meetings
Resignation of Balfour government (December) and formation of
Liberal administration with Campbell-Bannerman as PM

1906 Liberals win landslide victory at general election (January)
Parliamentary Labour party formed
Trades Disputes Act

1907 Anglo-Russian entente
Qualification of Women Act

Jarrow and Colne Valley by-elections
Rail strike narrowly averted

1908 Asquith succeeds Campbell-Bannerman as PM
Old Age Pensions introduced
'Women's Sunday' (June)
Strikes in various industries, including cotton, engineering and
shipbuilding

1909 'People's Budget' introduced (April)
Budget rejected by House of Lords (November)
Dissolution of parliament (December)
Osborne Judgement

1910 General election (January) deprives Liberals of independent
majority
Conciliation Committee formed and Conciliation Bill introduced
Budget passes Lords; Parliament Bill introduced (April)
Death of Edward VII; accession of George V (May)
Constitutional conference (June–November)
South Wales miners' strike; Tonypandy riots
Tom Mann founds Syndicalist League
Carson elected leader of Irish Unionist MPs

1911 Parliament Act passed (August)
National Insurance Act
Dock and rail strikes; riots at Liverpool and Llanelli
Agadir crisis
Bonar Law succeeds Balfour as Unionist leader

1912 Miners' strike (February–April); Minimum Wage Act
Third Home Rule Bill introduced (April)
London dock strike
Ulster Covenant signed (September)
Manhood Suffrage Bill introduced
Suffragette militancy

1913 Home Rule Bill twice rejected by Lords (January and July)
Ulster Volunteers formed
Manhood Suffrage Bill withdrawn
Emily Davison dies at Epsom Derby
'Cat and Mouse' Act
Dublin transport strike
Trade Union Act reverses effects of Osborne Judgement
Lloyd George launches Land Campaign

1914 'Triple Alliance' of miners, railwaymen and transport workers
Curragh 'mutiny' (March)
Buckingham Palace conference (July)
Britain enters First World War (August)

APPENDIX 2

General Election Results

	Votes	% share	Candidates	Seats	Returned unopposed
1906					
Liberal	2,751,057	49.4	536	399	27
Unionist*	2,422,071	43.4	556	156	13
Labour	321,663	4.8	50	29	0
Nationalist	35,031	0.7	87	83	74
January 1910					
Liberal	2,866,157	43.5	511	274	1
Unionist	3,104,407	46.8	594	272	19
Labour	505,657	7.0	78	40	0
Nationalist	126,647	1.9	105	82	55
December 1910					
Liberal	2,293,869	44.2	467	271	35
Unionist	2,420,169	46.6	548	272	72
Labour	371,802	6.4	56	42	3
Nationalist	131,720	2.5	106	84	53

* includes Conservative and Liberal Unionist figures.
Source: F. W. S. Craig, *British Electoral Facts, 1885–1975* (London, 1976), pp. 6–8.

NOTES

PREFACE

1. Elie Halevy, *The Rule of Democracy, 1905–1914* (revised edn, London, 1952).
2. For a more detailed consideration of the context of Dangerfield's study, see C. W. White, 'The Strange Death of Liberal England in its time', *Albion* 17 (1985), pp. 425–47.
3. For example, Martin Pugh, *State and Society: British Political and Social History, 1870–1992* (London, 1994), pp. 143–4.

INTRODUCTION: THE VICTORIAN LEGACY

1. Gordon Brooke-Shepherd, *Uncle of Europe: the social and diplomatic life of Edward VII* (London, 1975), p. 94.
2. A guide to general works on the period is provided in the notes on Further Reading.
3. On the background to British foreign and imperial policy, see Paul Kennedy, *The Realities Behind Diplomacy* (London, 1981).
4. J. A. Thomas, *The House of Commons, 1832–1901* (Cardiff, 1939) explores the social background of Members of Parliament. For other changes in the political system, see H. J. Hanham, *Elections and Party Management: Politics in the time of Disraeli and Gladstone* (2nd edn., Harvester, 1978); Martin Pugh, *The Making of Modern British Politics, 1867–1939* (Blackwell, 1982, 1993).
5. The importance of the press in the politics of the period is analysed in two stimulating studies: Alan J. Lee, *The Origins of the Popular Press, 1855–1914* (London, 1976) and Stephen

Koss, *The Rise and Fall of the Political Press in Britain* (London, 1990).

6. The relationship of gender conflicts to conventional party politics is a more complex subject, although the women's movement tended to be closer to the Liberals than the Conservatives.

7. A. Sykes, *Tariff Reform in British Politics, 1903–13* (Oxford, 1979).

8. There is a useful discussion of the crisis theme in Mary Langan and Bill Schwarz (eds), *Crises in the British State, 1880–1930* (London, 1985), pp. 8–12.

1 THE SOCIAL CRISIS: POVERTY, SOCIAL REFORM AND THE STATE

1. L. G. Chiozza Money, *Riches and Poverty* (London, 1905), p. 42 and frontispiece.

2. *Ibid.*, p. 72.

3. Extracts from the writings of the late-Victorian 'social explorers' will be found in Peter Keating (ed.), *Into Unknown England, 1866–1913* (Manchester, 1976).

4. The respective figures for 'primary' and 'secondary' poverty were 9. 91 per cent and 17. 93 per cent.

5. Seebohm Rowntree, *Poverty, A Study of Town Life* (London, 1914 edn), p. 72, quoted in D. Read (ed.), *Documents From Edwardian England* (London, 1973), p. 205.

6. M. E. Rose, *The Relief of Poverty, 1834–1914* (London, 1972), p. 53.

7. A good overview of these developments is provided by Sydney Checkland, *British Public Policy, 1776–1939* (Cambridge, 1983).

8. Some historians have, rightly, pointed out that the idea of a sudden switch from 'individualism' to 'collectivism' is an over-simplification, since neither policy was ever pursued in an absolute form. An acknowledgement of the more 'collective' impulses behind public policy in the early twentieth century is nevertheless indispensable to an understanding of governmental attitudes in the Edwardian period.

9. N. Soldon, 'Laissez-Faire as Dogma: the Liberty and Property Defence League, 1882–1914', in K. D. Brown (ed.), *Essays in Anti-Labour History* (London, 1974), pp. 234–261.

10. This is necessarily a bald summary. For a fuller discussion, see Henry Pelling, *Origins of the Labour Party* (2nd edn, Oxford, 1965).

11. To say this is not to endorse the view that the Webbs, or the Fabians as a whole, were alone responsible for the spread of

collectivist ideas, since recent research has placed their efforts in a more realistic perspective. On the role of the Fabians, see F. M. McBriar, *Fabian Socialism and English Politics, 1884–1918* (Cambridge, 1962) and Norman and Jeanne McKenzie, *The First Fabians* (London, 1977).

12. Sidney Webb, 'Lord Rosebery's Escape From Houndsditch', *Nineteenth Century*, September 1901, pp. 366–86.
13. R. J. Scally, *The Origins of the Lloyd George Coalition: The Politics of Social Imperialism, 1900–1918* (Princeton, 1975), Chapter III, gives a good account of the 'Coefficients'. See also G. R. Searle, *The Quest for National Efficiency* (Oxford, 1971).
14. The most detailed study of the election is A. K. Russell, *Liberal Landslide* (Newton Abbot, 1973). For the full results of the election, see Appendix 2.
15. Russell, *Liberal Landslide*, pp. 65, 79, 83.
16. He reported to colleagues that he had spoken only of 'enquiry and experiment'. Campbell-Bannerman to Asquith, 1 December 1905, Bodleian Library, Asquith papers, MS Asquith 10, f. 173.
17. For a fuller discussion of their ideas, see Michael Freeden, *The New Liberalism* (Oxford, 1978), Peter Clarke, *Liberals and Social Democrats* (Cambridge, 1978), Stefan Collini, *Liberalism and Sociology* (Cambridge, 1979).
18. On Masterman, see Edward David, 'The New Liberalism of C. F. G. Masterman', in K. D. Brown (ed.), *Essays in Anti-Labour History*, pp. 17–41.
19. Churchill to Asquith, 29 December 1908, in Randolph Churchill, *Winston S. Churchill*, companion volume 2, part 2 (London, 1969), p. 863.
20. Rose, *Relief of Poverty*, pp. 19–20.
21. See Chapter 2.
22. Winston Churchill, 'The Untrodden Field of Politics', *Nation*, 7 March 1908. The text is quoted in Kenneth O. Morgan (ed.), *The Age of Lloyd George* (London, 1971), pp. 147–8. Churchill also delivered and published an important collection of speeches on *Liberalism and the Social Problem* (London, 1909).
23. A recent study of the factors leading to the passage of this Act is Sheila Blackburn, 'Ideology and Social Policy: the origins of the Trade Boards Act', *Historical Journal*, 1991, p. 43ff. Churchill's contribution to the Liberal social reforms has been authoritatively analysed in Paul Addison, *Churchill on the Home Front, 1900–1955* (London, 1992).
24. The basic text on the handling of the problem of unemployment is José Harris, *Unemployment and Politics: a study in English Social*

Policy, 1886–1914 (Oxford, 1972), but see also Kenneth D. Brown, *Labour and Unemployment, 1900–1914*, (Newton Abbot, 1971).

25. Ian Packer, 'Lloyd George and the Land Campaign, 1912–14', in Judith Loades (ed.), *The Life and Times of David Lloyd George* (Bangor, 1991), pp. 143–52; Bentley B. Gilbert, *David Lloyd George, Organizer of Victory, 1912–16* (London, 1992), chapters 1 and 2.
26. Churchill, 'Untrodden Field'.
27. The schemes introduced were, though, sufficiently flexible to be extended, as they were during and after the First World War.
28. Rose, *Relief of Poverty*, p. 53.
29. *Ibid.*, p. 51.
30. It should also be noted, however, that the tax changes in the 1909 budget, and the proposed land valuation, had temporarily inhibited new house building schemes.
31. T. R. Gourvish, 'The Standard of Living, 1890–1914', in Alan O'Day (ed.), *The Edwardian Age: Conflict and Stability, 1900–1914* (London, 1979), pp. 13–33.
32. This aspect is considered more fully in Chapter 4.
33. Some New Liberals like Hobson were prepared to consider state ownership of certain industries and the creation of a 'mixed economy' as a means of redistributing the rewards of labour and giving the government a more managerial economic role. But, apart from some measures of reorganisation such as the Port of London Act (1907) and the 1909 Development Act, the government's policies remained more market-orientated than collectivist.
34. The Commission had been appointed by the outgoing Balfour government in 1905. The Minority Report was largely ignored by the Liberals, who preferred to concentrate on their own welfare measures.
35. See Chapter 4.
36. Henry Pelling, 'The Working Class and the Origins of the Welfare State', in Pelling, *Popular Politics and Society in Late-Victorian Britain* (2nd edn., London, 1979), pp. 1–18; Pat Thane, 'The Working Class and State "Welfare" in Britain, 1880–1914', *Historical Journal* xxvii, 4, 1984, pp. 877–900.
37. Ironically the Liberals believed that the insurance principle, as well as being financially attractive for the taxpayer, would appeal to working-class instincts of providence and self-protection, already in evidence in trade union benefit clubs and Friendly Societies.
38. At least they were apparent to the middle classes. Working-class families did not necessarily receive any direct benefit from government spending, however, while the regressive effect of increases in

indirect taxes may actually have left them worse off. In any case, social spending absorbed only part of the increase in total expenditure, which was the result of the Boer War and the naval rearmament programme as well. Pugh, *State and Society*, pp. 117–18.

39. This question receives fuller discussion in Harold Perkin, *The Rise of Professional Society* (London, 1989), Chapter 5.

40. C. F. G. Masterman, *The Condition of England* (repr. , London, 1959), p. 88.

41. Status might be even more important where middle-class incomes were only on a par with, or even below, those of skilled workers.

42. Space precludes a more detailed treatment of these themes. There are some interesting reflections on working-class attitudes in R. McKibbin, *The Ideologies of Class* (Oxford, 1990). For more general works of social history, see the guide to Further Reading.

2 THE CONSTITUTIONAL CRISIS, 1909–11

1. For the structure of the system, see Norman Gash, *Politics in the Age of Peel* (2nd edn., Hassocks, 1977). On the Reform crisis and its background, see Michael Brock, *The Great Reform Act* (London, 1973) and John Cannon, *Parliamentary Reform, 1640–1832* (Cambridge, 1972).

2. It was the rejection of this measure which prompted Gladstone, as Chancellor of the Exchequer, to introduce the first 'modern' budget in 1861, with the paper duty proposals incorporated into the Finance Bill (which, conventionally, the Lords did not amend). Richard Shannon, *Gladstone, volume 1, 1809–1865* (London, 1982), pp. 416–7.

3. Similarly in the early nineteenth century the Tory majority in the House of Lords (largely the product of the many peerages created under the Younger Pitt) matched the Tory ascendancy in the Commons. It is worth noting, however, that after 1832 the Tories used their majority in the Lords to obstruct measures proposed by the Whig governments of Grey and Melbourne – a strategy which foreshadowed that employed by Balfour and Lansdowne after 1906. The split in Peel's Conservative party over the repeal of the Corn Laws in 1846 led to a more even division of the Lords between the main party groupings. E. A. Smith, *The House of Lords, 1815–1911* (London, 1992) gives a good analysis of the changing function and composition of the Lords in the nineteenth century.

4. Roy Jenkins, *Mr Balfour's Poodle* (London, 1954), p. 24. This is the best narrative account of the constitutional crisis, its title deriving from a famous remark by Lloyd George denying that the House of Lords was the 'watchdog of the constitution'.

5. Quoted in G. H. LeMay, *The Victorian Constitution* (London, 1979), p. 170.

6. See Chapter 4.

7. This was perhaps a recognition that the Lords' claim to be acting in line with public opinion had at least some foundation, although the Liberals' reluctance to face another election and endanger their majority after such a short time in office is also understandable.

8. On Lloyd George's career in this period, see John Grigg, *Lloyd George, the People's Champion* (London, 1978) and Bentley B. Gilbert, *David Lloyd George, The Architect of Change* (London, 1987). The most detailed account of the budget crisis is Bruce Murray, *The People's Budget* (Oxford, 1980).

9. The full text of both speeches is reprinted in H. Du Parcq, *The Life of David Lloyd George*, vol. 4 (London, 1913), pp. 678–96.

10. Jenkins, *Mr Balfour's Poodle*, p. 84.

11. N. Blewett, *The Peers, the Parties and the People: the General Elections of 1910* (London, 1972) gives a full account of the campaigns. Before 1914 not all constituencies went to the polls simultaneously and the actual process of voting was spread out over several weeks.

12. Quoted in Jenkins, *Mr Balfour's Poodle*, p. 122.

13. The figures, and those used subsequently, are taken from F. W. S. Craig, *British Electoral Facts, 1885–1975* (London, 1976).

14. Jenkins, *Mr Balfour's Poodle*, p. 136. See also, Philip Magnus, *King Edward VII* (London, 1964), chapters 22 and 23.

15. H. H. Asquith, *Fifty Years of Parliament*, quoted in Jenkins, *op. cit.*, p. 146.

16. For a study of the new King's role in the crisis, see Kenneth Rose, *King George V* (London, 1983), pp. 113–31.

17. J. D. Fair, *British Inter-Party Conferences: a study of the procedure of conciliation in British politics, 1867–1921* (Oxford, 1980).

18. For the differences within the Liberal party over Lords' reform see C. C. Weston, 'The Liberal Leadership and the Lords' Veto, 1907–1910', *Historical Journal* 11 (1968), pp. 508–37. Whether Asquith intended the conference to fail from the outset is a moot point. His acceptance of the idea (suggested by the Unionist, J. L. Garvin, editor of the *Observer*) could have been designed to prove to the King that the government had done all it could to find a compromise, thereby strengthening Asquith's hand if he needed to

request the creation of peers as a last resort. At the same time, if an agreement had been possible, the Liberals would have been spared a second election and further conflict with the Lords. To have insisted on a summer election so soon after the new King's accession would in any case have been impossible and might have alienated public opinion, sections of which already felt that the strain of the crisis had contributed to Edward's death.

19. The full text of the memorandum is printed in Grigg, *The People's Champion*, pp. 362–8. Lloyd George's own version of events is given in his *War Memoirs* (London, 1938), pp. 20–24. See also, Searle, *Quest for National Efficiency*, Chapter VI; Scally, *Origins of the Lloyd George Coalition*, Chapter VII; G. R. Searle, 'Balfour's Coalition Memorandum of 1910', *Historical Research* 66 (1993), pp. 222–9.

20. This is not to say, however, that the leaders themselves were necessarily in favour of coalition, which was far from being the case.

21. Knollys did not reveal the details of the Lambeth Palace meeting of 29 April to the King, on the grounds, he claimed later, that Balfour had since changed his mind about taking office. When the King found a record of the meeting in 1913, however, he admitted that he might have acted differently if he had known the full story in 1911. Whether, by November, Balfour would indeed have been willing to form a government is unclear.

22. King's diary, 16 November 1910, quoted in Jenkins, *Mr Balfour's Poodle*, p. 178.

23. G. H. L. Le May, *The Victorian Constitution* (London, 1979), Chapter 7, provides a good summary of the constitutional issues.

24. King's diary, 16 November 1910, quoted in Jenkins, *Mr Balfour's Poodle*, p. 260.

25. Interestingly, A. J. P. Taylor recalls that the main issue in his part of Lancashire was Land Reform. A. J. P. Taylor, *A Personal History* (London, 1983), p. 17.

26. Jenkins, *Mr Balfour's Poodle*, pp. 199–204.

27. Quoted *ibid.*, p. 210.

28. Gregory D. Phillips, *The Diehards* (Harvard, 1979).

29. Quoted in Jenkins, *Mr Balfour's Poodle*, p. 260.

30. King's diary, 10 August 1911, quoted *ibid.*, p. 265.

31. No further changes affecting the House of Lords were made until after the Second World War, when the Parliament Act of 1949 reduced the delaying power of the Lords from two years to one. The next important change was the introduction of life peerages in 1958.

32. Jenkins, *Mr Balfour's Poodle*, p. 272. In fact, only twelve of the 29 Finance Bills between 1913 and 1937 were certified as 'money bills' under the Parliament Act.
33. See Chapter 5. On the general question of aristocratic power, see David Cannadine, *The Decline and Fall of the British Aristocracy* (Yale, 1990).
34. This of course was the situation which Lloyd George had tried to prevent with his coalition proposal in 1910.
35. In Dangerfield's words, the Liberals' 'victory' over the Lords was the victory from which 'they never recovered', *The Strange Death of Liberal England* (London, 1935, repr. 1983), p. 20.
36. The original candidates for the succession were Walter Long and Austen Chamberlain. Bonar Law's leadership of the party is considered more fully in Chapter 5.
37. The Conference was viewed with considerable suspicion by the partisans on both sides for precisely this reason. G. R. Searle, *Country Before Party: Coalition and the Idea of 'National Government' in Modern Britain, 1885–1987* (London, 1995), pp. 70–7.
38. It has also sometimes been argued that, for the Liberals, the House of Lords was a 'necessary enemy', without which they lost part of their *raison d'être* as the party opposed to aristocratic privilege. In a convoluted way, therefore, they had a vested electoral interest in not stripping it of all of its remaining powers.

3 SUFFRAGISM AND FEMINISM

1. For further statistical and other material on these topics, see Jane Lewis, *Women in England, 1870–1950* (Harvester, 1984).
2. Since working-class families tended to remain larger than middle-class families the workload for working-class women, without servants, was proportionately greater. Elderly parents could help with child-minding and other tasks, but they could also be an additional strain on the family budget.
3. Lewis, *Women in England*, p. 112.
4. *Ibid.*, p. 8.
5. *Ibid.*, p. 169. For more extensive treatment of women's trade unionism, see S. Lewenhak, *Women and Trade Unions* (London, 1977) and N. Soldon, *Women in British Trade Unions, 1874–1976* (London, 1978).
6. As the eighteenth-century jurist Sir William Blackstone succinctly

put it, 'In marriage husband and wife are one person, and that person is the husband'.

7. The intricacies of this question are unravelled in Lee Holcombe, *Wives and Property* (London, 1983).

8. Previously the law had recognised only divorces secured by private Acts of Parliament.

9. This remains a largely unexplored subject, but some impression of this world can be gained from the 'parliamentary' novels of Anthony Trollope, in particular from the career of their principal heroine, Lady Glencora Palliser.

10. Food riots, of course, were not necessarily 'political' acts, although they did involve a form of 'direct action'. On Chartism, see David Jones, 'Women and Chartism', *History*, February 1983, pp. 1–21, and Dorothy Thompson, *The Chartists* (London, 1984), Chapter 7.

11. Beatrice Webb's experiences are described in her published diaries, edited by Norman and Jeanne MacKenzie, *The Diary of Beatrice Webb* (London, 1982).

12. Martin Pugh, *The Tories and the People* (Oxford, 1985), p. 49.

13. Patricia Hollis, *Ladies Elect* (Oxford, 1987), p. 486.

14. *Ibid.*

15. There had been earlier attempts to secure women's suffrage, for example Orator Hunt's petition in the House of Commons in August 1832 'that every unmarried female possessing the necessary pecuniary qualification should be allowed to vote'. Roger Fulford, *Votes for Women* (London, 1957), p. 28.

16. Such views were expressed even by Radicals like John Bright, who believed that 'to introduce women into the strife of political life would be a great evil to them' and would produce no compensating benefit for the nation at large. Bright to T. Stanton, 21 October 1882, quoted in H. J. Hanham (ed.), *The Nineteenth Century Constitution* (Cambridge, 1969), p. 280.

17. Even Beatrice Webb took this view at one stage, although she later became a supporter of women's suffrage.

18. There was some pressure, too, from foreign example: women in New Zealand gained the vote in 1893, those in Australia in 1902.

19. Another sister, Adela, also participated in the activities of the WSPU.

20. Martin Pugh, *Women's Suffrage in Britain, 1867–1928* (London, 1980), p. 6.

21. The limitations of the WSPU in this respect are demonstrated by studies of working-class suffragism, notably Jill Liddington and Jill Norris, *One Hand Tied Behind Us* (London, 1978).

22. In 1913, 63 per cent of WSPU members were unmarried (or at least identified themselves as 'Miss').
23. Whether the use of the label 'militancy' is fully justified given the relatively low level of violence is debatable, but the conventional attribution is followed here for the sake of clarity.
24. See above, pp. 77–8.
25. There is no evidence that suffragette intervention was responsible for the loss of the seat, however.
26. Keir Hardie was one of those who attacked the government for its treatment of the suffragette prisoners.
27. Martin Pugh, *Electoral Reform in War and Peace, 1906–1918* (London, 1978), p. 187, provides an analysis of the relative strength of these views.
28. In this he was representing the opinion of the government.
29. Pugh, *Electoral Reform*, p. 188.
30. *Ibid.*, p. 41.
31. Asquith to Venetia Stanley, 27 January 1913, quoted in Michael and Eleanor Brock (eds), *H. H. Asquith, Letters to Venetia Stanley* (Oxford, 1985), p. 27.
32. For the Labour party's relations with the suffrage movement see, Martin Pugh, 'The Labour Party and Women's Suffrage', in K. D. Brown (ed.), *The First Labour Party* (London, 1985), pp. 233–53.
33. The Irish Nationalists, for example, had supported women's suffrage before 1912 but swung against reform after 1912 because they thought it might impede the progress of Irish Home Rule.
34. Some historians challenge the significance, or even the fact, of Asquith's admission. For example, Andrew Rosen, *Rise Up, Women! The militant campaign of the Women's Social and Political Union, 1903–1914* (London, 1974), pp. 236–7.
35. Kenneth O. Morgan, *Keir Hardie, Radical and Socialist* (London, 1975), p. 169.
36. It is possible that an extended franchise might also have benefited the Labour party as well. This issue is discussed more fully in Chapter 4.
37. Emmeline Pankhurst, *My Own Story* (London, 1914), p. 51.
38. The WSPU was notoriously prone to splits. Even Sylvia Pankhurst broke away to form her own East London Federation because of disagreements with her mother and sister.
39. The text is reprinted in Jane Marcus (ed.), *Suffrage and the Pankhursts* (London, 1987), pp. 187–240.
40. The doctrine of 'free love' was in vogue in some of the more bohemian radical and socialist circles of the 1900s; militant

suffrage campaigners were often assumed to have lesbian orientations.
41. H. G. Wells was one of those to advocate the 'Endowment of Motherhood', in his novel *The New Machiavelli* (London, 1911) and elsewhere. The romantic novelist, Marie Corelli, predicted 'darker days . . . for the nation' if 'the mothers of the British race decide to part altogether with the birthright of their simple *womanliness* for a political mess of pottage'. *Woman or Suffragette? A Question of National Choice*, quoted in Donald Read (ed.), *Documents from Edwardian England*, p. 298.

4 THE CHALLENGE OF LABOUR

1. The GNCTU was founded in 1833 but collapsed within a year. For the early history of the Labour movement, and its development in the later nineteenth century, see Henry Pelling, *A History of British Trade Unionism* (London, 3rd edn, 1976) and E. H. Hunt, *British Labour History, 1815–1914* (London, 1981).
2. David Powell, *British Politics and the Labour Question, 1868–1990* (London, 1992), pp. 7–11.
3. The background to this is described in John Vincent, *The Formation of the Liberal Party* (London, 1966). See also, F. M. Leventhal, *Respectable Radical: George Howell and Victorian Working Class Politics* (Harvard, 1971); Royden Harrison, *Before the Socialists* (London, 1965); H. J. Hanham, *Elections and Party Management*. A recent detailed treatment of working-class popular Liberalism is E. Biagini, *Liberty, Retrenchment and Reform* (Cambridge, 1992).
4. The eight hour day was seen as one way of reducing unemployment, by increasing the demand for labour.
5. H. A. Clegg, A. Fox and A. F. Thompson, *A History of British Trade Unions Since 1889, vol. 1, 1889–1910* (Oxford, 1964) provides a full account of the new unionism in all its aspects.
6. W. Thomas Lewis to T. E. Ellis, 10 March 1890, National Library of Wales, T. E. Ellis papers, f. 1421.
7. Henry Pelling, *Social Geography of British Elections, 1885–1910* (London, 1967), pp. 419–20 identifies 89 'predominantly' working-class constituencies, but this may underestimate the working-class vote.
8. Cyril Parry, *The Manningham Mills Strike* (Hull, 1975); E. P. Thompson, 'Homage to Tom Maguire', in Asa Briggs and John Saville (eds), *Essays in Labour History* (London, 1967), pp. 276–316; Keith

Laybourn and Jack Reynolds, *Liberalism and the Rise of Labour, 1890–1918* (London, 1984), chapter 3.

9. Henry Pelling, *Origins of the Labour Party*, chapter VI.
10. Barry McGill, 'Francis Schnadhorst and Liberal Party Organisation', *Journal of Modern History*, vol. xxxiv, 1962, pp. 19–39.
11. David Powell, 'The Liberal Ministries and Labour, 1892–1895', *History*, October 1983, pp. 408–26.
12. An Employers' Liability Bill was introduced in 1893 but withdrawn after suffering amendments at the hands of the House of Lords. Payment of MPs and a Mines Eight Hours Bill were proposed by private Members but did not receive government backing.
13. T. R. Threlfall, 'The Political Future of Labour', *Nineteenth Century*, February 1894.
14. Meanwhile, three new Lib–Lab MPs were returned at by-elections in 1897–8.
15. Clegg, Fox and Thompson, *British Trade Unions*, pp. 161–8.
16. The Liberals' difficulties in this respect are explored in David Powell, 'The New Liberalism and the Rise of Labour, 1886–1906', *Historical Journal*, June 1986, pp. 369–93, and, on a broader canvas, in Michael Freeden, *The New Liberalism*.
17. Duncan Tanner, *Political Change and the Labour Party, 1900–1918* (Cambridge, 1990) is the fullest recent discussion of these complex issues, incorporating much new evidence.
18. The progressivist case, in effect, maintains that Liberal–Labour cooperation transferred easily to the new conditions of Edwardian politics. For a fuller guide to the historiographical debate, see the notes on Further Reading.
19. K. D. Brown, *Labour and Unemployment*, chapters 3 and 4.
20. Henry Pelling, 'The Politics of the Osborne Judgement', *Historical Journal* 25, December 1982, pp. 889–909.
21. Martin Pugh, *The Making of Modern British Politics, 1867–1939*, p. 139.
22. This may, of course, have owed more to the marginality of some of the Liberal gains than to Labour's stronger appeal for traditional Tory voters.
23. Labour's freedom of action was further curtailed by the fact that, for financial reasons, Labour could not afford to provoke another election until the Osborne Judgement had been reversed. Also, if Labour MPs had helped to bring down a Liberal government, their action would have made the electoral pact difficult to sustain.
24. Pugh, *Modern British Politics*, p. 140.

Notes

25. The situation at Hanley was complicated because Outhwaite was regarded as being too radical by some sections of the national Liberal leadership. The by-elections are analysed more fully in Roy Douglas, 'Labour in Decline, 1910–14', in K. D. Brown (ed.), *Essays in Anti-Labour History*, pp. 105–125. See also, P. F. Clarke, 'The Electoral Position of the Liberal and Labour Parties, 1910–1914', *English Historical Review*, October 1975, pp. 828–36; Martin Petter, 'The Progressive Alliance', *History*, vol. 58, 1973, pp. 45–59.

26. Henry Pelling, 'Labour and the Downfall of Liberalism', in Pelling, *Popular Politics and Society*, p. 117; Pugh, *Modern British Politics*, has some slightly different figures.

27. It was, however, higher than the percentage increase in TUC-affiliated membership.

28. Chris Wrigley, 'Labour and the Trade Unions', in K. D. Brown (ed.), *The First Labour Party*, p. 152.

29. Tanner, *Political Change*, chapter 11.

30. Rodney Barker, 'Socialism and Progressivism in the Political Thought of Ramsay MacDonald', in A. J. A. Morris (ed.), *Edwardian Radicalism, 1900–1914* (London, 1974), pp. 114–30.

31. Tanner, *Political Change*, provides the most balanced assessment. Attempts have been made to show that Labour's growth before 1914 was artificially hampered by the restrictions of the electoral system, notably in H. C. G. Matthew, R. McKibbin and J. Kay, 'The Franchise Factor in the Rise of the Labour Party', *English Historical Review* xci, June 1976, pp. 723–52. This view has been rebutted by P. F. Clarke, 'Liberals, Labour and the Franchise', *EHR* xcii, October 1977, pp. 582–90, and again by Duncan Tanner, 'The Parliamentary Electoral System, the "Fourth" Reform Act and the Rise of Labour in England and Wales', *Bulletin of the Institute of Historical Research* 56 (1983), pp. 205–19.

32. Cited in John Wilson, *CB. A Life of Sir Henry Campbell-Bannerman* (London, 1973), p. 475. To be fair, Balfour had described the echo as 'faint' and was in any case trying to find excuses for his party's defeat.

33. David Clark, *Victor Grayson, Labour's Lost Leader* (London, 1985), chapter 6.

34. Discussed below.

35. The Labour movement, like the Liberals, strenuously opposed Tariff Reform, fearing the imposition of 'food taxes' which would raise the cost of living.

36. Henry Phelps Brown, *The Origins of Trade Union Power* (Oxford, 1983), chapters 2 and 3.

37. Pelling, *British Trade Unionism*, pp. 293–4.

38. See Further Reading.
39. Indeed, industrial militancy could be seen as an *alternative* to parliamentary action, and consequently a sign of dissatisfaction with a too-moderate Labour party.
40. B. Holton, *British Syndicalism, 1900–1914: Myth and Reality* (London, 1976) is a good introduction.
41. C. J. Wrigley, *David Lloyd George and the British Labour Movement* (Brighton, 1976), Chapter III.
42. Pelling, *British Trade Unionism*, p. 143. G. R. Askwith's memoir, *Industrial Problems and Disputes* (London, 1920) provides a vivid first-hand account of these years.
43. The Workmen's Compensation Act of 1906 might be added to this list.
44. Roy Jenkins, *Asquith* (London, 1978), p. 234. Asquith was suspect in Labour eyes, moreover, because he had been Home Secretary at the time of the Featherstone shooting.
45. Anthony Mòr O'Brien, 'Churchill and the Tonypandy Riots', *Welsh History Review* 17: 1, June 1994, pp. 67–100; Paul Addison, *Churchill on the Home Front* (London, 1992), pp. 140–51. On the government's policing policies generally, see Jane Morgan, *Conflict and Order: the Police and Labour Disputes in England and Wales, 1900–1939* (Oxford, 1989) and Roger Geary, *Policing Industrial Disputes* (London, 1985).
46. Pelling, *British Trade Unionism*, p. 294.
47. On the concept of 'corporatism', see Keith Middlemas, *Politics in Industrial Society* (London, 1979).
48. As Lloyd George recorded in his *War Memoirs* (London, 1938), p. 1141: 'in the summer of 1914 there was every sign that the autumn would witness a series of industrial disturbances without precedent. ' On the Triple Alliance, see G. A. Phillips, 'The Triple Industrial Alliance in 1914', *Economic History Review* vol. XXIV, February 1971, pp. 55–67.
49. Standish Meacham, 'The Sense of an Impending Clash', *American Historical Review* vol. 77, December 1972, pp. 1343–64.

5   IRELAND AND THE CRISIS OF NATIONALISM

1. E. J. Hobsbawm, *Nations and Nationalism Since 1780* (Cambridge, 1990).
2. Keith Robbins, *Nineteenth Century Britain: England, Scotland and Wales, the Making of a Nation* (Oxford, 1988) is a stimulating introduction

to the complexities of the topic. Attempts to inculcate 'Britishness' and the resistance provided by alternative nationalisms are described in Linda Colley, *Britons* (Yale, 1993) and Eric Hobsbawm and Terence Ranger (eds), *The Invention of Tradition* (Cambridge, 1983), especially in the essays by Hugh Trevor-Roper, Prys Morgan and David Cannadine.

3. Important general works on Irish history are R. F. Foster, *Modern Ireland, 1600–1972* (London, 1988); D. G. Boyce, *Nineteenth Century Ireland* (Dublin, 1990) and F. S. L. Lyons, *Ireland Since the Famine* (London, 1973). On Irish nationalism, see D. G. Boyce, *Nationalism in Ireland* (London, 1982) and Robert Kee, *The Green Flag* (London, 1972).

4. Parnell's career is brilliantly described in F. S. L. Lyons, *Charles Stewart Parnell* (London, 1977).

5. Christopher Harvie, *Scotland and Nationalism* (2nd edn, London, 1994). On the relationship between the land question and nationalism, see D. W. Crowley, 'The "Crofters' Party", 1886–92', *Scottish Historical Review*, October 1956, pp. 110–26.

6. Kenneth O. Morgan, *Wales in British Politics, 1868–1922* (3rd edn, Cardiff, 1980), and the same author's *Rebirth of a Nation: Wales, 1880–1980* (Oxford, 1981).

7. Pugh, *State and Society*, chapter 5; Checkland, *British Public Policy*, chapters 2 and 10; Keith Robbins, *The Eclipse of a Great Power, 1870–1992* (London, 1994), chapter 1.

8. The crisis was precipitated by the results of the 1885 election, which gave the 86 Irish Nationalists the balance of power between the 249 Conservatives and the 335 Liberals. Gladstone's conversion to Home Rule facilitated Liberal–Nationalist cooperation to defeat Salisbury's caretaker government, returning the Liberals to power. The high-politics of this crisis are recounted in A. B. Cooke and John Vincent, *The Governing Passion: Cabinet Government and Party Politics in Britain, 1885–86* (Brighton, 1974), which emphasises Gladstone's use of Home Rule as a means of reasserting his control over the Liberal party. On the defeat of the Home Rule Bill and the arguments for and against it, see D. G. Boyce, *The Irish Question and British Politics, 1868–1986* (London, 1988), pp. 28–34, 147; Grenfell Morton, *Home Rule and the Irish Question* (London, 1980), pp. 33–41.

9. Michael J. Winstanley, *Ireland and the Land Question, 1800–1922* (London, 1984), pp. 39–41; Lyons, *Ireland Since the Famine*, pp. 202–23.

10. Lyons, *Ireland Since the Famine*, pp. 224–60. Nationalist politics were disrupted in this period by the after-effects of Parnell's involve-

ment in the O'Shea divorce case which, even after Parnell's death in 1891, left his party deeply divided. The defeat of the second Home Rule Bill in 1893 further encouraged nationalists to seek alternatives to parliamentary action.

11. Ian Machin, *Disraeli* (London, 1995), pp. 136–51.

12. This movement was actively promoted by Conservative organisations such as the Primrose League, for which see Martin Pugh, *The Tories and the People, 1880–1935*, especially chapter 4.

13. Childers' book was only one of a number of popular novels on the 'future war' theme, another notable example of the genre being William Le Queux, *The Invasion of 1910* (London, 1906). The background to this phenomenon is discussed in I. F. Clarke, *Voices Prophesying War* (Oxford, 1966).

14. A. J. A. Morris, *The Scaremongers: Advocates of War and Rearmament, 1896–1914* (London, 1984).

15. On Roberts, see, R. J. Q. Adams, 'Field Marshal Lord Roberts: Army and Empire' in J. A. Thompson and Arthur Mejia (eds), *Edwardian Conservatism: Five Studies in Adaptation* (London, 1988), pp. 41–76. (The volume also contains valuable essays on Lord Hugh Cecil, Willoughby de Broke, George Wyndham and Lord Halsbury. Baden-Powell's activities are discussed in Michael Rosenthal, *The Character Factory: Baden-Powell and the Origins of the Boy Scout Movement* (London, 1986).

16. One exception to this rule was Erskine Childers, who supported the Nationalist side in the Home Rule controversy.

17. Birrell's term of office is analysed in L. Ó. Broin, *The Chief Secretary: Augustine Birrell in Ireland* (London, 1969). The fullest account of Liberal policy generally is Patricia Jalland, *The Liberals and Ireland* (Brighton, 1980).

18. Boyce, *Irish Question*, pp. 37–41; Alan O'Day, 'Irish Home Rule and Liberalism', in O'Day (ed.), *The Edwardian Age*, pp. 113–32.

19. Morton, *Home Rule*, pp. 59–60; Vernon Bogdanor, *Devolution* (Oxford, 1979), chapter 2.

20. The text of Randolph Churchill's pronouncements is given in Morton, *Home Rule*, pp. 94–5, and their context more fully outlined in R. F. Foster, *Lord Randolph Churchill* (Oxford, 1982), pp. 252–68. The best narrative account of the Ulster dimension of the pre-war conflict is A. T. Q. Stewart, *The Ulster Crisis: Resistance to Home Rule, 1912–14* (London, 1967), but see also Patrick Buckland, *Irish Unionism 2: Ulster Unionism and the Origins of Northern Ireland, 1886–1922* (Dublin, 1973).

21. For Carson's career, see H. Montgomery Hyde, *Carson* (London, 1953), a sympathetic account from a Unionist perspective.

22. Stewart, *Ulster Crisis*, pp. 50–4.
23. For the text, see Morton, *Home Rule*, p. 107.
24. Kipling also wrote a poem, 'Ulster 1912', in support of the Unionist cause.
25. The Conservative and Liberal Unionist parties formally merged in 1912 to create the Conservative and Unionist Party.
26. *The Times*, 29 July 1912, quoted in Read (ed.), *Documents from Edwardian England*, pp. 305–7. See also, Robert Blake, *The Unknown Prime Minister. The Life and Times of Andrew Bonar Law* (London, 1955).
27. In fairness to Asquith, the six-year opt-out would have given time for at least one, and possibly two, general elections to take place, with an incoming Unionist government having the power to make exclusion permanent. Another problem, though, was the government's proposal for county-by-county voting. Of the nine Ulster counties, only four (Antrim, Armagh, Down and Londonderry) had Protestant majorities; three (Donegal, Cavan and Monaghan) were Catholic; the remaining two (Fermanagh and Tyrone) evenly split. County ballots were thus likely to result in the exclusion of less than half the historic province of Ulster.
28. Asquith to Venetia Stanley, 16 March 1914, quoted in M. and E. Brock (eds), *Asquith Letters*, p. 55.
29. *The Times*, 16 March 1914.
30. I. F. W. Beckett (ed.), *The Army and the Curragh Incident, 1914* (London, 1986); Stewart, *Ulster Crisis*, chapters 12 and 13.
31. I. F. W. Beckett, *Johnnie Gough, VC* (London, 1989), chapter 8.
32. Stewart, *Ulster Crisis*, chapter 16.
33. Roy Jenkins, *Asquith*, pp. 319–23.
34. Winston Churchill, *The World Crisis* (London, 1938), vol. 1, p. 155.
35. Stewart, *Ulster Crisis*, pp. 237–43.
36. See Chapter 3.
37. Stewart, *Ulster Crisis*, pp. 86–7.
38. Dan McDermott, 'Labour and Ireland' in K. D. Brown (ed.), *The First Labour Party*, pp. 254–67; Lyons, *Ireland Since the Famine*, pp. 270–86.
39. For Liverpool, see P. Waller, *Democracy and Sectarianism* (Liverpool, 1981).
40. Morgan, *Wales in British Politics*, pp. 255–9.
41. Quoted *ibid.*, p. 258.
42. *Ibid.*, pp. 259–74.
43. It has been argued, however, that the result was the opposite of what the Liberals had intended. The point is summarised in Donald Read, *The Age of Urban Democracy: England, 1868–1914* (London, 1994), pp. 468–9.

44. Asquith was a leading Liberal Imperialist. Even former 'pro-Boers' like Lloyd George were strong supporters of the Empire.
45. G. R. Searle, 'Critics of Edwardian Society: The Case of the Radical Right', in O'Day, *The Edwardian Age*, pp. 79–96; A. Sykes, 'The Radical Right and the Crisis of Conservatism Before The First World War', *Historical Journal*, 26, 1983, pp. 661–76. See also Phillips, *Diehards*, chapter 7.
46. Searle, *Country Before Party*, pp. 79–81.
47. Gregory D. Phillips, 'Lord Willoughby de Broke: Radicalism and Conservatism', in Thompson and Mejia, *Edwardian Conservatism*, pp. 77–104; Searle, 'Critics'.
48. The counter argument here is that resistance was justified because the Liberals were overriding the rights of Ulster Protestants by not providing adequate protection for minority interests in a Home Rule Ireland, but this kind of special pleading simply emphasises the extremities to which the opponents of Home Rule were being driven.
49. Jeremy Smith, 'Bluff, Bluster and Brinkmanship: Andrew Bonar Law and the Third Home Rule Bill', *Historical Journal* 36, 1 (1993), pp. 161–78; Richard Murphy, 'Faction in the Conservative Party and the Home Rule Crisis, 1912–14', *History*, 1986.
50. Blake, *Unknown Prime Minister*, pp. 173–210.
51. *The Times*, 27 July 1914.

CONCLUSION

1. Zara Steiner, *Britain and the Origins of the First World War* (London, 1977) provides a good overview of this process from a British perspective and also contains some valuable insights about the relationship between foreign policy and domestic politics.
2. Richard C. Thurlow, *The Secret State: British Internal Security in the Twentieth Century* (Oxford, 1994).
3. The differences between the two varieties of interventionism, and the balance between the state's roles of reform and control, caused concern to a number of 'New Liberal' thinkers, among them L. T. Hobhouse, whose ideas are discussed in Stefan Collini, *Liberalism and Sociology* (Cambridge, 1979), chapter 4. For comparisons between Britain and other countries, see R. J. Goldstein, *Political Repression in 19th Century Europe* (London, 1983).
4. A guide to this debate is provided in the notes on Further Reading.
5. In many areas, of course, the Liberals were the working-class party

by default, because Labour had no separate presence. Perceptions of class were in any case subjective and the Liberals could draw upon their traditional identity as the party of anti-aristocratic protest.

6. E. H. H. Green, *The Crisis of Conservatism: The Politics, Economics and Ideology of the British Conservative Party, 1880–1914* (London, 1995). (Unfortunately this major study appeared too late to be used in the preparation of the present work.)

7. A more optimistic view of the benefits of the Land Campaign is taken in Ian Packer's essay on this topic in Loades, *Life and Times of David Lloyd George.*

8. Controversy arose because Lloyd George and some of his ministerial colleagues were accused of misleading parliament over their dealings in the shares of the American Marconi Company.

9. For a summary of recent writing about the influence of domestic factors on foreign policy, see James Joll, *The Origins of the First World War* (London, 1984), chapter 5. According to some accounts, the Liberal government actually expected the outbreak of war to increase rather than alleviate domestic unrest, especially on the part of organised Labour.

10. Pugh, *Electoral Reform in War and Peace.*

11. Powell, *British Politics and the Labour Question*, pp. 58–63. This was despite, or perhaps partly because of, the powers which the government had taken to prohibit strikes and control labour through the Munitions of War Act, one example of the more coercive use of state power prefigured by some of the developments of pre-1914.

12. The most important difference between what was conceded in 1921 and what was proposed in 1914 was that only the North of Ireland remained within the United Kingdom, whereas the Free State eventually became the independent Irish Republic. Boyce, *Irish Question and British Politics*, chapter 2.

13. The more authoritarian use of state power was exemplified not only by the measures of labour control referred to above but by the introduction of military conscription and the severe restrictions imposed on civil liberties by the 1914 Defence of the Realm Act. On the wider impact of the war, see Arthur Marwick, *The Deluge* (2nd edn, London, 1991) and Trevor Wilson, *The Myriad Faces of War* (Oxford, 1986).

14. Strictly speaking, the electoral truce applied only to by-elections and did not preclude preparations for post-war activity. Moreover, a degree of partisanship persisted even under the coalitions, and a wartime election was always a possibility. John Turner, *British*

Politics and the Great War (Yale, 1992) emphasises the element of partisanship, while G. R. Searle, *Country Before Party: Coalition and the Idea of 'National Government' in Modern Britain, 1885–1987* (London, 1995) takes a more optimistic view of the ability of politicians to sink their differences in a common cause.

15. Chris Wrigley, *Lloyd George and the Challenge of Labour: the Post-War Coalition, 1918–1922* (Hemel Hempstead, 1990); Kenneth O. Morgan, *Consensus and Disunity: The Lloyd George Coalition Government, 1918–1922* (Oxford, 1979).

16. For a brief account of the Reform crisis, see John Stevenson, *Popular Disturbances in England, 1700–1870* (London, 1979), pp. 218–28.

17. France was a partial exception, because of the way in which hereditary elites had been weakened by successive revolutions since the late eighteenth century, although there was social and industrial unrest before 1914, accompanied by the growth of political extremism. A broader perspective on these developments is provided in Norman Stone, *Europe Transformed, 1878–1919* (London, 1983) and Arno J. Mayer, *The Persistence of the Old Regime: Europe to the Great War* (New York, 1981).

FURTHER READING

The best starting point for further reading is provided by the two classic texts to which frequent reference has already been made: the two-volume epilogue to Elie Halevy's *History of the English People in the Nineteenth Century*, translated as *Imperialism and the Rise of Labour* (London, 1951) and *The Rule of Democracy* (London, 1952); and George Dangerfield, *The Strange Death of Liberal England* (London, 1935, repr. 1983). Halevy's work, despite being completed more than half a century ago, is still a remarkably accurate, scrupulously academic account, although of course lacking the fruits of subsequent research. Dangerfield should perhaps be read more for its provocativeness of interpretation than any claim to objectivity or detachment, but deserves to be read all the same. Both books, however, need to be supplemented by more recent general texts and by specialist studies of particular topics.

Those books which focus on the Edwardian period alone are comparatively few in number. Donald Read, *Edwardian England, 1901–15* (London, 1972) is a good thematic survey, with some excellent illustrations. Read has also edited a collection of essays on various aspects of *Edwardian England* (London, 1982) and a selection of *Documents from Edwardian England* (London, 1973) as a companion to his general volume. Another useful compilation of essays, which addresses the 'crisis' theme, is Alan O'Day (ed.), *The Edwardian Age: Conflict and Stability, 1900–1914* (London, 1979). Paul Thompson, *The Edwardians* (London, 1975) draws extensively on material from oral history archives. J. B. Priestley's book of the same title provides an illustrated eye-witness view of the period as seen by one of the century's most respected novelists. Robert Cecil, *Life in Edwardian England* (London, 1969) and Ronald Pearsall, *Edwardian Life and Leisure* (Newton Abbot, 1973) deal straightforwardly with social aspects, while Samuel Hynes, *The Edwardian Turn of Mind* (London, 1968, new edn 1991) is a post-Dangerfieldian attempt by a literary historian to distil the spirit of the age through a study of topics such a Fabianism, theatrical censorship and the life and works of H. G. Wells.

Most of the other available textbooks follow Halevy's lead in presenting the Edwardian period as an 'epilogue' or extension of the Victorian age which preceded it. With some slight variation in their terminal dates, these works include E. J. Feuchtwanger, *Democracy and Empire: Britain, 1865–1914* (London, 1985), Richard Shannon, *The Crisis of Imperialism, 1865–1915* (London, 1976) and Donald Read, *The Age of Urban Democracy: England, 1868–1914* (London, 1994). The same approach is taken by the older, but recently reprinted, volume in the Oxford History of England, R. C. K. Ensor, *England, 1870–1914* (Oxford, 1936) and in José Harris, *Private Lives, Public Spirit: A Social History of Britain, 1870–1914* (Oxford, 1993). J. F. C. Harrison, *Late Victorian Britain, 1875–1901* (London, 1990) deals only briefly with the Edwardian decade, but its treatment of the Victorians is influenced at least in part by Edwardian preoccupations. By contrast, some works deliberately adopt a longer perspective which challenges the assumptions of conventional chronological boundaries. In this category are Keith Robbins, *The Eclipse of a Great Power: Britain, 1870–1992* (London, 1994), Martin Pugh, *State and Society: British Political and Social History, 1870–1992* (London, 1994), Bernard Porter, *Britannia's Burden: The Political Evolution of Modern Britain, 1851–1990* (London, 1994) and Mary Langan and Bill Schwarz (eds), *Crises in the British State, 1880–1930* (London, 1985).

On the political history of the period, there are a number of general surveys. Martin Pugh, *The Making of Modern British Politics, 1867–1939* (2nd edn., Oxford, 1993) is an excellent analytical study which incorporates much of the latest research on major themes. Robert Rhodes James, *The British Revolution: British Politics, 1880–1939* (London, 1978) covers the same ground in a more elegant, narrative format, while David Brooks, *The Age of Upheaval: Edwardian Politics, 1899–1914* (Manchester, 1995) specifically targets the developments of the early 1900s, supported by extracts from documentary sources. The two main parties are well covered in the secondary literature. George Bernstein, *Liberalism and Liberal Politics in Edwardian England* (London, 1986) is a reliable introduction to its topic and there are several studies, of varying length, of the Campbell-Bannerman and Asquith administrations. G. I. T. Machin, *The Liberal Governments, 1905–1915* (Bangor, 1991) is the briefest, yet packs a great deal of sense into a small compass. Colin Cross, *The Liberals in Power, 1905–1914* (London, 1963) is a solid narrative. Peter Rowland has produced a monumental two-volume book on *The Last Liberal Governments* (London, 1971). For the Conservatives, Robert Blake, *The Conservative Party from Peel to Thatcher* (London, 1985) is useful for background but needs to be read in conjunction with more detailed works such as John Ramsden, *The Age of Balfour and Baldwin, 1902–1940* (London, 1978), E. H. H. Green, *The Crisis of Conservatism: The Politics, Economics and Ideology of the British Conservative Party, 1880–1914* (London, 1995) and David Dutton, *'His Majesty's Loyal Opposition': The Unionist Party in Opposition, 1905–1915* (Liverpool, 1992). Some of the more specialist articles and monographs are referred to in the chapter notes above or in the bibliographies of the works cited. There are standard biographies of most of the prominent political figures of the period, as well as published collections of primary material in the form of diaries, letters, etc., for example, Edward David (ed.), *Inside Asquith's Cabinet, from the diaries of Charles Hobhouse* (London, 1977) and Trevor Wilson (ed.), *The Political Diaries of C. P. Scott, 1911–1928* (London, 1970).

Sources for the individual themes addressed by the present study have mostly been mentioned in the references to particular chapters, but it may be helpful to recapitulate the most important titles and to list any additions. The subject of poverty and social reform is well served by both secondary accounts and documentary reprints. J. H. Treble, *Urban Poverty in Britain* (London, 1979) looks at the extent of poverty and its causes; M. E. Rose, *The Relief of Poverty, 1834–1914* (London, 1972) examines strategies for dealing with poverty, from the Poor Law Amendment Act of 1834 onwards. *The Evolution of the British Welfare State* is treated in overview by Derek Fraser's volume of that title (2nd edn, London, 1984) and the reforms introduced by the Liberal governments are considered in J. R. Hay, *The Origins of the Liberal Welfare Reforms, 1906–14* (London, 1975) and Bentley B. Gilbert, *The Evolution of National Insurance in Great Britain* (London, 1966). Standish Meacham, *A Life Apart: the English Working Class, 1890–1914* (London, 1977) provides an evocative reconstruction of working-class life, based partly on oral testimony, and there are extracts from the observations of middle-class witnesses of working-class poverty in Peter Keating (ed.), *Into Unknown England, 1866–1914* (Manchester, 1976). Other primary sources, in the form of recent reprints of contemporary Edwardian accounts, are Maud Pember Reeves, *Round About A Pound A Week* (1913, repr. London, 1979) and Lady Bell, *At The Works* (1907, repr. London, 1985), the latter being a study of life in the working-class districts of Middlesborough. There is at present (1995) no current edition of Rowntree's *Poverty*, but Keating gives lengthy extracts, as does the documentary collection edited by Read. Asa Briggs, *Seebohm Rowntree* (London, 1961) gives a biographical account of Rowntree's life and work. Another contemporary source of value, especially for its enlightened Liberal perceptions of social crisis, is C. F. G. Masterman, *The Condition of England* (1909, repr. London, 1959).

The constitutional crisis of 1909–11 is fully dealt with in the general texts. The standard narrative account is Roy Jenkins, *Mr Balfour's Poodle* (London, 1954), and additional light is thrown on the part played by individual politicians in the various biographical studies, including Jenkins' *Asquith* (London, 1978) and the best lives of the two monarch's involved, Philip Magnus, *King Edward the Seventh* (London, 1964) and Kenneth Rose, *King George V* (London, 1984). The constitutional aspects of the crisis are explored in G. H. Le May, *The Victorian Constitution* (London, 1979) and H. J. Hanham, *The Nineteenth Century Constitution* (Cambridge, 1969). Hanham's book contains substantial documentary extracts introduced by an incisive editorial commentary. On the wider topic of aristocratic power and its adaptation or resistance to democratising pressures, see David Cannadine, *The Decline and Fall of the British Aristocracy* (Yale, 1990), Andrew Adonis, *Making Aristocracy Work: the Peerage and the Political System in Britain, 1884–1914* (Oxford, 1993) and E. A. Smith, *The House of Lords, 1815–1911* (London, 1992). Gregory D. Phillips, *The Diehards* (Harvard, 1979) is a detailed study of one particular aristocratic subgroup. The elections of 1910 and their significance are discussed in Neal Blewett, *The Peers, the Parties and the People* (London, 1972).

The women's movement in Edwardian Britain has received considerable attention from historians and the suffrage campaign has been an obvious focus of interest. Martin Pugh, *Women's Suffrage in Britain, 1867–1929* (London, 1980) is a concise introduction to the major debates. There are many other studies of aspects of the suffrage agitation and responses to it, among which must be mentioned Constance Rover, *Women's Suffrage and Party Politics in Britain, 1867–1914* (London, 1967); Antonia Raeburn, *The Militant Suffragettes* (London, 1973); Andrew Rosen, *Rise Up, Women! The militant campaign of the Women's Social and Political Union, 1903–1914* (London, 1974); David Morgan, *Suffragists and Liberals* (Oxford, 1975) and Jill Liddington and Jill Norris, *One Hand Tied Behind Us* (London, 1978). Sandra Holton, *Feminism and Democracy: Women's Suffrage and Reform Politics in Britain, 1900–1918* (Cambridge, 1987) emphasises the role of the NUWSS; Martin Pugh, *Electoral Reform in War and Peace, 1906–1918* (London, 1978) establishes the broader context of franchise reform; Brian Harrison, *Separate Spheres* (London, 1978) concentrates on the phenomenon of anti-suffragism. Primary source material is readily accessible, notably in the volumes of the Women's Source Library, published by Routledge, especially Jane Marcus (ed.), *Suffrage and the Pankhursts* (London, 1987). The Pankhursts themselves have left their own autobiographical accounts of their activities, the fullest of which is Sylvia Pankhurst, *The Suffragette Movement* (1931, repr. London, 1984). An interesting biographical study is Ann Morley with Liz Stanley, *The Life and Death of Emily Wilding Davison* (London, 1988). The social background to the women's movement is covered in Jane Lewis, *Women in England, 1870–1950* (Brighton, 1984). Lucy Bland, *Banishing the Beast: English Feminism and Sexual Morality, 1885–1914* (London, 1995) highlights other issues of feminist concern.

If the women's movement is well-documented, the place of organised Labour in Edwardian society has been even more thoroughly assessed. H. Clegg, A. Fox and A. F. Thompson, *A History of British Trade Unions Since 1889, vol. 1, 1889–1910* (Oxford, 1964) and H. A. Clegg, *A History of British Trade Unions, vol. 2, 1910–1939* (Oxford, 1985) are the standard works. B. Holton, *British Syndicalism 1900–1914: Myth and Reality* (London, 1976) is the most complete study of its subject. James Hinton, *Labour and Socialism* (London, 1983) effectively links industrial and political themes. Keith Burgess, *The Challenge of Labour* (London, 1980) has a good chapter on 'The Edwardian Crisis, 1906–14' and there are important essays on the period in Henry Pelling, *Popular Politics and Society in Late Victorian Britain* (2nd edn, London, 1979). The response of the government to industrial unrest can be studied in E. H. Phelps Brown, *The Growth of British Industrial Relations* (London, 1959), C. J. Wrigley, *David Lloyd George and the British Labour Movement* (Brighton, 1976) and Jane Morgan, *Conflict and Order: the Police and Labour Disputes in England and Wales, 1900–1939* (Oxford, 1985). There is also a first-hand account of the industrial troubles written by the Liberal government's Chief Industrial Commissioner, published as Lord Askwith, *Industrial Problems and Disputes* (London, 1920).

The political dimension of Labour's challenge, and Liberal reactions to it, has similarly generated a vast literature. Kenneth D. Brown (ed.), *The First Labour Party, 1906–1914* (London, 1985) explores the characteristics of the Labour party in its formative period. The two poles of the 'progressivist' versus 'inevitabilist' debate are presented, respectively, in P. F. Clarke, *Lancashire and the New Liberalism* (Cambridge, 1971) and Ross McKibbin, *The Evolution of the Labour Party, 1910–1924* (Oxford, 1974). The most comprehensive survey of the electoral politics of the Edwardian left, which attempts not only to synthesise but to move beyond the generalisations of earlier accounts, is Duncan Tanner, *Political Change and the Labour Party, 1900–1918* (Cambridge, 1990). For those wanting a fuller historiographical guide, Keith Laybourn, *The Rise of Labour* (London, 1988) provides a clear summary of the key controver-

sies. The question 'Did the Liberals still have a future in 1914?' is posed by Geoffrey Searle's 'Update' in *The Historian*, Summer 1992, pp. 10–12, which comments on all the recent writings, as does the same author's *The Liberal Party: Triumph and Disintegration, 1886–1929* (London, 1992).

Ulster's revolt against Home Rule was the last of the pre-war rebellions in Dangerfield's schema, although he correctly perceived this as being bound up with the more general 'Tory rebellion' against the policies of the Liberal government. The student therefore needs an awareness both of the Irish and British dimensions of the conflict, as well as their imperial implications. General histories of Ireland include, R. F. Foster, *Modern Ireland, 1600–1972* (London, 1988), F. S. L. Lyons, *Ireland Since The Famine* (London, 1973) and D. G. Boyce, *Nineteenth Century Ireland: the Search for Stability* (Dublin, 1990). Boyce has also written a history of *Nationalism in Ireland* (London, 1982) and a book on *The Irish Question and British Politics, 1868–1986* (London, 1988). Grenfell Morton, *Home Rule and the Irish Question* (London, 1980) is an accessible introductory text which contains a useful selection of primary sources. Patricia Jalland, *The Liberals and Ireland: the Ulster Question in British Politics to 1914* (Brighton, 1980) is the fullest study of Liberal policies, albeit one highly critical of Asquith's handling of the Irish problem. Events in Ulster are narrated in A. T. Q. Stewart, *The Ulster Crisis* (London, 1967) and further considered in Patrick Buckland, *Irish Unionism 2: Ulster Unionism and the Origins of Northern Ireland, 1886–1922* (Dublin, 1973). More detailed references on the British dimension, especially the links between Unionism and the 'radical right' will be found in the notes to Chapter 5 of this book, but on the role of the British Unionist leadership particular attention should be drawn to Robert Blake, *The Unknown Prime Minister: The Life and Times of Andrew Bonar Law* (London, 1955). Biographies of other leading figures such as Carson, Redmond and the members of the Liberal cabinet also contain valuable information. The United Kingdom context of the 'crisis of nationalism' is placed on a broad canvas in Hugh Kearney, *The British Isles: A History of Four Nations* (Cambridge, 1989).

Finally, there are facets of the Edwardian period which have not been considered at length in the present work on which additional background material might be desirable. On foreign policy, Zara Steiner, *Britain and the Origins of the First World War* (London, 1977) is a good summary. Robert K. Massie, *Dreadnought* (London, 1992) is a discursive, though readable, study of Anglo-German rivalries, and much else besides. Further guidance on this and other themes will be found in the general texts referred to above.

INDEX